a People and its Faith

a People and its Faith

COPYRIGHT, CANADA, 1959
by UNIVERSITY *of* TORONTO PRESS
PRINTED *in* CANADA
Reprinted in 2018
ISBN 978-1-4875-7312-6 (paper)

CONTRIBUTORS

GERALD M. CRAIG is Assistant Professor of History, University of Toronto. He was editor of *Early Travellers in the Canadas, 1791-1867* (1955), and has been Associate Editor of the *Canadian Historical Review*.

BEN KAYFETZ is Director, National Joint Public Relations Committee of the Canadian Jewish Congress and B'nai B'rith.

SIDNEY S. SCHIPPER is a business man in Toronto. He is a Vice-President of Holy Blossom Temple.

DENNIS H. WRONG is Assistant Professor of Sociology, Brown University, Providence, Rhode Island. He is the author of *American and Canadian Viewpoints* (1955).

ALBERT ROSE is Professor of Social Work, University of Toronto. He is the author of *Regent Park: A Study in Slum Clearance* (1958).

JOHN R. SEELEY is an Associate, Department of Psychiatry, University of Toronto. He is the senior author of *Crestwood Heights: A North American Suburb* (1956); and *Community Chest: A Case Study in Philanthropy* (1957).

EMIL L. FACKENHEIM is Associate Professor of Philosophy, University College, University of Toronto. He was formerly the Rabbi at Temple Anshe Sholom, Hamilton, Ontario.

AARON M. KAMERLING is Director, B'nai B'rith Hillel Foundation at the University of Toronto. He was ordained at the Hebrew Union College–Jewish Institute of Religion, and has held congregations in Williamsport, Pennsylvania, and Chicago, Illinois.

LOU H. SILBERMAN is Hillel Professor of Jewish Literature and Thought, Vanderbilt University, Nashville, Tennessee.

FERDINAND M. ISSERMAN is the Rabbi at Temple Israel, St. Louis, Missouri. He was the Rabbi at Holy Blossom Temple from 1925 to 1929.

JACOB J. WEINSTEIN is the Rabbi of congregation Kehilath Anshe Mayriv, Chicago, Illinois.

HENRY E. KAGAN is the Rabbi at Sinai Temple, Mt. Vernon, New York. He was founder of the Committee on Religion and Psychiatry of the Central Conference of American Rabbis, and is consultant on Judaism to the Joint Commission on Mental Health, appointed by the United States Congress.

ABRAHAM L. FEINBERG is the Rabbi at Holy Blossom Temple, Toronto. He has been the spiritual leader of the congregation since 1943. His writings, addresses and public appearances have made him well known throughout Canada.

PREFACE

In the fall of 1956, Holy Blossom Temple, a Reform Jewish congregation in Toronto, celebrated its hundredth anniversary. For the oldest Jewish congregation in the city, founded little more than twenty years after the Town of York became the City of Toronto, a centennial celebration was a memorable event which its officers and members deemed worthy of genuine commemoration. The development of a book of essays which would add substantially to the understanding, both by Jews and by non-Jews, of certain aspects of the evolution and faith of the Canadian Jewish community, was thought to be such a commemorative act.

This book was initiated, in fact, some months before the actual observance of the centennial. Its conception was, at first, sufficiently limited in scope that its protagonists believed that it could be prepared and published within the centennial year. As with many projects which seem relatively simple and circumscribed at first, later examination revealed a programme which was far from simple and relatively unlimited. The task of rounding out the contributions which it seemed essential to include was one which required not a few months but several years.

The essence of the approach to the preparation of this collection of essays was an attempt to place the Jewish community in its proper perspective in Canadian life and the non-Jewish community in its proper perspective with respect to Jewish life in one part of Canada. These essays, therefore, include some that are frankly historical in nature, some which deal with contemporary issues in historical perspective, some which reveal the essence of Jewish existence, and some which deal with the faith of Reform Judaism and its probable direction in the second half of the twentieth century. Four words have been chosen carefully to describe the major parts of this publication: history, relations, existence, and faith.

Gerald Craig introduces the historical section and the book with an essay in which the major trends and lines of development in the history of Canada are presented in order to describe the fertile soil in which the Jewish minority group grew and developed and came to fruition as Canada has come to fruition in the twentieth century. This broad outline is followed by a detailed description and analysis of the evolution of the Jewish community of Toronto over the past century by Ben Kayfetz. His descriptive analysis is further documented by Sidney Schipper's essay on the contribution of Holy Blossom and its lay and spiritual leaders to the development of the social institutions of the Jewish and wider community in Metropolitan Toronto.

All of this may be conceived as a vast backdrop against which the Jewish minority in Toronto and in Ontario sought to establish its place in the economic and social development of a growing nation. The development of such relationships was not without its major pitfalls and severe barriers. Dennis Wrong discusses the changing relations between Jews and non-Jews in Ontario since the early years of the nineteenth century in the first essay in this group. This is followed by Albert Rose's analysis of the role of Holy Blossom in drawing attention to and dealing with the various threats, both direct and indirect, to the freedom of the Jewish and other minority groups in the larger community. John Seeley completes this section with an essay in which he raises a series of vitally important questions concerning the nature and programmes of intergroup relations in our modern Western society.

In the third part of the book Emil Fackenheim considers the whole question of Jewish existence and ascribes it to the faith of Jews in a "living God." His discussion is followed by Aaron Kamerling's essay describing in intricate detail the spiritual roots of the State of Israel from pre-Biblical times. Lou Silberman completes this section with an analysis of contemporary trends in Jewish theological thought with particular reference to Martin Buber and other pioneers of our lifetime.

Reform Judaism receives careful examination in the final portion of this collection of essays. Rabbi Ferdinand Isserman deals with the essentials of Reform Judaism as an introductory statement. This is followed by Rabbi Jacob Weinstein's analysis of the development of Reform Judaism in North America, particularly since 1885. Rabbi Henry Kagan considers the influence of psychology upon religion and the role of the spiritual counsellor in contemporary society. The final essay in the book by Rabbi Abraham Feinberg constitutes essentially a summary of the material which precedes it through his development of the principles upon which Reform Judaism, and Holy Blossom Temple in particular, have been founded and have progressed.

As well, it is equally important to state clearly what this book is not. It is not a history of the Jewish community in one part of Canada. It is not an exposition of Reform Judaism in Western society. It is not an historical tribute to the contribution of Holy Blossom Temple to the development of Jewish life in Canada. Nor is it a treatise on anti-Semitism or pro-Semitism. It is not a consideration of what are sometimes called "modern Jewish problems." Nor is it a source book in which answers will be found to the many questions raised by younger and older people concerning the meaning of life in an atomic or space age.

On the contrary, this collection of essays is intended to raise some of the fundamental questions of our time rather than to provide simple or more difficult answers. Each contributor to this book was given complete freedom to develop his own subject in his own way within the over-all framework and objectives of the programme. Several writers have treated the historical material from different points of view. Each essayist has written what he wished to write about a subject which was of interest and concern to him. The views of these writers do not necessarily represent the views of the members of Holy Blossom Temple or the editor of the book.

A project of this nature and scope obviously cannot be completed and brought to fruition without the assistance and co-operation of many people. The programme has, from the beginning, been under the general supervision of a small committee of volunteers who acted in a capacity of liaison between the Board of Directors of Holy Blossom Temple on one hand, and the editor and the contributors on the other. This so-called "Centennial Publication Committee" considered and approved the general outline of the book in the early stages and fostered its development through the long gestation period. The members of Holy Blossom are pleased to see it appear with the imprint of the University of Toronto Press which will present the volume to the wider public beyond the congregation.

The "Centennial Publication Committee" was composed as follows:

ABBEY A. MUTER, *Chairman*

MRS. JUDITH BOHNEN
MAX E. ENKIN
EMIL L. FACKENHEIM
ABRAHAM L. FEINBERG
JOSEPH L. KRONICK
BORA LASKIN
SIDNEY S. SCHIPPER
LESTER SUGARMAN
HEINZ WARSCHAUER

ALBERT ROSE, *Editor*

The editor has had, throughout the entire exercise, the generous assistance and co-operation of the Rabbis and administrative staff of Holy Blossom Temple. The

Chairman of the Committee has been a constant source of encouragement. The friendly aid of all these persons and many others is freely acknowledged. As well, the senior officers of the University of Toronto Press have been most generous in their encouragement and technical assistance at all stages in the process of development of this project.   A.R.

TORONTO, AUGUST, 1959

xi / Preface

HISTORY
3 / The Canadian Setting / GERALD M. CRAIG
14 / The Evolution of the Jewish Community in Toronto / BEN KAYFETZ
30 / The Contribution of Holy Blossom to its Community / SIDNEY S. SCHIPPER

RELATIONS
45 / Ontario's Jews in the Larger Community / DENNIS H. WRONG
60 / The Price of Freedom / ALBERT ROSE
85 / Some Radical Problems of Intergroup Relations / JOHN R. SEELEY

EXISTENCE
105 / Jewish Existence and the Living God / EMIL L. FACKENHEIM
119 / The Religious Roots of the State of Israel / AARON M. KAMERLING
134 / The Search for Relevance / LOU H. SILBERMAN

FAITH
153 / The Essentials of Reform Judaism / FERDINAND M. ISSERMAN
163 / Reform Judaism Reconsidered / JACOB J. WEINSTEIN
173 / Psychology and Religion / HENRY ENOCH KAGAN
187 / A Liberal Synagogue Today: Its Purposes and Principles / ABRAHAM L. FEINBERG

Contents

History

Craig /

Kayfetz / Schipper

THE CANADIAN SETTING / *Gerald M. Craig*

If we try to view Canadian history in the widest possible perspective, we must observe the manner in which the expansion of Europe led to the growth of new nations with distinctive ways of life in the Western hemisphere. From the end of the fifteenth century down to our own day, that is, for over 450 years, men, women, and children have been streaming out of the Old World to start life again in the New World across the Atlantic Ocean. Spaniards and Portuguese were the first to come, to Central and South America. After nearly a century they were followed by Englishmen who settled along the eastern seaboard of the North American mainland and by Frenchmen who penetrated the interior of the continent by way of the broad St. Lawrence. Soon afterward, the Dutch established themselves at the mouth of the Hudson River, and it was in this colony of New Netherland (later New York) that the first Jewish settlers found a home in the New World, in 1654.

After 1700 the Scotch-Irish and Germans began to arrive in large numbers. The defeat of Napoleon in 1815 was followed by another outpouring from the British Isles, soon joined by a vast movement from Germany and Scandinavia. Finally, in the years from about 1890 to 1914 came the greatest migration of all, with the influx of many millions from eastern and southern Europe. Thus, we on this continent are all immigrants or the descendants of immigrants. We and our ancestors were drawn or driven by a great variety of circumstances and motives while participating in this stupendous folk wandering. The hopes and fears, the joys and tears, of all these people, most of them very poor in this world's goods when they came here, form an epic of modern world history.

For many years the lands that are now Canada did not figure significantly in the great population movements. French power was established on the St. Lawrence by a few hundred men and women, and then by a few thousand. The population of New France did not grow rapidly as did that of the English colonies to the south. The fur trade did not need, indeed could not survive with, a large population. Moreover, the French government forbade the entry into New France of any non-Catholic settlers, a regulation that helped to check the colony's growth. Some non-Catholics, including an occasional Jew, did evade the edict, but the population of the colony on the St. Lawrence remained remarkably homogeneous: French, Catholic, and about one-twentieth as numerous as the English colonists. The story of New France's expansion into the interior, to the Mississippi and Saskatchewan river valleys, is a stirring one, but one that was doomed to end in defeat, as the struggle for North America reached a climax. In 1763 France was forced to cede Canada to Great Britain.

It was the opinion of Guy Carleton, the British governor after the conquest, that the advent of British rule in Canada would bring little real change to the colony. He believed that its population would and should remain predominantly French. To be sure, it was now legal for non-French and non-Catholic people to settle along the St. Lawrence, and a few hundred English-speaking merchants and government officials soon did so. Among these was Aaron Hart, the founder of the Montreal family of that name; as early as 1768 a handful of Jewish residents had founded their first congregation, "Shearith Israel," in Montreal. But Carleton rightly believed that, "barring catastrophe shocking to think of," Canada was not likely to attract a non-French population in the foreseeable future.[1] In consequence, every effort must be made to turn the French Canadians into loyal British subjects by guaranteeing to them the preservation of their language, religion, and laws. The result was the Quebec Act of 1774.

Within a few years, however, the "catastrophe" had occurred. In 1775 the American colonists rose in rebellion against British authority, provoking war that resulted in the establishment of the United States of America. The War of the American Revolution was a civil war that in many instances turned father against son, and brother against brother. In Canada there were a few, both French and English, who showed sympathy for the revolutionary cause, while in the American colonies there were a great many who remained loyal to the British cause. The tiny Jewish population, whether to the south or to the north, was as much divided as any other group. As the war ended in American independence many thousands of Loyalists left the new republic to find homes within the British Empire. Canada now acquired an unexpected but substantial English-speaking population, stretched along the shores of the upper St. Lawrence, Lake Ontario, and Lake Erie, and some Jews were included among the migrants. The old province of Quebec was divided in 1791 to form two provinces, Lower Canada (now Quebec) and Upper Canada (now Ontario).

For the next thirty years the provinces grew very slowly. During the long war between Britain and France, which ended only with the defeat of Napoleon in 1815, there was little chance of immigration from Europe. Within the provinces there was a growing conflict between the mercantile and the agricultural interests.

In Lower Canada the French Canadian majority, in control of the representative Assembly, became increasingly suspicious of the executive branch, which was sympathetic to the ambitions of the English-speaking merchants. This conflict led to a notable event when in 1807 Ezekiel Hart was elected to the Assembly as a member for Three Rivers. The majority in the Assembly expelled him from that body on the ground that a Jew could not take the oath prescribed for members. This episode is usually set forth as an early example of intolerance and discrimination, but it is probably more correct to see it in the larger perspective of economic conflict, since the majority in the Assembly objected to Hart at least as much because he represented English-speaking mercantile interests as because he was a Jew. In any case the controversy served a useful purpose, leading eventually as it did to the granting in 1832 of full political rights to Jews in the British North American colonies. It was not until 1858 that Jews could sit in the British House of Commons.

This passing reference to the British attitude towards the Jews should not, however, be allowed to stand by itself. If we are to see the Canadian setting in its full clarity, we must put it in the still larger perspective of the British background. For out of the British background emerged an attitude towards the Jews which was something new in the modern world. When the Jews began to re-settle in England in 1656, after their expulsion more than three hundred years earlier, they embarked upon a way of life that they had hitherto not known in the Old World. As Cecil Roth, the leading historian of British Jews, has written, the Jews in England lived in "an atmosphere of almost unqualified freedom."[2] On the continent of Europe, with the exception of Holland, Jews at this time lived in ghettos, as an enclave sharply separated from the rest of society and forbidden to engage in many lines of endeavour. In this situation the concept of "the mysterious Jew" could easily develop, with rumours and suspicion always in the air about the unknown and probably sinister happenings in the ghetto. In England, however, the ghetto system never developed, and Jews could live normally within the larger community. Needless to say, England's practice in this matter spread to her dependencies across the seas, including Canada. Just as Canadians generally inherited a rich tradition of freedom from Britain, so did Canadian Jews share in a liberating tradition emanating from the mother country. Undoubtedly the environment of the New World would in any case have proved unfriendly to the restrictive customs of the Old; nevertheless, it was of enormous value to have the weight of British practice working in the same direction. It is important to recall this long tradition, now that the fate of Diaspora Jewry is largely bound up with that of the English-speaking countries. The United States, too, shared in this tradition during its colonial period.

With this background in mind, we must turn now to look at certain dominant features of the growth of Canada in the nineteenth century. At first, as we noticed earlier, this growth had been slow, but from the 1820's onward there was a noticeable quickening of the Canadian pulse. In particular, Upper Canada was to emerge as a bustling, vigorous community. A large immigration from the British Isles arrived to mingle with the old Loyalist and American population. Agriculture, particularly wheat-farming, began to flourish. Roads were improved, and the 1850's saw the beginnings of an elaborate railway network. The province was coming out of the pioneer stage, with the basic work of settlement completed and the economy growing more diversified.

Such a period of expansion usually involves tensions and discord, and Upper Canada was not free of these. A main source of unrest lay in the dual role of the province as a loyal British colony and at the same time a North American community open to every manner of pressure from the neighbouring republican states. Many Upper Canadians were so envious of the rapid progress of these states that they demanded an early end of colonial restraints as an essential for achieving similar progress themselves. Other Upper Canadians were so fearful of American expansionism that they clung the more closely to the British connection as an insurance against annexation by the United States. Out of these divisions came the abortive rebellions of 1837, to be followed in the 1840's by the firm establishment of local self-government within the British orbit. Finally, in 1867 the maritime provinces of Nova Scotia and New Brunswick joined in Confederation with Upper and Lower Canada to form the Dominion of Canada. The modern British Commonwealth of free nations was foreshadowed in the Canadian achievements of these years. Canadians were pioneering in the political sphere as well as on the land.

It is remarkable how directly the history of the Jews in Canada parallels that of the country as a whole. Included among the immigrants of the pre-Confederation period were a few hundred Jews from England and from Germany, clearly part of the larger movement from these countries to North America. The earlier Jewish community in Canada, centred mainly in Montreal, had been almost entirely Sephardic[3] in background. With the arrival of immigrants from England and Germany, Ashkenazic[4] congregations were founded, the first in Montreal and then one in Toronto celebrated by the present volume. Thus there were in Canada by the end of the 1850's a few hundred German and English Jews, living mainly in Montreal and Toronto, the forerunners of the much larger immigration to come.

Another interesting feature of Jewish life in these years was its relation to the larger English-speaking world of Great Britain and the United States. Just as Canadians generally looked to these countries for intellectual stimulus, for material assistance, and for skilled people, so too did Canadian Jews. Spiritual leaders came from both Britain and the United States, and the Canadian congregations frequently advertised in the Jewish papers of New York when seeking to hire teachers and other trained people. Similarly, the population movements of Canadian Jews paralleled those of the general population. Immigrants from Britain and Europe frequently came to the United States, lived there for a while, and then settled down permanently in Canada. There were others who reversed the process by coming first to Canada, and then moving on to the United States. Jewish settlers, too, moved in both directions.

The decades immediately following the Confederation of 1867 were a period of hope deferred for Canada. The country did not grow as rapidly as the optimists of the 1860's had expected. The long depression following the financial panic of 1873 cast a heavy shadow over economic activity. After some delay the first transcontinental railway was completed in 1885, but the anticipated filling-up of the Canadian West did not at once follow this great accomplishment. Instead, Canada suffered a continuous drain of population to the expanding American economy. National unity was shaken by the Riel Rebellions in the West, which in turn led to bitter feeling between Protestant Ontario and Catholic Quebec. The political fabric was rent by the provincial rights movement which sought to limit the authority of the federal government. In this period of Sir John A. Macdonald's leadership, secure foundations for later Canadian growth were laid, but it was also a time of trial and disappointment.

In the last years of the century the picture suddenly became brighter, and shortly the new prime minister, Sir Wilfrid Laurier, asserted that the twentieth century belonged to Canada. The long depression lifted, gold was discovered in the Yukon, farm prices began to rise, and the Canadian West at last began to attract large numbers of settlers, both from the United States and from Europe. In this mood of exuberant optimism Canada's railway system was expanded, indeed over-expanded, by the building of two additional transcontinental lines.

It was at the end of the time of pessimism and at the beginning of the time of optimism, that is, in the 1880's and 1890's, that Canada began to receive a new type of immigration from Europe. Immigrants were continuing to come from the British Isles in considerable numbers, but they were now supplemented by an ever-mounting human flood from central and eastern Europe, especially from Germany, Austria-Hungary, and Russia. The countries of southern Europe, particularly Italy and the Balkan countries, were likewise being abandoned by millions of their inhabitants. Taken altogether, this emigration from Europe in the thirty years or so before the outbreak of the First World War was the mightiest movement of people in modern history. The great majority, at least twenty millions, came to the United States, but substantial numbers also went to Latin American countries, particularly Argentina and Brazil, and to Canada.

Like immigrants in other times and places, these millions of people were both pulled and pushed from the Old World across the Atlantic to the New. On the one hand, the countries of the Western hemisphere were vigorously competing for immigrants. Employers wanted cheap labour, farmers were needed on still empty prairies, and railway and steamship companies were anxious for passenger traffic. As a result, government and private agents were busy across Europe seeking to attract settlers to their countries. Very often their methods and their propaganda were none too scrupulous, but obviously they were effective. On the other hand there were factors at work which drove the millions of immigrants to leave their old homes with the desperation of people escaping from a sinking ship. Most important, in the opinion of Oscar Handlin, a leading historian of immigration, was the destruction of Eastern European society that occurred in the decades after 1870. Landholding was concentrated into fewer hands, with the result that peasants were forced off their small plots. The Jewish middlemen, who had served the needs of the peasants, were deprived of their traditional economic functions as well.[5] There was further disintegration when industry began to penetrate this region. In short, the cake of centuries-old custom was abruptly broken; when cholera and hatred of military service are added to the list, it becomes easy to understand the dimensions of the movement.

The impact on Canada of her share of this immigration was a minor demographic revolution. Hitherto Canada's population had been almost entirely comprised of two groups: the French-speaking Canadians, who made up just over 30 per cent, and the Anglo-Celts from the British Isles and the United States, who made up nearly 60 per cent of the population. The only other group of any size were the residents of German origin, most of whom had been in the country for many years. But now there were the first signs of a challenge to the Anglo-Celtic and French predominance in the population. The time was coming when these two groups would together number no more than about 80 per cent of the population, with a probability that the percentage would eventually decline still further.

The Jewish element was a relatively small part of the pre-First World War immigration, being far outnumbered by the British, and also by the Ukrainians and the Scandinavians. Yet it was in these years that Canada for the first time received a Jewish population of any size. By 1914 there were over 100,000 Jews living in the country, and they represented just over 1 per cent of the total population of the country. They had of course come mainly from central and eastern Europe, particularly from the sections of Poland then dominated by Russia, and from Roumania. Jews emigrated for the same reasons that sent millions of others forth to the New World, but they had an additional and pressing need to seek shelter across the Atlantic. As East European society disintegrated in the ways outlined above, the Jew was made to serve as a scapegoat. Bewildered peasants, encouraged by the Czarist government, looked upon the Jews as the cause of their troubles. At periodic intervals after 1870 Jewish lives and property were destroyed in a series of bloody pogroms. Under these circumstances Jews saw no alternative but to flee to the west as rapidly as possible. Thus to the small number of German and English Jews, and the much tinier Sephardic community, were now added many tens of thousands of Jews from eastern Europe, coming to Canada after centuries of ghetto life and fleeing from bitter persecution.

It was natural that many of these unhappy refugees should find a haven within the little Jewish communities of Montreal and Toronto, which at times felt almost overwhelmed by this large and in many ways alien influx. There were problems of adjustment not only as between the newcomers and the population as a whole, just as there were for the much larger non-Jewish immigration, but also as between westernized Jews and the newly arrived easterners, fresh from what was literally another world. Yet within a short time shelter and jobs were found for these as well as for other immigrants. In the case of Toronto, the Jewish population grew from just over 500 in 1881 to nearly 1500 in 1891. In 1901 it had risen to over 3,000 and then catapulted to more than 18,000 by 1911. This figure was nearly doubled in another decade. By 1921 Jews represented just over 5½ per cent of Toronto's population, and were second to the Anglo-Celts (to be sure, a very small second) among the city's ethnic groups, a percentage and a position which they have since approximately maintained. (When the full results of the current immigration from Europe become clear, it is likely that the Jewish percentage of Toronto's population will have declined somewhat.)

Although a large proportion of the Jewish immigrants went to Montreal and Toronto, many of them ventured farther afield. A third sizable community developed at Winnipeg, and Jews otherwise found homes in most parts of the country. Since many of Canada's best opportunities in these years lay on the farms, it was natural that Jews should seek to revive their long-lost agricultural heritage on the prairies of western Canada. But this experiment was not a success. For centuries Jews had been forbidden to engage in agriculture; moreover, farming in western Canada posed special problems which only experienced farmers were likely to solve. Like most of the urban immigrants from England of this period, the great majority of the Jewish newcomers found homes in Canada's cities. By 1921 the Jews constituted about 1½ per cent of Canada's population, again a percentage that has remained substantially constant since that time.

The immigrants from central and eastern Europe were received with mixed feelings by the older Canadian population. By and large, the newcomers were welcomed, because it was generally believed that Canada needed more people. Nevertheless, many old-stock Canadians, both of French and of Anglo-Celtic origin, were troubled by the dimensions of the influx. French Canadians assumed, and rightly so, that as the immigrants were gradually absorbed into the mainstream of the national life they would serve to increase and strengthen the English-speaking cultural group. As this happened, the relative weight and power of French Canadians in the country as a whole was likely to decline. Already a minority, the French Canadians feared that continuing immigration would lead to a further weakening of their position.

Among English-speaking Canadians there was the fear that the newcomers could not be absorbed. There were too many of them and they were too alien. Earlier immigrants from the British Isles and from northern Europe had readily taken to the Canadian way of life, but what could be expected of these strangers, with their odd customs, their low standard of living, and their almost complete ignorance of constitutional government? Canada was still a young country, with the gristle not yet hardened into bone, striving to maintain its identity against a gigantic and expansive neighbour. Canada needed a population that would foster and strengthen Canadian traditions; but as immigrants arrived from central Europe, native-born Canadians drifted off to the United States. Immigration did not increase the country's population nearly as much as had been expected; yet it was certainly changing the composition of that population, and it was a change for the worse as far as many old-stock Canadians were concerned.

The Jewish immigrants from eastern Europe received their full share of the distrust arising out of these nativist fears and misgivings. There were, however, specific shafts aimed at the Jews that were not intended for the general run of immigrants. It was a time when the farming population was growing increasingly suspicious of the expanding power of the cities and of the control by bankers over the economy of the country. With the aid of a few ardent publicists, it was not hard to identify Jews with city life (thought to be immoral and materialistic) and with the supposed conspiracy of the international bankers. The actual controversies surrounding this subject were confined largely to the Populist agitation in the United States, but in them lay the origins of anti-Semitism in its modern form on this continent. The infection inevitably spread to Canada, and the stereotype of the clever, ambitious, and grasping Jew, who lived off the work of other people, was soon widely held. Not far in the future lay Henry Ford's dissemination of the Protocols of Zion and the activities of the revived Ku Klux Klan, to be followed in the 1930's by fascist-tinged silver shirt movements and the outbursts of Father Charles E. Coughlin.

It would not be accurate to write of all this in any tone of exaggeration. Canada never suffered as directly from the anti-Semitic sickness as did her American neighbours. Moreover, if Canada had to do some importing in this matter, at least she could also do some exporting, as in the instance of Father Coughlin and W. J. Cameron (who worked for Henry Ford).

One aspect of Canadian-American relations is sometimes forgotten: that proximity to the great republic acts as a safety valve for the elimination of our more ardent spirits, a process that sometimes works to our advantage. But if we are not to exaggerate in our discussion of Canadian attitudes, we have nevertheless to admit that the early years of the twentieth century saw Canadians imitating their contemporaries in many petty practices, such as restrictive covenants in real estate transfers, unstated "quotas" in some aspects of university admission, restrictive arrangements at places of entertainment and recreation, a whole complex of social exclusion, and an undetermined amount of discrimination in employment.

The most extreme situation, which can receive only brief mention here, existed in the province of Quebec. French Canada went through a period of abrupt change as the valley of the St. Lawrence became industrialized. This painful process was then exacerbated by the onslaught of the great depression of the 1930's. French Canadians began to assert that they were becoming "hewers of wood and drawers of water" in their own province, while control of their economy was being gathered into the hands of a few outsiders. Such control was real enough, but the outsiders were little known and rarely observed. On the scene, however, in the city of Montreal, was Canada's largest Jewish community, a ready target for feelings of frustration and bitterness. As Jews became active in several lines of small business and of trade, they became the objects of distrust and suspicion.

Such feelings were strongest during the depression and lessened with the advent of prosperity.

In the last couple of decades there has been a general improvement in the atmosphere. A tightening-up of immigration regulations in the 1920's meant that the influx of strangers was diminished to a trickle. Meanwhile the children of the immigrants discarded those customs of their parents that were widely regarded as foreign, and became largely indistinguishable from the middle-class Canadians generally. In short, they were less visible on the social scene than their parents had been. Another factor of importance was the anti-Jewish horror set loose in Nazi Germany. Many Canadians who had never given much thought to the subject felt a wave of sympathy for European Jews and a deep sense of disgust that such barbarities could occur in the twentieth century. Many were led to re-examine their general outlook, and to purge themselves of vague feelings that might once have seemed fairly harmless but had now been shown to be the stuff on which demagogues could feed. Moreover, the war against Hitler seemed to be a mockery if discrimination against religious and racial minorities was allowed to persist at home. Out of this background grew a demand for legislation ensuring fair employment practices, and a general increase in understanding.

And so the relations of Jews and Gentiles within the Canadian setting gradually changed. On the one hand the Jews bcame more "Canadianized" and more closely identified with the whole community. The old immigrant culture all but disappeared in the bright but rather thin atmosphere of the New World. Jews joined fully in the sense of nationalism that pervaded Canada as the twentieth century reached its half-way point. At one time it was largely an accident whether a central European Jew came to the United States or to Canada; but his son or grandson was a self-conscious Canadian patriot who had fought in Canada's wars and looked at the world through Canadian spectacles. Those Jews who supported the doctrines of Zionism denied strongly that they were any less firmly loyal to Canada than their fellow-citizens. In short, Jews were becoming as Canadian-centred as any group in the country.

On the other hand the Anglo-Celtic and French-speaking majority became willing to accept a diversity that once had seemed dangerous to them. It was now accepted that the central European ethnic groups would remain as a permanent element in the Canadian population, that they would make valuable contributions to Canadian society and civilization, which would as a result be richer and more varied. This new willingness to see the virtues of diversity came of course more readily as that diversity became less striking. As the children of the immigrants learned English, as they became North American in outlook and ambition, the much-touted diversity seemed to be largely a matter of interesting foods, folksongs, and a voting tendency on particular public questions. Above all, it was accepted that there should be diversity in the religious sphere, in the sense of Protestant, Catholic, and Jew, but within each broad religious framework cultural and even sometimes denominational variations became less marked. And all three groups found it increasingly easier to work together for civic and public purposes than in former times.

NOTES

[1] Carleton to Shelburne, November 25, 1767, quoted in Adam Shortt and Arthur G. Doughty, *Documents relating to the Constitutional History of Canada*, Part One (Ottawa, 1918), p. 284.

[2] Cecil Roth, "Two Cradles of Jewish Liberty"; *Commentary*, vol. XVII (February, 1954), p. 111. See also Cecil Roth, *A History of the Jews in England* (Oxford, 1941).

[3] *Sefarad* is the name given in Hebrew to Spain. Jews of Spanish and Portuguese origin are termed *Sefardic* or *Sephardic*.

[4] The word *Askhenaz* meant Germany in Hebrew; hence Jews whose origin loosely derived from Germany, including those who lived in Poland, were called *Askhenazim* and their congregations *Askhenazic*.

[5] Oscar Handlin, *Adventure in Freedom: Three Hundred Years of Jewish Life in America* (New York: McGraw-Hill, 1954), p. 80.

THE EVOLUTION OF THE JEWISH COMMUNITY IN TORONTO /

Ben Kayfetz

The Toronto Jewish community was formally founded more than one hundred years ago with the establishment of Holy Blossom Congregation in 1856, and its composition at that time forms a striking contrast to the community we know today. From the earliest records one gets a picture of a quiet, respectable, God-fearing community of small merchants following the traditional middle-class virtues and living up as best they can to the duties enjoined by Judaism, a community striving to make the adjustment to the New World and its mores. The adjustment was not too drastic as most of Toronto's early Jewish settlers were not newcomers to the Western way of life. They came from the United Kingdom, from the United States, from the Rhineland, Bavaria, or the western marches of the old Hapsburg Empire. Even those who stemmed from Galicia and the old Russo-Polish Pale of Settlement[1]—and there was from the beginning a sizable portion of them in Toronto's first congregation—were not utter strangers to the English language, having lived in England or America for some years before their arrival in Upper Canada.

The year 1856 is something of an "anniversary year" in modern Jewish history in other ways. It marks the birth in Rochester, New York, of Louis Marshall, American constitutional lawyer and communal leader; in Louisville, Kentucky, of Louis Dembitz Brandeis, the renowned American jurist; and turning to eastern Europe, of Morris Winchesky, the proletarian agitator and pamphleteer; of Achad Ha'am, the philosophic founder of cultural Zionism; of Aaron David Gordon, theoretician of the Jewish back-to-the-soil movement; in Galicia, of Naphtali-Herz Imber, the vagabond Hebrew songster who penned the words for *Hatikvah*[2]; and in Moravia, of one of the giants of our time, Sigmund Freud. The year 1856 also saw the death in Paris in his "mattress-grave" of Heinrich Heine who spent his life in the effort to reconcile his Jewish, German, and European heritages; in the republic to the south of Canada, Isaac Mayer Wise, who had already lived in the United States for ten years, had recently left Albany for a post in Cincinnati after making the first cautious innovations in ritual that were destined to revolutionize the religious development of American Jewry. The holding, in a rented room at Yonge and Richmond streets in Toronto, of the city's first recorded Jewish High Holy Day services, truly took place at an auspicious time.

Moving to the wider scene, in Damascus in that decade the world was to be shocked by a blood libel which was not the first and would not be the last in a long and tragic history of accusations. It was the period of the Second Napoleonic Empire in France, of rash military adventures in the Crimea, of the Indian Mutiny. Europe had fallen back into the doldrums after the abortive and short-lived uprisings of the Glorious Year, 1848. Stern and brutal repression had triumphed throughout the Continent. In Rome, Vienna, Prague, Berlin, Warsaw, and Budapest the ideal of civil and national freedom had been suffocated by the rifleman's jackboot. Kossuth and Garibaldi were both in exile, far from their homelands, waiting for a favourable sign that would bring them back.

In eastern Europe, Jewry in 1856 lay for the most part under the knout of Czarist repression. It was less than a year since the death of Nicholas I, the Czar who had introduced the terrorization of the edict whereby Jewish ten- and eleven-year-olds were snatched from their families and sent for twenty-five years' service in the army. Nine years were to elapse before the Russian peasant was to be freed from serfdom. From this group of Jews were to come leaders in literature, but the grandfather of Yiddish literature, Mendele Mocher S'forim, had yet to publish his biting satires on the sordidness and narrowness of the *shtetl* (the East European Jewish town). Of the other two classic writers of Russo-Polish Jewry, I. L. Peretz was a child of six and Shalom Aleichem was not yet born. Russian and Polish Jewry was as yet untouched by the *Haskalah* (the "enlightenment") or by the Jewish national and cultural renaissance or by political emancipation which in France may be dated from the time of Napoleon.

Hebrew was still a sacred tongue to be used only in prayers and sacred commentaries and Yiddish was the homely jargon of the market-place and street, not considered fit for learned or dignified usage. Zionism, even the non-political pre-Herzlian *Hovevei Zion* movement, was something still far off in the unpredictable future. The revolutionary impulse among Jews in Russia had not yet attained the kaleidoscopic variation it was to reach in later decades and had not developed the divergent ideologies that are based on the realities of ghetto life such as Bundism, Territorialism, Borochovism, Folkism, etc.[3] Russo-Polish Jewry, and its closely related Galician and Roumanian counterparts, lay seemingly asleep but it was to explode into turbulent intellectual and political activity about thirty or forty years later.

II Against this background we may place the Jewish community of 1856 in Toronto, a community whose Judaism may seem somewhat one-dimensional when we compare it with the many colourings and divergencies of later years. It had, however, the corresponding virtue of clarity of definition. All Jews knew without speculation what was meant by being a Jew—there was no quibble about affiliation or ideological refinements that detracted from or limited one's Jewish obligations or commitments.

The first group had to provide the three indispensables for a Jewish congregation: burial, the ritual bath, and worship. Even *kashruth* (food prepared in accordance with ritual demands) was not as important as these, for, if need be, meat could always be replaced by a vegetarian or dairy diet. We have no exact date for the actual beginning of the *mikvah* (ritual bath), but we know that a cemetery was provided some years before the synagogue was organized.[4] The features of congregational activity we see in the minutes of those early days are wholly in keeping with the trend of congregational organization in Jewish history. The multi-functional nature of the synagogue officiant was apparent. He had to be a factotum—learned enough in the law to answer queries, competent to teach the young, efficient as a slaughterer of fowl and cattle, and a master of some vocal talent, as well, to officiate at the Sabbath service. The difficulty of reconciling all these capacities in the person of one official is a constant theme of the business of the early meetings as we find them recorded in the minutes that have survived. A good *shochet* (ritual slaughterer) might be a bad *chazan* (cantor); a good *chazan*, on the other hand, would not necessarily be an effective teacher, and so the story went on until the nineties when the long and irregular succession of transient religious functionaries gave way to men who had not only received proper *smichah* (ordination) but who had, in addition, some familiarity with worldly studies.

Isaac Mayer Wise, writing his *Reminiscences* in the middle decade of the last century, has a word to say about this kind of community servant:

There was antipathy at that time in America to rabbis and preachers in general. . . . There was no room in the synagogue for preachers and rabbis. The chazan *was the Reverend. He was all that was wanted. The congregations desired nothing further. The* chazan *was reader, cantor and blessed everybody for* chai pash,[5] *which amounted to 4½ cents. He was teacher, butcher, circumcizer, [*shofar*][6] blower, gravedigger, secretary. He wrote the amulets with names of all the angels and demons on them for women in confinement, read* shiur *[appropriate prayer] for the departed sinners, and played cards or dominoes with the living; in short he was a* Kol-bo, *an encyclopaedia, accepted bread, turnips, cabbage, potatoes as a gift and peddled in case his salary was not sufficient. He was* sui generis. . . .

[*The*] *congregations were satisfied and there was no room for preacher or rabbi.*[7]

Toronto's Jewry avoided to a great extent the clear and sharp division between what was later called "up-town" Jewry and what was known as the *Yiddishe gass* (that is, the area of interests and tastes of the more newly arrived immigrant element) and the consequent harsh clash of interests which was a feature for so long of the communal structure and development of United States Jewry and the effects of which are still visible today in an American Jewry with sharply split leadership. True, the senior congregation, Holy Blossom, was known as the *deitshishe shul* (German synagogue) but it was never identified with the parentalistic ideology of a stratum in North American Jewish life which was referred to somewhat disparagingly as the "yehudim."

The word "German" in the popular name for the synagogue (*deitsh*) suggests far more than a mere ethnic tag descriptive of a country of origin. It connoted an attitude, an approach to Jewish life and could be applied to Jews wherever they came from. In this sense the term was a legacy of the early *Haskalah* period initiated in Germany by Moses Mendelssohn which proclaimed that Jews could speak the language of their country of residence, read widely in western European literature and participate in secular activities, without damage or loss to their Jewish tradition. "A Jew at home, a man [*Mensch*] abroad," was the watchword. The term applied to such features as style of clothing, method of worship, and personal habits far more than to any Rhenish or Bavarian area of origin. There were "Germans" in this sense who had never left Galicia or Lithuania.

The very gradualness of the transition from traditional worship to Reform in this congregation reflects the development characteristic of Toronto's Jewry. The writer has not made a detailed study but it seems likely that there are few other Jewish congregations on the continent where the process of transition from Orthodoxy to Reform took such a long period, from about 1880 when the auctioning of *aliyoth*[8] was dropped—a forbidding omen to some—to 1920 when official affiliation took place with the Union of American Hebrew Congregations. Forty years, equivalent to the Pentateuchal period of wandering in the wilderness, elapsed before the congregation made up its mind definitely as to the direction it was going. Not that there were no squabbles or disputes—the records and minute books of the congregation show a considerable number of serio-comic episodes of this kind—but the congregation would not take a definite step to break with tradition until such time as there was full consent and unanimity within its membership.

Not until after 1920 was mixed seating for all services introduced to Toronto.

Praying with uncovered head came only in the thirties. This does not say that Toronto's community was unaware that such reforms were going on elsewhere. Edmund Scheuer, Mark Cohen, and others persevered for years from the late eighties in the hope of effecting these and other alterations. But change came slowly in Toronto.

This "gradualness" in Holy Blossom also had the effect of helping to absorb the socio-cultural differences between West and East European Jews. There never arose in Toronto the sharp distinctions of certain Jewish communities in the United States between German and Russo-Polish Jews, distinctions that plagued American Jewish communal development and that in a sense still bar effective unity at a national level through the respective successor organizations (the American Jewish Committee, American Jewish Congress, etc.). An impressive number of families originating in Galicia and Lithuania entered the Holy Blossom family and were taken into its mainstream. Without minimizing the element of class distinction or family pride that nevertheless did exist, Toronto, it must be stated, was singularly free of the almost tribal "cold enmity" between East European and German Jews—an enmity that in some American cities caused the discharge of a rabbi for "fraternizing" with East European Jews, that created country clubs restricted in membership to Jews of German descent. Such an animosity was also responsible for an incident in which the venerable Rabbi Jacob Joseph, who for a while was the first (and last) Chief Rabbi of New York City, was derided as "an immigrant and prejudiced rabbi reared among the bigotries of the Eastern countries."

A revealing contrast to Toronto Jewry's development is that of a close-by American community—the city of Rochester, New York, almost directly across Lake Ontario—whose first Jewish congregation was founded a little more than a decade before Toronto's and whose economic development, based primarily on the clothing trade, followed a similar pattern.[9] Reform, from the outset, made rapid headway in Rochester. Though it too started as an Orthodox congregation, as early as 1857 the B'rith Kodesh of Rochester had instituted Confirmation services at *Shavuoth* (the Feast of Weeks in the spring), had abolished the "unaesthetic" practices of using rattles and noisemakers during the reading of the Book of Esther, the tossing about of nuts and raisins at *Simchath Torah* (the last day of the Feast of Tabernacles in the fall), and other such folk customs "not suited to the age." By 1863 the *Kol Nidrei* prayer was dropped from the Day of Atonement Service and the calling up of male worshippers to the Reading of the Torah had likewise been omitted. Before the end of the American Civil War there was a mixed choir (mixed in a dual sense as it was open to women *and* Christians). In 1869 candidates were running for the Board of Officers on a platform of "radical reform," though what radical reform was left after these innovations is hard to say. By 1882 the Rochester congregation was a member of the newly formed Reform Union of American Hebrew Congregations and in the same year its rabbi announced the abolition of the Bar Mitzvah ceremony in favour of the "more sensible custom of Confirmation." Toronto, it seems, was quite untouched by these developments. In 1882 the four-decade-long process was just beginning and innovations that Rochester had left behind in the sixties and seventies were not to be made in Toronto till after the turn of the century and some not until the twenties and thirties of the new century; some, in fact, not at all.

The factors behind this slowness of pace are not hard to determine. Toronto's Jewish community was a very small one until after 1900. The membership of Holy Blossom as late as 1937 never exceeded 300. In a small close-knit community of this size radical change would not be easy to achieve. Toronto Jewry's line of communication was with London either through Montreal or directly, not with Cincinnati or New York.[10] When Holy Blossom gave up the long succession of untrained spiritual leaders and looked about for a rabbi and preacher, or, as the phrase went then, "a lecturer," it sought its spiritual leaders from Jews' College in London—a seminary which to this day requires from its students a formal commitment of adherence to traditional Orthodoxy. These rabbis were willing to make certain modifications in ceremony and ritual and favoured a kind of social acculturation to the Canadian (as to the English) scene, but in religious matters, despite their seeming adaptability, they were essentially conservative.

An anthropologist writing of Toronto's early Jewish settlers says the following: *Many of them were British-educated, and certainly most of them were Anglophiles. They imported British rabbis for their synagogues, sent their sons to Britain to be educated and to fight in British wars, wore British woolens, and in many cases returned to Britain in their old age. Such patriotic immigrants were welcomed with open arms in the capital of the colony of Upper Canada.*[11]

The Anglophile characteristics (if the term may be used) of the early Jewish settlers in Toronto were of great importance in the acceptance of Jews both as individuals and as a group after their arrival in Toronto. Rabbis Elzas and Lazarus were of English birth and training, schooled at Jews' College. Rabbi Solomon Jacobs, an Englishman by birth and training and a devout Jew in the Anglo-Jewish pattern of piety, moved in the top circles of Toronto society and established Toronto Jewry as part of the scene in British and Tory Toronto where the

Loyalist strain still dominates culturally and socially. Though Holy Blossom, since its affiliation with the Union of Amerian Hebrew Congregations in 1920, has recruited its rabbis from the United States of America, the orientation set in the nineteenth and early twentieth centuries still remains. Yankee rabbis have come to admire and emulate the attachment to the Crown and the steadying institution of a constitutional monarchy.

The line of communications of the Toronto community, however, has changed direction. In the last twenty years the establishment of the Canadian Jewish Congress has given Toronto Jews a sense of a Canadian Jewish identity arising out of problems they have in common with other Jews in Vancouver, Montreal, and Winnipeg. The community, to an extent, still leans on New York for professional guidance and technical advice. In its religious forms it has departed from the common British institutions such as the Chief Rabbinate and the specifically English pattern of religious practices retained in South Africa, Australia, and other parts of the Commonwealth: in terms of religious denomination, Canadian synagogues have United States affiliations. Nevertheless, Canadian Jewry has attained a status of total independence of either the United States or Great Britain.

Despite its pro-English orientation and external social conformity—or perhaps because of this—Toronto's Jewish leadership at no time sought to minimize any basic differences or grievances with its neighbours or with various elements in the majority community. When the Anglican Church attempted to introduce religious teaching in the Toronto public schools in 1897, the Toronto Hebrew Congregation (the corporate name of Holy Blossom) submitted a reasoned, cogent brief which might well be a model for similar submissions. Shorn of a few stylistic devices peculiar to the nineties, it could be used today without any essential change of text. The intriguing fact about it is that brief succeeded. The Protestant churches of that day were still militant enough and consistent in their teaching to oppose giving to the state such a precious duty as instruction of the young in their faith. The Baptists and others rose to the assistance of the Jews, "hotfooting it," as the newspaper headline of the day had it, "after the Anglicans."[12] The community of today has a good deal to learn from the fearless stand taken in 1897 by a Jewish community as young as that in Toronto.

III   Jewish education in Toronto was from the beginning directed along various ideological lines. There is no ideology in Jewish life which at one time or other has not had its representative Talmud Torah or school (*shule*) for the instruction of the young. The traditional *cheder*, the old-fashioned Jewish school—and a much maligned institution—was for many years the most common. In fact, its decline set in only in the twenties and thirties and even today it is not totally extinct though it has not been the norm in Jewish education for twenty-five or thirty years. When East European immigrants started arriving here en masse in the nineties they found the Holy Blossom Sabbath School operating under the personal supervision of Edmund Scheuer—a German-born French-taught jeweller who was a pioneer of Jewish education in Toronto. But the style of this pedagogy—its use of English as the language of instruction, its deviations from strict tradition—made it less attractive to them, and Toronto's first Talmud Torah went up on Simcoe Street in 1907, the ancestor of the present *Ivrit-b'Ivrit* school system (learning Hebrew by the "direct method" without the aid of translation into Yiddish or English), known as the Associated Hebrew Schools which has branches on St. Clair Avenue and a new building on North Bathurst Street.

It is interesting and somewhat characteristic of the spirit of militant independence of Toronto that just as the Russian Jewish followers of the late Rabbi Jacob Gordon did not recognize Holy Blossom's Bond Street Sabbath School, so about a decade later, their school system was in turn ignored by a third influx of Jews, this time mainly from Poland. In the years of the First World War a group of these, deploring "the absence of proper Jewish education" and apparently ignoring the school on Simcoe Street, came together to found what was to become the Eitz Chaim Talmud Torah. The cultivation of *Ivrit b'Ivrit* was somewhat suspect to the founders of the Eitz Chaim (literally, this name means "the living tree"). For one reason it seemed to look upon the acquisition of Hebrew as an end in itself rather than a means for learning of holy lore; it smacked of the "heretical" approach of Hebraist secularism and hence was forbidden. As one of the spiritual heads of Eitz Chaim, the late Rabbi J. L. Graubart, expressed it: "*Ivrit b'Ivrit* would be acceptable. It is important, however, that those who teach it be God-fearing Jews and I don't know whether teachers with both qualifications can be found in this country."[13]

There could be no compromise or union, therefore, between the Orthodox Talmud Torah on Simcoe Street with its slight tendency towards *Haskalah*, "the enlightenment," and the Eitz Chaim system of D'Arcy Street dedicated to the unchanging past of the Polish *shtetl*. How closely the latter system sought to emulate its model can be gleaned from passages in its own annals. It was only in 1930 that the Board of the Eitz Chaim reluctantly accepted a proposal that blackboards be introduced as teaching aids; they had been considered a peculiar innovation inconsistent with traditional Jewish pedagogy. The principal's report for that year recommended, incidentally, that they be dropped as the experiment had not proven successful.[14] Even the ubiquitous *pushka* (coin-box) of the Jewish National Fund had a difficult time penetrating this school as it too represented an "ideology" or an "ism"—it was "modern"—and was therefore outside the framework of historic Judaism as the Eitz Chaim's leaders had known it and wanted to preserve it. Today Eitz Chaim schools not only co-operate with Zionist causes like the Jewish National Fund but have long since reconciled themselves to blackboards and make use of other up-to-date pedagogical equipment and aids.

Toronto shares with Montreal the distinction of being among the first communities in North America to institute the Yiddish secularist school. The Peretz School started in 1911 and was the result of the combined effort of a group of Poale-Zion (Labour Zionists), Territorialists (S.T.'s they were then called, being known in Russia as Socialist-Territorialists), and socialists of the Bundist wing, who felt the need to train the rising generation in the kind of Jewish life and ideals they wanted to see flourish: a Jewish community bound by the tie of a common language and culture (the Yiddish tongue), maintaining those traditions, festivals, and customs which had a "national-cultural" value, with some flavouring of a socialist ideal for mankind. Because the sponsorship was non-partisan (there was an uneasy alliance between Zionists, Galuth (diaspora) nationalists, and anti-Zionists), political ideology was minimized in favour of a common cultural orientation, but here too the partnership broke down. There was the expected *Kulturkampf* as to whether Hebrew was to be relegated to a secondary position or given equality with Yiddish. By 1919 the Poale-Zion had withdrawn from the Peretz School leaving it to be maintained solely by the *Arbeter Ring* (the Workmen's Circle). The non-partisan school experiment had not lasted long and the phenomenon of a secular Yiddish-Hebrew school unattached or uncommitted to a particular ideology vanished.

Now once again each ideology sponsored its own *shule*. Just to complicate matters further, after the historic *Arbeter Ring* convention of 1926, the left wing broke away and it too set up its own schools, borrowing for this purpose the name of Morris Winchevsky, the socialist poet and pamphleteer. In 1932 a fourth group, the Left Poale-Zion, founded its own school system—the Borochov School —which is still flourishing today and like the others draws children of parents who are not necessarily political followers. The result of these splits and fragmentations is that today there are four systems of secular Yiddish schools operating in Toronto.

These, of course, have followed the trend of this type of school throughout Canada and the United States. Both the recasting of Jewish life after two generations in America and the consequent reassessment of values have restored a good deal of the religious and much of the Hebraic element to these schools which in the beginning were militantly, almost dogmatically, secularist. Paradoxically even the most doctrinaire of these groups and one which has stood in increasing isolation from the mainstream of Jewish life—the Communist-sponsored schools—have had to give some hesitant recognition to the abiding religious basis of Jewish life and culture.

IV   The organizational and communal life of Toronto's Jewish community has been vigorous and complex. The most ubiquitous feature has been the proliferation of *landsmanshaften* (literally, associations of persons from the same place of origin), sick benefit societies, and *hilfsfareins* (associations for overseas relief). The list of Toronto's benefit and fraternal associations sounds like a roll-call from the old Czarist Pale of Settlement: the Kiever-Podolier, the Minsker Farband, the Mozirer Sick Benefit Society, the Litvish-Latvisher Farband, the Ovrutch-Volyner, the Linitzer, and others. But the full wealth of Toronto's *volkstumlichkeit*, its folkish quality, becomes apparent with the list of the specifically Polish-Jewish *landsmanshaften*: the Wierbznicker, the Czenstochower, the Ostrowtzer, the Tsouzmerer, the men of Chmielnik, of Kielce, of Warsaw and Lodz, of Radom, of Apt, of Ivansk, of Lagow, of Chentshyn, of Stashow, Drildz, Ozherow, Zaglembia, Shidlow, Slipia—it reads like a gazetteer of the place names of central Poland. The fraternal order—whether it be *landsmanshaft,* insurance order, or sick benefit society—was the order of the day. Louis Rosenberg, Canadian Jewry's statistician, has estimated that in 1941, 57 per cent of the adult males of the Jewish community of Toronto belonged to one or another of these organizations.

Communal life has also been characterized by the variety of small religious groups outside the major congregations. Many of the immigrants who arrived after the first influx from eastern Europe did not join the already existing synagogues such as the McCaul St. or University Avenue congregation but formed their own *shtiblech* (literally, "small rooms," thus, tiny congregations) and conventicles. There was no end of such splinterization. Today within one-quarter of a mile of Spadina Avenue and Dundas Street there are still about thirty congregations, each one fully autonomous and independent of the others—a figure that is almost increased by half at the season of the High Holy Days. The total number of congregations in Toronto today is somewhere in the neighbourhood of sixty.

The social milieu of the immigrants swarming to Toronto may be seen in an unusual way by examining the ballot of the Canadian Jewish Congress's first Plenary Session in 1919. It was not until 1934, in its second phase, that assistance in leadership of the Canadian Jewish Congress came from Holy Blossom Temple; in 1919 few if any of its membership placed their names for election on the ballot. There were 100 names of candidates for 40 places. They included students, pressers, Hebrew teachers, one *shochet,* a dentist, cloakmakers, small merchants, labour organizers. On the reverse side of the ballot are given the instructions to voters. It is characteristic that though the rest of the ballot was printed in two languages, these instructions were given in Yiddish only, it being presumed that those well versed enough to read English needed no basic enlightenment on the how and why of casting a ballot.

Immigrants after 1919 brought new streams, this time from Poland and the Ukraine, swelling the numbers of *landsmanshaften* and *Anshei*[15] synagogues, bringing even newer ideologies—Borochovism, Torah V'Avodah (literally, the Bible and labour), the Yiddish theatre: the whole richness and versatility of the multi-coloured cultural flower that was East European Jewry in its last phase before the final destruction.

In transplanting this, something fell by the wayside and something remained. It is revealing to study the pages of the *Proletarisher Gedank,* an organ of an oppositionist Zionist group, the Left Poale-Zion (for some reason Toronto was one of the three or four cities in North America with an active Left Poale-Zion movement). This group today, as a Toronto organization, is barely distinguishable from other such movements, co-operates with the United Jewish Welfare Fund, with the Canadian Jewish Congress, the other parties in Zionism, and with the Jewish community in general for the benefit of local welfare, education, and causes overseas. In those days (1934), however, it took an intransigent "class-conscious" position. Commenting on the Canadian Jewish Congress then undergoing reorganization, the paper's editor wrote: "Our stand in opposition to all-Jewish conferences and in opposition to the Canadian Jewish Congress . . . has saved the Jewish working class from being yoked into the service of the Jewish 'Yahudim'-bourgeoisie."[16]

This was the militancy and the dogmatism that characterized the *Yiddishe gass* in those days. It applied along religious lines as well as political. In 1912 from the pulpit of the "Great Synagogue" on McCaul Street, Rabbi Jacob Gordon proclaimed a *cherem* (an excommunication) upon the National Radical school (ancestor of the Peretz School of the Workmen's Circle) for having organized a Saturday afternoon picnic in Lambton Park in desecration of the Sabbath.

V   Schematically the history of Toronto Jewry can be divided into three stages of development.

The first extends from the earliest days to the turn of the century when a small acculturated middle-class Jewish community lived in a state of more or less integration with its neighbours, a community deriving its inspiration and standards from a British source and fulfilling its modest needs as a group on the West European pattern.

The second period, extending from about 1900 to the time of the Second World War, is the dynamic stage historically and its effects are still quite visible today. It was the period of the mass immigration from eastern Europe, the time of storm and stress, of economic struggles for the individual and the group, of the perplexing problem of how to transplant the practices and values of Judaism in its East European form (or Jewishness, if the distinction can be made) to a totally new environment. It was an age of *gerangel* (a word dear to Yiddish poets), of struggle between the values of the *shtetl* and of the New World; an age when the social leaders of the *shtetl* became proletarians and upstarts grew wealthy, a period when the foundations of the Jewish communal structure of today were first laid, a period of conflict between two generations who spoke different languages figuratively and literally.

It was, with all this, a period of rich, cultural activity that extended into all phases of Jewish life. The synagogue was left behind in the complex sprouting of Jewish life in this period. In the trade unions, in the Yiddish theatre, the *landsmanshaften,* sick benefit societies and credit unions, existing institutions were given a Jewish form and meaning and often totally new vessels and forms were created in response to the new situation.

A sub-period can be defined within this category—the years from 1930 to 1945 comprising the time of the Great Depression and the Second World War. This has been called the "static" period in the development of Toronto's Jewish population. Immigration stopped; the community had a chance to pause; very little movement took place outside the boundaries set by the population shift in the twenties—west to Dovercourt Road and north to Bloor Street. While the community itself was active and vibrated with all the aches and pains of Jewish life, it did not expand socially and demographically. It was a community which in its own view and in that of the outside world was introverted.

The third period is the one in which we find ourselves today, one of transition from an eastern European immigrant community to a Jewish community composed of persons who have been raised in Canada, who are products of Canadian schooling and Canadian environment, adjusting their Jewish interests and needs to the familiar scene about them. It exists in a Toronto vastly different from the Toronto of thirty or for that matter of fifteen years back. The Toronto whose symbols were the Lord's Day Alliance and the Orange Order has given way to a quite different, sophisticated, cosmopolitan centre and it is in this context that its Jewry is finding its way. The sharp edges of ideologies have been blurred, partisans of divergent philosophies of Jewish life find they are not so far apart. The synagogue has been restored to the centre of Jewish life though it is not the synagogue of a generation back and its leadership is totally different. It represents a suburbanized community with an interest in Judaism much more self-conscious and articulate than that of twenty or twenty-five years ago, though not as confident and as assured of its goals.

The history of the Toronto community corresponds to some extent to that of other comparable communities but has its special characteristics. With its sister community of Montreal it shares the distinction of being one of the only two Jewish communities in North America outside of the metropolis of New York which still publishes a Yiddish daily. Conversely, it has the distinction of being the only community of its size that has no Jewish weekly of its own in the English language. Why a community less than one-third its size such as Winnipeg can maintain three Jewish weeklies in English is also an interesting question. Does this mean that Toronto is so firmly attached to the Yiddish tongue that it has no need to seek its Jewish news and its Jewish mental nourishment in the pale reflection of the official vernacular? Far from it. Yiddish, despite its golden age in Toronto and its long history of secular *shule* progress, regrettably does not have before it any bright prospect for survival in the future.

Toronto's community also shares the dubious distinction of having more than other comparable communities a greater proportion of chaos on the subject of kosher meat and slaughter. Of the sixty reputedly kosher butchers in the city, less than two dozen have supervision; the remainder flaunt the kosher label but give no official evidence of adherence. The history of *bossor-kosher* (kosher meat) in Toronto goes back to interminable squabbles in the twenties culminating in 1932 in a public court hearing (always a greatly to be feared *chillul-hashem*[17]), the repercussions of which eventually led to the total collapse of the *kehillah* structure (community council).

Orthodoxy in Toronto has not completely left behind its East European wrappings. The pattern known in England, and to some extent in New York, of an orthodoxy native and in harmony with its environment, has not yet taken root in Toronto where it is still identified with the Jewish folkways of eastern Europe. Perhaps it is Toronto's long history of congregational splinterization that helps explain the failure to achieve unity in orthodox ranks. Montreal and Winnipeg have had for many years *kehilloth* that have succeeded in imposing some semblance of unified action and authority in matters of *shechitah* (ritual slaughter) and *kashruth* (food prepared in accordance with ritual demands). In Toronto in the early twenties there were two authorities, one so-called Russian and the other so-called Polish. In the thirties and forties each rabbi or group of rabbis would set up its own authority and sanctions. At present the Canadian Jewish Congress is making a constructive attempt to bring together the various factions.

While Toronto has produced a number of distinguished writers in Yiddish and Hebrew and some in English, it lacks the literary circles and groups that Montreal has produced; yet this is perhaps an unfair comparison, for many of Montreal's features have no parallels in Jewish communal life in North America. Montreal's French Catholic–English Protestant polarity may be the key to its Jewish development. It has given the impetus perhaps to a day-school system that encompasses fully half of all Jewish children who get any Jewish education, to large institutions like a Jewish Public Library, a Jewish General Hospital, and a Young Men's Hebrew Association, some of which are more than a generation older than Toronto's corresponding establishments. It is with cities such as Detroit and Cleveland that Toronto must be compared, bearing in mind again its relatively new arrival on the scene. In the background of a monolithic Anglo-Saxon Protestant royalist culture Toronto Jewry must find a way of development different again from that in cities like Winnipeg which were cosmopolitan from the beginning and in the cities south of the border where republicanism gave the Jewish community still another flavour.

Within the historical time-periods which have been outlined there has been wide variation in interest in a national approach to Jewish problems. The "Congress movement" was an expression of the Jewish conscience that welled up in the years 1914 to 1919 and sought to come to grips with the manifold problems of world Jewry in the war years: the need for organization and co-ordination, the collection and distribution of funds to war-stricken European Jews, the need to speak with a united voice for minority rights for the Jews in what were then the new succession states in East Europe, and the wish to confirm and back up the newly won right to a Jewish homeland in Palestine. After the initial excitement and enthusiasm of the war years there was an abrupt let-down in the twenties. Abraham Rhinewine, writing in 1925, said: "Interest in the Canadian Jewish Congress has fallen and is gradually dying. Nothing happened after the first conference. The Congress has ceased to function. Nothing but apathy exists."[18] Interest was to rise again to an unprecedented peak, however, and to remain there thanks to the unending chain of Jewish losses and tragedies in the thirties. The Canadian Jewish Congress revived in 1934; and in 1937 the Federation of Jewish Philanthropies, an organization started twenty years before with Edmund Scheuer at its head, gave way to the United Jewish Welfare Fund, a community instrument that has led the way in communal planning and fund-raising ever since.

This is the tentative outline of the story of a community—a community whose life in its relatively short and modest span reflects fully and sensitively the many impacts that have shaped its development: the Anglo-Saxon and monarchic tradition; North American frontier egalitarianism; the aggressive despotisms of the Czarist autocracy and later of the central European succession states; the many movements—in varied political and cultural manifestations—which drew their inspiration directly from the prophetic tradition, the promise of Zion and this promise fulfilled; both rationalist religious and secular emancipation and a new conservatism that seeks out the past again. The expanding and dynamic community we know today is a community that has experienced a century of full Jewish living and experience and that has accumulated a wealth of resources it can use to advantage in the promising years that lie ahead.

NOTES

[1]This form was applied to sections of Czarist Russia to which settlement of Jews was restricted; they were legally excluded from such cities as Moscow and St. Petersburg (Leningrad).

[2]The song which has been adopted as the official anthem of Israel and sung since Imber's time by Jews throughout the world as a song of hope, which is the literal meaning of the word *"hatikvah."*

[3]Bundism may be defined as a Jewish socialist movement; Territorialism was the name given to the programme of the group of Jews who sought areas of settlement for the Jews outside of and in addition to Palestine; Borochov was the Jewish philosopher (1881–1917) who sought to reconcile socialism with Jewish nationalist aspirations; Folkism was a movement which sought to isolate Jewish distinctiveness through its folkways, its language, its distinctive culture, rather than through nationalist aspirations in a specific territory—one of the principal leaders was Dubnow (1860–1941).

4See the essay by Sidney Schipper which follows this analysis.
5*Chai pasch*, literally 18 farthings.
6The traditional ram's horn which is blown on the High Holy Days.
7Isaac Mayer Wise, *Reminiscences*, p. 45.
8The honour bestowed upon a worshipper by his being called up to the reading of the Torah (Hebrew *aliyah*, ascent).
9For the references to Rochester, N.Y., the writer is indebted to *The Jewish Community in Rochester, 1843–1945* by Stuart E. Rosenberg (Columbia University Press, 1954).
10Cf. the earlier essay in this volume by Gerald Craig.
11Margaret Pirie, "A Study in Social Mobility of the Toronto Jewish Community," unpublished doctoral dissertation, Department of Anthropology, Yale University, 1957.
12Toronto *World*, October 22, 1897.
13*Eitz Chaim Jubilee Book* (Toronto, 1943), p. 144.
14*Ibid.*, p. 154.
15*Anshei* is the Hebrew for "men of"; thus, synagogues named after the European *shtetl* from which the members came to Canada.
16*Proletarisher Gedank* (Toronto-Chicago), October 1, 1934, p. 3.
17A public controversy with scandalous implications; literally, desecration of the (divine) Name.
18Abraham Rhinewine, *Der Yid in Canada* (privately published), I (1925), 238–239.

THE CONTRIBUTION OF HOLY BLOSSOM TO ITS COMMUNITY /

Sidney S. Schipper

At the Regional Conference of the Canadian Jewish Congress held in Toronto in January, 1956, Dr. Isidore Goldstick emphasized that, "It is Jewish survival that has always been the essential objective of every Jewish organized activity—the survival of the Jewish people and the survival of distinctive Jewish patterns."[1] In the same vein, Reform Jews in Canada emphasize that they aim for ". . . the productive union of the best in Canada with the best in Judaism." This can be achieved through their concept that "God-belief is personal commitment and covenant" and thus can be preserved the ". . . meaningful, valid traditions of Jewish history and thought, [adapted] to the twentieth century," and new forms created for their expression. Reform Judaism, therefore, feels that today it is maintaining "a vigorous, flexible, dynamic, progressive Jewish life" that shares in "Canada's destiny . . . in a common effort with non-Jews for social and civic betterment and the promotion of goodwill based on mutual respect and equality."[2]

These were the identical principles and objectives of that pioneer group of seventeen people who began the Toronto Hebrew Congregation, and, indeed, the Toronto Jewish community in 1856. There was one difference and one only. The pioneers, in 1856, practised the Orthodox ritual and knew little or nothing, as yet, of any organized liberal Jewish movement although their Judaism, influenced by some years in England, was more liberal than elsewhere.

Deep within them were the philosophies of Judaism, the basic and original and traditional *religious values* of Judaism. The achieved a fuller expression of these values over the century by changing the traditional ceremonies and ritual gradually as the need arose, so that they could concentrate more on the moral values their religion offered. For them this was the best means of achieving the survival of their people in Toronto and the survival of their distinctive and traditional moral and social patterns; these people came to Canada in freedom and not in flight.

The Holy Blossom Congregation was founded by a mixed group of English and German Jews who came to Canada, not in escape from persecution, but in pursuit of economic success and independence. They came to a country in its pioneer phase, to a country that was bilingual and bicultural, a country that was just beginning to learn how two cultures could live together and build together in strength. The environment was one where tolerance was "built in," so to speak, and where slight differences were partly understood and accepted. It was their great fortune, therefore, that the founding families of Holy Blossom were all English-speaking. In fact, many of them could speak several other languages as well, including French, and so their first introduction to the community at large was not hindered by any language barrier.

Many other of the "culture facts" that the social scientist studies when analysing an ethnic group were common to the community into which they had transplanted themselves. Just as their speech and writing were the same as those of the non-Jewish community, so were their shelter, dress, and occupations. They had similar tastes in art and music, having been influenced in England and Germany by the cultural standards of that time. Their concepts of government and law were similar, and their great emphasis on ethics and morals according to the Biblical code was an added asset in a society whose religion stemmed from the same source and in which neither Protestantism nor Catholicism was a state religion. With no one predominant religion jealously establishing a pattern for all, the Jew was able to fit himself into the community as a quiet adherent of the original Biblical law. It was only when, three decades later, the East European Jew arrived in Toronto with a markedly different culture, a strange language, and in foreign dress that the problem so common with minorities arose, that of being understood and of being accepted in an alien world, which included their co-religionists to a lesser degree.

But in 1856, this was not yet a problem. The seventeen families who began their first congregation were Jews by religion and not by culture. Judah and Henry Joseph were Anglo-Jews whose families had emigrated to England from the Netherlands. Judah was born in England and Henry in Sorel, Quebec, and of course both spoke English while Henry spoke French as well. Abraham and Samuel Nordheimer, though born in Germany, had come to New York and then lived and worked in Kingston, Ontario, for three years prior to taking up residence in Toronto and had learned their English there. Alfred Braham arrived in 1844 from England, as did later Lewis Samuel, the Lumleys, the Davis's, and the Aschers. At the same time others like the Simpsons and the Sterns came up from the United States, while the Benjamins came from Australia. With this nucleus it was not difficult for the new congregation, both as individuals and as a group, to fit into the social pattern of the community to which they had come.

In each case these new arrivals brought with them some money and certain talents which allowed them to set up shop without putting any strain or inconvenience upon the non-Jewish community. In fact, many of the businesses which they opened filled a need in the mercantile pattern of the city. The Toronto Jewish community was thus fortunate to begin with a measure of financial stability and with the respect due the merchant class of that day. Because of this respect and the pride of self-reliance that these pioneers were gradually able to enjoy, it was possible for later waves of East European immigrants to settle in Toronto without causing too much of a dislocation in the city. By the time they arrived, the Jewish community had already become organized into a religious and social group that was able to look after the emergency needs of new arrivals without calling upon the non-Jewish community for help. Indeed, the atmosphere was so co-operative that a large portion of the Gentile community exhibited sympathy and offered financial aid voluntarily through the civic government.[3]

II The first community responsibility that this budding Jewish group felt was for the burial of their dead. In 1849 Mr. Joseph and Mr. Nordheimer had purchased a lot for use as a cemetery and it is interesting to note that in the deed they are referred to as "Trustees of the Hebrew Congregation of Toronto." Obviously there was a congregation before 1856 but it was not until September 7, 1856, that the "Sons of Israel" officially banded together for worship. Then in 1858 the tract of land was turned over to the congregation and became its burial ground. But the desire to worship together and to practise the religion of Judaism as a group, because of the precepts of their faith, automatically made these people assume the first responsibility for communal requirements: in 1858 the cemetery; in 1859 the "cheder" (Hebrew School).

All of the members of Toronto's young Jewish community were well aware of the great responsibility which Judaism places on every Jewish community and on every Jewish person; traditionally, the care of the sick, of the poor, of the widow, and the education of the young are community responsibilities. Indeed, many of these members came from families who, in their native countries, figured prominently in Jewish communal affairs. The Benjamins and the Samuels especially had grown up in an atmosphere of dedicated charity and compassion. In 1859 they set up a religious school of ten children which was, in time, to become a pattern for the rest of the community. In the meantime, more Jews were arriving in Toronto and some of those who were already settled were running into the kinds of difficulty that one meets every day in every group—financial, physical, and domestic. At first these personal problems were met by individual help: cash gifts, clothing, personal advice. It was the custom for each family to invite a new arrival to the city for Friday evening dinner. Many other hospitable services were given until it became too much of a drain on any one individual and in 1868 the ladies of the congregation got together to form the "Ladies' Benevolent Fund" which looked after helping the needy financially. The president of the congregation generally made the attempt to find the newcomer work and lodging but if this was impossible, transportation was provided to another town.[4] In many cases the civic government aided in these efforts and it is significant that the friendly relationship that existed between the Jewish citizens and the civic leaders made this possible. In 1875 Mr. Samuel Stern organized the "Toronto Hebrew Benevolent Society" and it was also in this year that the first B'Nai B'Rith lodge was founded in Toronto. In 1878 the Ladies' Benevolent Fund became the "Ladies' Montefiore Hebrew Benevolent Society," composed mainly of women of Holy Blossom Congregation.

In the 1880's, as has been described in earlier essays, came the first great wave of immigration from Russia. These people *were* fleeing from persecution. They were destitute, sick, tired, and strange. They spoke no English, knew little of British or North American customs; they dressed in strange costumes and had no feeling of equality with other, non-Jewish citizens, having lived all their lives in ghetto-like communities. They had learned to draw themselves within their own spheres and to exist as part of closely knit kinship groups whose cultural and social patterns were influenced only in a minimum way by the non-Jewish community in which they found their homes. In other words, they were geographically Russians but culturally Jews. These groups arrived in a community that was geographically Canadian, culturally British, and Jewish by religion only. These immigrants looked inward, with little reference to the community in which they found themselves, while their brethren who welcomed them looked outward at "their" city. The newcomers were dependents who had to look to their brethren for help. They were soon to become employees in a community where there had been little employer-employee consciousness because the whole community up to that time was more or less a stable group made up of the same class in the same area, a merchant class with status in the community, both in their own minds and in the view of their neighbours.

Since these newcomers brought with them their own culture and their own ritual, their presence in the community gave rise to strains and tensions, but these soon were resolved in the organization of other synagogues and social groups of like tastes and customs, and of certain welfare groups designed to meet the new needs presented by the coming of people who spoke another language. However, because all were adherents of the same faith each synagogue or group had the same spiritual basis for the development of community services, and though each strived to retain its own religious ceremonials and cultural identity, the overall sense of social and communal responsibility was highly developed. Thus where, at first, most charity took the form of personal appeals to wealthy citizens, there now developed the need for co-operative effort in fund-raising and welfare work. So, for instance, arose the "Dorcas Society"[5] in 1883 to make clothes for the poor and to teach children sewing.

The Goel Tzedec Synagogue was one of the new religious groupings. It was formed mainly by Russian Jews but numbered also a few who had withdrawn from Holy Blossom because of certain reforms that had been instituted there, reforms in ritual and ceremony and ancient customs: such as the separation of female worshippers from the male by a veil which was later abolished upon protest of the women; the introduction of instrumental music to some religious services; and the abolition of the sale of honours at Torah reading. In the new traditionally orthodox Goel Tzedec Synagogue began the fascinating, competitive, divided partnership that was to be the spark and the strength of institutional development in Toronto.

The transfer of these dissatisfied people from Holy Blossom was the reason, sociologically speaking, for the original congregation's maintaining strength, since it helped to maintain its homogeneity. At the same time it brought to the young Goel Tzedec group a certain amount of "know-how" and familiarity with the new Canadian environment that was vital for instant efficiency and success. It gave to an immigrant congregation that stemmed from the Russian political and cultural sphere a handy core-group already trained in British parliamentary procedure and possessing a recognized status, assets that were to become of much value in the development of Toronto's other great congregation. It also gave to Goel Tzedec a group who understood Holy Blossom and who had much the same view of the position of Jewish citizens of Toronto, the same desire for common effort with non-Jews for social and civic betterment and the furtherance of Jewish welfare in concert with other Jewish institutions. Had this sharing not happened, there is every reason to believe that an inward-looking, non-English-speaking group might have been maintained in Goel Tzedec which would have tried to preserve intact its old-country standards, to build a more elaborate body of ritual around its beliefs in a manner typical of self-conscious immigrants. This might have upset the existing equilibrium of the Toronto Jewish community and might have resulted in the members of the established synagogue having to justify publicly their beliefs and ritual to a confused non-Jewish community to ensure the survival of their own status. Instead, and happily so, a ready-made group of advisers became members of Goel Tzedec, not in order to maintain their status or to avoid disintegration of the community, but to ease their own conscience in the practice of orthodox ritual and ceremony.

The years have proven that this sharing was Toronto Jewry's second greatest stroke of fortune—next to the ability of members to speak English. As we see in the development of many of the institutions, the approach to community responsibility was very much the same on the part of both congregations and led to an unofficial yet potent competitive partnership in all communal projects. Indeed many of the workers involved enjoyed, finally, membership in both organizations.

III The emphasis of the Holy Blossom leaders upon redefining their religious and social values from time to time; the conscious attempt to adjust their religious practices to the changing environment; the intensely patriotic desire to develop a Canadian Jewish community and not just another Polish, Russian, or Lithuanian group residing in a Canadian city: all these things led Holy Blossom Congregation from reform to reform, including the reading of prayers in English and the holding of services at times more convenient to the members who had to make their living in a non-Jewish milieu. There developed the realization that, through a *personal* commitment to God, the Holy Blossom Jew could be as good a Jew in a modern sense as were his forefathers in their traditional ways. This was the vitality of the congregation, the force that gave it flexibility, and this progressive attitude made easy the sharing in the destiny of the country in which it thrived. With this attitude it was imperative that the congregation obtain an English-speaking rabbi so that the full benefit of its relation with the rest of the community could be maintained and expanded.

In 1886, one of the greatest forces for reform, education, and accomplishment arrived in Toronto via Hamilton, Ontario, in the person of Edmund Scheuer, whose name has already been introduced. His constant sense of the modern, his feeling for the Canadian interpretation of traditional things, his zeal for the revision of ritual and custom to make them conform to contemporary needs, supplied the drive that was to steer Holy Blossom into the camp of liberal Judaism and eventually, in 1920, into the Union of American Hebrew Congregations, the organization of the Reform Jews of North America. In 1890, at last, the first English-speaking rabbi was installed at Holy Blossom. With the help of Mr. Scheuer and Mr. A. D. Benjamin, Rabbi Dr. Barnett Elzas was able to institute many changes in ritual and custom but, most important, he became the spokesman for Toronto Jewry and helped to maintain a better equilibrium within the community. This was the beginning of the present-day institutional structure of the community, resting on an almost paternal desire to make sure that the Jewish community of Toronto maintained an ordered social life not in isolation but in friendly co-operation with fellow Jews and non-Jews alike.

This is not to say that the only influence on the institutional development in this city was that of Holy Blossom. It is simply a statement regarding the basis upon which the entire community developed its services and an attempt to pinpoint the source from which the trend towards integrated welfare services developed. The ferment of reform and revision meant that the spiritual values of the Holy Blossom Congregation would not develop in isolation within the total community, and the development in that congregation of a broad community-wide outlook had important consequences later. Nevertheless, while it is true that this liberal spirit is the spirit of the Reform movement of today, it is by no means peculiar to the Reform movement, but is shared by many groups within the Conservative movement as well, to which Goel Tzedec (now Beth Tzedec after amalgamation with the McCaul Street synagogue) is now affiliated.

It was this sharing that, in 1897, influenced the establishment of the first co-operative community-wide institutions, notably the Council of Jewish Women (dedicated to faith and humanity through religious education and philanthropy), the Anglo-Jewish Association (protecting the civil rights of Jews), the Zion Society (relating to early Zionism), and the Talmud Torah Association (for Jewish education). It was this sharing and the leadership supplied by both Holy Blossom and Goel Tzedec that enabled the Jewish community, through Holy Blossom and its pulpit, to present in unity a memorandum to the Board of Education in June, 1897, expressing its opposition to religious education in the public schools, and to block it for almost another fifty years. It was this sharing that resulted eventually in the establishment of a Young Men's Hebrew Association, a Mount Sinai Hospital, a Federation of Jewish Philanthropies, and a Toronto Hebrew Free Loan Association.

Without this sharing the United Jewish Welfare Fund would not have joined the rest of the community of Toronto in 1943 in a common effort, later the Community Chest, and later still the United Community Fund, since the Orthodox group maintained its traditional attitude that Jews could go it better alone. With the agreement of the Conservative group a vote of the Board of the United Jewish Welfare Fund on April 4, 1943, went slightly in favour of joining in the community-wide project on the resolution that "a non-sectarian appeal is the ideal of unity." This small majority helped to keep intact the Jewish community's membership in the greater Toronto picture.

Without this sharing the Canadian Jewish Congress could not have become the national spokesman of the Canadian Jewish people. Congress, by helping the community keep in touch with Jewish developments in Canada and elsewhere, gave the Toronto group liaison with the national community and helped it to express the patriotism it had developed. Where there are smaller Jewish groups in smaller towns and villages the inter-group and inter-faith relationships even today approximate the happy picture that was Toronto's during its first thirty years of existence, because the Jew, as anyone else in a small group, is easier to get to know. Congress soon assumed the responsibility of public relations which were developed out of the principles of a free interchange of ideas and the encouragement of joint activity.

And finally, without this sharing there would be no Bureau of Jewish Education to supply standards of teaching and a curriculum for all the Jewish schools in the city. It is significant that although neither Holy Blossom nor Beth Tzedec receive financial support from the Bureau, maintaining their own schools at their own expense, these congregations supply between them most of the leadership for the Bureau's administration and planning.

But despite this emphasis on sharing in many cases of institutional development, there can be seen the influences of Reform Jewish values as passed on both by the rabbis and by the lay leaders of Holy Blossom Congregation. For example, the Jewish school system of today in Toronto is a direct outgrowth of an educational pattern developed by Holy Blossom Temple. The first schools were conducted in the synagogue for the education of the children of the members. Although the teaching of religion was the main function, the curriculum developed by virtue of a broad outlook along general lines giving an appreciation of Jewish history and culture and ritual as it exists today in all its phases. This is in direct contrast to the teaching in some of our local religious and Jewish schools which attempt to slant their curricula in accordance with their own beliefs, sometimes to the detriment of the children's understanding of other Jews. Some Orthodox schools ignore the Reform position entirely with the result that their children are relatively uninformed and sometimes misinformed about their fellows. Some nationalistic groups slant their material away from religion and towards politics. It is a fact that Holy Blossom has always attempted to show Reform Judaism as a movement within the larger Jewish sphere so that its children are not unaware of what other

Jews are like and of how they worship and what they believe and why. Because of this liberal outlook, Holy Blossom and Rabbi Brickner were asked in 1920 to operate religious schools in other parts of the city and maintained three schools open to all: a regular school, a high school, and—stimulated by the Zionists—a free school for girls in the Orthodox Hebrew Men of England Synagogue.[6] Today, under the Bureau of Jewish Education, a beneficiary of the United Jewish Welfare Fund, all Jewish schools in the city are gradually being brought together under one liberal and general curriculum and towards a better understanding of all Jews no matter what their ritual.

IV Institutions in any community arise only when there is a great need. With the need comes agitation and this usually follows on a crisis of some sort, often economic. The people then must be united in the project so that they can develop the morale, the momentum, and the operating tactics that will supply the answer to the need. Old institutions often break up in times of crisis to give way to new ones which are designed to supply better and more efficient answers to the problems. Such was the case in the years from 1900 to the First World War. Social planning in these years was simply a solution to a problem of crisis, and crises came often to Toronto.

A great influx of European Jews fleeing oppression and war was experienced by the Toronto community. The equilibrium of the community was almost shattered. There were too many people in need and not enough money to go round. There were too many groups springing up to service the same people in a fragmented way, and these were draining the limited finances in duplicated administrations and fund-raising costs. The Jewish Benevolent Society of Toronto, founded by Edmund Scheuer in 1892, was bankrupt in 1905 when the wave of Polish refugees arrived. The Associated Hebrew Charities, its successor, was bankrupt in 1915–16 when the World War wave of immigrants descended upon Toronto.

The crisis brought reactions from the Jewish community and from the non-Jews. The Jewish community reorganized its "Associated Hebrew Charities." Under the leadership of Edmund Scheuer and his friends at Holy Blossom, and Abraham Cohen and his friends at Goel Tzedec, the Federation of Jewish Philanthropies of Toronto was formed in 1916 "to remove the evil of indiscriminate and unauthorized forms of solicitation . . . and . . . to provide for the COMMUNITY an organization to represent it in various spheres of philanthropic endeavour in all possible directions commensurate with its funds." Eleven organizations pledged their membership.[7] Here was community consciousness based upon spiritual values, for as the president, Edmund Scheuer, said in his 1917 report, "It is the right and duty, and it is just for those who have, to give to those who have not." Charity being a fundamental part of Jewish faith it is not suggested that this attitude was a Reform Jewish influence. This influence was rather in the development of a community conscience for the self-respect of the Jews as a group.

Just prior to the setting-up of the Federation, in 1914 in fact, the Jews were beset with the problem of juvenile delinquency, which was to reach its height in 1922. Here the community, under the leadership of Abe Lewis first, then Ralph Raphael, M. M. Cohen, and Rabbi Brickner of Holy Blossom Temple, reached out to the non-Jewish community to borrow the Big Brother technique and develop it in its own way; there was a reduction in the rate of juvenile delinquency by more than 70 per cent, from 1922 to 1924, through the "Jewish Boys in Training" scheme. First the need was recognized by Mr. Lewis who lived in the troubled area. His successful techniques showed the rest of the community the way and the community assumed responsibility.

In 1913 it was necessary to form the "Ezras Noshem Society" to look after the sick who suffered from lack of care even in hospital because of such difficulties as language barriers. This developed, in 1923, into the Mount Sinai Hospital which, under the influence of Reform Jewish thinking and leadership—notably that of E. F. Singer—but always sympathetic towards orthodox views and customs, strove to maintain a non-sectarian medical service in spite of the fact that one of the reasons for its establishment was that Jewish sick and Jewish doctors found it difficult to get enough beds in other hospitals.

This was the period in which the non-Jewish community, for the first time, got a really intimate look at the truly East European Jew *before* he had a chance to become even partly assimilated into the Jewish-Canadian group. The non-Jew thought him a strange character, the living counterpart of the literary stereotype of a Jew, and so he imagined him to be a heathen. It became the self-appointed duty of a group of non-Jews to save these poor souls by converting them, and active missionary work using relief and welfare aid as incentives, was carried on. Certain Jewish workers, notably Ida (Lewis) Siegel, hastened to the defence. The Jewish community conscience could not ignore the situation and counteracted the missions by setting up training and interest groups such as the "Sewing School for Girls." It was forced to step up its welfare work and keep these people busy so that they would have less time on their hands and a diminishing need for the service of the missions. This was the first major open clash with any non-Jewish section of the community and it proved the wisdom of the original approach to the problem of integrating the immigrant into the Jewish community first. But money was scarce then for the Jewish community.

The same pattern of fund-raising reorganization repeated itself in the now classical manner following the depression and with the wave of refugees from Naziism in the 1930's. The Federation of Jewish Philanthropies went bankrupt and the United Jewish Welfare Fund was formed in 1937, again under the leadership of men and women whose religious ties were in Holy Blossom and Goel Tzedec synagogues.

But it is in the development of the B'Nai B'Rith and of the Young Men's and Young Women's Hebrew Association that we see most clearly the results of the broad community consciousness that was developed over the years. The statements of the principles of B'Nai B'Rith and of the Y.M. and Y.W.H.A. in Toronto read like the principles of Reform Judaism, and it is difficult to believe that this is coincidental. It is far more logical to conclude that, since many of the men and women, and all of the chief leaders, who helped to organize these institutions were brought up in Holy Blossom and Goel Tzedec, and some in both synagogues, they were subject to the influences presented by the liberal minds of Toronto's first congregation, and that the only way they could live was as part of a broader community and by the principles laid down by their fathers and grandfathers.

B'Nai B'Rith proclaims in the preamble to its constitution that it has the "mission of uniting Israelites in the work of promoting their highest interests and those of humanity; of developing and elevating the mental and moral character of the people of our faith; of inculcating the purest principles of philanthropy, honour and *patriotism*; of supporting science and art; alleviating the wants of the poor and the needy; visiting and attending the sick; coming to the rescue of victims of persecution; providing for, protecting and assisting the widow and the orphan on the *broadest principles of humanity*."

The Y.M. and Y.W.H.A. aims "to provide a community centre for the Jewish youth where it will obtain recreation under proper supervision; where a healthy Jewish esprit de corps may be developed under suitable environment and opportunities; a healthy *self-reliant* and *self-respecting* Jewish generation will add credit to OUR COMMUNITY, to OUR CITY, and to OUR COUNTRY."[8] These were expanded to read, in 1940, "to preserve, foster and develop the highest ideals of Judaism and of Canadian Citizenship"[9] and revised in 1955 to add "co-operate with other civic bodies in advancing the welfare of the entire community and in furthering the democratic way of life."[10]

Thus the thread of Jewish philosophy is unbroken even under the influence of Reform Jewish practice. In order to encourage understanding and acceptance by the community-at-large, members of the Jewish community must have the talent of understanding, developed from the broadest outlook. To achieve this they must change with the times, not in basic truths but in surface practices; they must be "flexible, vigorous, dynamic, and progressive in Jewish life," because Judaism is a way of life and not just ritual and ceremony and custom. The Jewish community must be a functioning part of the larger community for, in the words most often repeated by one who was most charitable to all at all times, Rabbi Jacobs, leader of Holy Blossom from 1901 to 1920, "Have we not all one Father, has not one God created us all?"[11] By setting the example in community living, in community conscience, in institutional development, Holy Blossom Temple has served the Jewish people, assisting it to achieve survival with respect, survival with self-reliance, survival with a future and in freedom. This liberal approach is the strength of its institutions and the life of its community.

This is why the present mayor of the City of Toronto and its first mayor of the Jewish faith, Mr. Nathan Phillips, can publicly say without contradiction: "From its inception a century ago, Toronto Jewry has pursued the course of constructive co-operation with their fellow citizens. Over the years, religious and communal organizations were established which enabled Jews to retain their own spiritual heritage, and contribute to the traditions of Canadian democracy. Thus a pattern was created wherein diverse ethnic and religious groups have joined together to make Toronto a great cosmopolitan city in which unity and mutual respect prevail."[12] In this area lies the contribution of Holy Blossom Congregation to the institutional development of Toronto. This was the practical application of the principles of its Reform Judaism.

NOTES

[1] I. Goldstick, "Congress as a National Pattern," address to Fourteenth Regional Conference, Canadian Jewish Congress, Toronto, January 28–29, 1956.
[2] A. L. Feinberg, "The Holy Blossom Heritage: Its Second Century," *100th Anniversary: Holy Blossom Temple Bulletin*, November, 1956, p. 5.
[3] The minutes of the "Ladies' Benevolent Fund" for 1876 acknowledged that the "late and present Worshipful Mayors of the city had rendered valuable services in granting railway passes for those who were desirous to leave Toronto" to try their luck elsewhere. A few years later the City of Toronto made an annual grant of $150.00 to the Toronto Hebrew Benevolent Society towards relief work among new immigrants.

[4] H. Warschauer, *The Story of Holy Blossom Temple* (experimental ed., mimeographed; Toronto, 1956), p. 115.

[5] "Dorcas" originates in Acts 10: 36—the name of a charitable woman. Most charitable groups in the 1880's and 1890's had "Dorcas" committees which later developed into sewing groups, as did that of Holy Blossom.

[6] A. D. Hart, *The Jew in Canada* (Toronto, 1926) p. 107.

[7] These were: Ladies Cooperative Board, Jewish Orphans Home, Jewish Girls' Club, Junior Council of Jewish Women, Hebrew Ladies Maternity Aid and Sewing Circle, Hebrew Young Ladies Boot and Shoe Society, Big Brother Movement—Jewish Branch, Hebrew Free Loan Society, The Sewing School, The Jewish Dispensary, Hebrew Burial Society.

[8] Hart, *The Jew in Canada*, p. 448.

[9] Young Men's and Young Women's Hebrew Association of Toronto, *Constitution and By-Laws* (June, 1940), Sec. 1d.

[10] *Ibid.* (April, 1955), Article II, Sec. 1c.

[11] Rabbi Solomon Jacobs, *Sermons*, Holy Blossom Temple, Toronto, 1901–1920.

[12] *Message of His Worship the Mayor of Toronto, Nathan Phillips, Q.C., on the Occasion of the Centennial Celebration of the Founding of the Jewish Community in Toronto*, City of Toronto, September 5, 1956.

Relations

Wrong /

Rose / Seeley

ONTARIO'S JEWS IN THE LARGER COMMUNITY / Dennis H. Wrong

The changing relations between Jews and non-Jews in Ontario, and specifically in Toronto, cannot be understood without describing the changes that have taken place in the Jewish community itself since the arrival of the first Jewish residents in the middle of the nineteenth century. Ideally, an account of the relations between two groups should devote equal attention to changes within each of them. Ethnic groups sharing a common community life influence and are influenced by one another and are subject to the same broad social and economic pressures. Everett Hughes has criticized the implicit ethnocentrism of "inter-group relations" studies that stress the patterns of adjustment of the minority group while ignoring or taking for granted changes within the majority group.[1] Yet, if only for reasons of space, it is often necessary to single out for attention a part of the whole, and this rather than any tendency to regard the Jewish group as having "adjusted" to a more stable non-Jewish community—let alone any conviction that Jews constitute a "problem" in Canadian life while non-Jews do not—accounts for the present essay's focus on the former.

I The story of the Toronto Jewish community is not strikingly different from the stories of other North American Jewish communities that trace their origins back no further than a century. For the purposes of this essay it is sufficient to remind the reader here of the pattern already outlined in preceding pages. In Toronto, as in Buffalo, Chicago, or Minneapolis, a few Jewish families from Germany and England arrived in the middle of the last century and became peddlers or opened retail stores in the central business district. In common with the other rapidly growing industrial and commercial cities of inland North America, Toronto lacked the long-established Sephardic Jewish communities of older cities like Montreal and several American cities on the Atlantic seaboard. Thus the first Jewish residents were a tiny proportion of the population and faced the task of creating an organized community life out of their own limited resources with only their non-Jewish fellow-citizens and the distant Jewish communities further east or overseas to turn to for assistance.

The former were prompt to lend a helping hand. The first Jewish community enterprise undertaken in Toronto was the obtaining in 1849 of a burial ground on behalf of the Toronto Hebrew Congregation, and it was purchased from John Beverly Robinson, later Mayor of Toronto and a scion of one of the powerful Conservative Protestant families making up the Family Compact. In 1859 leading Toronto citizens joined with the leaders of the Jewish community to raise funds in aid of Jewish refugees from pogroms in Morocco. Christians contributed to the building fund for the first Toronto synagogue on Richmond Street in 1875. And in 1894 such well-known Toronto family names as Eaton, Simpson, McLean, and Massey are found on the list of Christian contributors to the building fund for the Bond Street Synagogue.

The bulk of Jewish immigration to the New World before the 1880's was, as earlier essays have described, from western Europe and preponderantly from Germany and England. A somewhat larger proportion of the early Jewish settlers in Toronto appear to have been English rather than German in contrast to most of the American cities who received their first Jewish immigrants at this time. Statistical documentation of this difference is impossible. However, most of the "founding fathers" of organized Jewish life in Toronto were of English origin,[2] whereas histories of comparable American Jewish communities show their pioneers almost invariably to have been German.[3] American Jewish immigrants were in this period scarcely distinguished from other German immigrants in the popular mind.[4]

The Anglo-Jewish immigrants who played so large a part in the early history of the Toronto Jewish community—the Josephs, Lumleys, Samuels, and Benjamins—had a particular character in relation to the larger community, as has been referred to in other essays: they were probably less alien culturally to the society they entered than any other group of Jewish immigrants to North America in the past century. Toronto, although provincial and even "colonial" in outlook, was British and Victorian to the core and the Anglo-Jews had neither to learn a new language nor to change their political allegiance. As late as 1897 one finds A. D. Benjamin, in an address on the occasion of the opening of the Bond Street Synagogue, urging East European Jewish immigrants to become "Anglicized." It is hard to conceive of a prominent Canadian addressing himself to new immigrants in such a manner today, so conscious have we become of our bi-cultural destiny as a nation and of the continuous leavening of our dual cultural heritage with non-British and non-French immigrants from Europe. American Jews of Sephardic and German origin also certainly advised their newly arrived brethren from eastern Europe to "Americanize" themselves during the peak of the East European immigration at the turn of the century, but in the light of the lofty universalistic claims of what Gunnar Myrdal has called the "American Credo"[5] the phrase carries a lesser connotation of cultural exclusiveness than "Anglicization." Ontario in the nineteenth century was perhaps a more culturally homogeneous society than any in North America with the possible exception of New England. The fact that the Anglo-Jews were familiar with British traditions made them the natural leaders of the growing Jewish community and gave them an advantage in gaining assistance from prominent non-Jews that their counterparts in American cities lacked.

One also gains the impression—again impossible to document statistically—that the first Anglo-Jews to settle in Toronto were somewhat wealthier than most of the German Jews arriving at the same time in cities south of the border. More of the former seem to have established themselves at once as retail merchants without having had to spend several years peddling before accumulating the capital to open a store. The fact that coming to Canada meant no loss of British political allegiance undoubtedly facilitated the maintenance of close ties, commercial and otherwise, with English Jewry. Prominent English Jews, including Lord Rothschild and Sir Samuel Montagu, contributed to the building fund for the Bond Street Synagogue.

The children of the early immigrants often intermarried with Christians and disappeared from the Jewish community.[6] In part this was an inevitable result of the small numbers of Jews: today rates of Jew-Gentile intermarriage are higher in smaller North American communities with few Jewish residents than in the big cities where the bulk of the Jewish population is concentrated.[7] But frequency of intermarriage also attests to the relatively minor differences setting the early Jews apart from their non-Jewish neighbours.

Thus the first Toronto Jews were looked on by their fellow-citizens—and looked on themselves—as a group distinguishable only by religion. And there seems to have been little hostility towards them on religious grounds in spite of the bitter feuds between Protestant denominations and the uneasy awareness of French-Canadian Catholicism close at hand which played so large a part in shaping the mentality of nineteenth-century Ontario. Indeed Jews were viewed with respect as "The People of the Book." The proposal in the 1890's that the Christian religion should be taught in the public schools of Toronto, which was formally protested by Rabbi Lazarus of Holy Blossom and Mr. A. D. Benjamin, however it may have seemed to the Jewish community, was in no sense inspired by Christian intolerance of Judaism and appears to have been innocent of any intent to offend Jews.

Moreover, the small size of the Jewish community and the lack of sharp cultural and economic contrasts with the non-Jewish population encouraged the efforts, outlined above, to alter many features of the Orthodox religious service in order to bring it closer into line with the practices of Christian denominations. Reform Judaism was of German origin and in both Canada and the United States its leading advocates were highly educated immigrants from western Germany, long emancipated from the restraints of ghetto life, secure in their position in the larger community, and disposed to regard Judaism as a religion that was not unalterably at odds with liberal Protestantism.

The stability and prosperity of North American Jews and the close relations they had established with non-Jews seemed to many of them to be threatened by the huge Jewish immigration from eastern Europe that began in the 1880's after a succession of pogroms throughout European Russia. For the first time the existence of Jews with distinctive cultural and social traits going beyond commitment to an ancient and, in Christian eyes, attractively exotic religion impressed itself upon non-Jewish consciousness, and the new immigrants were seen to differ markedly from the well-acculturated[8] German and English Jews of the earlier migrations. With the East Europeans soon outnumbering the West Europeans, Jews could no longer be regarded simply as a religious group resembling their non-Jewish fellow-citizens in all other aspects. The East European Jews were either devoutly orthodox, religion permeating their daily activities, or else hostile or indifferent towards all religion; Yiddish was their mother-tongue; many of them had never before lived in close proximity to non-Jews; and their background, unlike that of the earlier immigrants, was predominantly rural or small-town rather than urban. As Nathan Glazer has pointed out,[9] they were conscious of themselves as a people or nation and not merely as a religious group; "Jewishness" and "Judaism" were no longer identical. It is easy to understand why the new immigration was viewed with misgivings by the older immigrants and seen as a possible threat to their established position *qua* Jews in the larger community.

In many American cities the German and East European Jews for a long time formed distinct communities, belonging to separate congregations, living in different parts of the city, and having few social contacts with one another.[10] In Toronto, however, the Jewish population numbered less than a thousand before the influx of East European immigrants, so the two groups could scarcely pursue a separate communal existence. The older residents, therefore, felt an immediate responsibility towards the newcomers, many of whom arrived penniless. This sense of obligation towards their fellow-Jews, which other essayists have described, was increased by the Christian missionary activities in connection with charitable work among immigrant Jews that drew sharp protests from Rabbi Jacobs of Holy Blossom in 1911. Similar incidents occurred in American cities and gave an impetus to the establishment of Jewish social service organizations.[11] It was during the period of greatest immigration from eastern Europe between 1880 and 1925 that most of Toronto's Jewish welfare agencies and charitable societies were founded.

Mass immigration also coincided with the revival of anti-Semitism in Europe. Much of the immigration was, of course, itself a direct response to Russian and Rumanian pogroms, but the 1880's and 1890's also witnessed the temporary prominence of anti-Semitic journalists and politicians in the countries of western Europe—Stoecker and Ahlwardt in Germany, Schoenerer and Lueger in Austria, Drumont in France—and the century closed with the Dreyfus case, that ominous harbinger of future events. Anti-Semitism overseas made North American Jews more aware of their kinship, although it also intensified the uneasiness with which the old residents regarded the foreign ways of the newcomers.

One can detect something of this uneasiness in the speeches made by Mr. A. D. Benjamin and Rabbi Lazarus at the opening of the Bond Street Synagogue in 1897. Referring to the new immigrants, Mr. Benjamin noted that the older Jewish residents "have always striven diligently to uplift these unfortunate brethren" and he went on to praise the children of Russian, Polish, and Galician Jews for their "wonderful aptitude for acquiring the English language" and for their good school records "notwithstanding the drawback of their foreign origin." The same slightly patronizing note is struck by Rabbi Lazarus in urging the Jews of Toronto to "abandon Oriental customs belonging to religion only by accident of Eastern birth." Not surprisingly, some of the newcomers resented the air of superiority sometimes adopted by the English and German Jews and their reaction appears in the phrase for Holy Blossom already met with in these pages, "the German shul," although by 1910 a majority of its congregants were of East European origin.[12]

The East European immigrants were themselves a highly diversified group. They included not only the religiously orthodox but also a smaller number of adherents to secular and even atheistic political and cultural movements such as Diaspora nationalism, Yiddish culturalism, the socialism of the Russian and Polish Bunds, and several brands and varieties of Zionism. Thus the Jewish community became internally differentiated along lines transcending the distinction between Jews of West and East European origin. And the continuation of mass immigration from eastern Europe until 1930, nearly a decade after it had fallen off in the United States,[13] added new contrasts between older, more acculturated residents and recent arrivals.

II As the first wave of East European immigrants became acculturated to Canadian life and moved up the socio-economic ladder, Anglo-Jews became less prominent as leaders and spokesmen of the Toronto Jewish community. Until 1920 all of the Holy Blossom rabbis were brought over from England and their British loyalties and background stood them in good stead in defending the interests of Jews before non-Jewish community leaders and in publicizing the contributions of Jews to Canadian life. Rabbi Jacobs played a particularly prominent role in this connection; from 1908 until his death in 1920 he was "*the* British Jew in Toronto" and was consulted by non-Jews on all matters touching the life and interests of Ontario Jewry.[14]

The East European immigrants, however, lacked any previous connection with England and thought of themselves first as Canadians and North Americans rather than as British subjects. As they began to emerge from the collective isolation of the immigrant community and move out of the "ghetto" area of first settlement, their ties with the larger American Jewish communities undergoing a similar evolution became closer. Many of their relatives and former *landsleute* had gone to the United States and they had no similar links to British Jewry. Since 1920 all of the Holy Blossom rabbis have been Americans, graduates of the Hebrew Union College in Cincinnati. The 1920's also witnessed the establishment of a Conservative synagogue in Toronto, another sign of the "Americanization" of the Jewish community, for Conservative Judaism is a movement indigenous to North America. As Marshall Sklare points out, "the signal contribution of Conservatism would seem to be that of offering an acceptable pattern of adjustment to the American environment for many East-European-derived Jews."[15]

Since there are fewer Jews in the whole of Canada than in any one of New York, Chicago, Philadelphia, or Los Angeles, it is not surprising that Canadian Jewish life should be heavily influenced by American models. Indeed, Canadian Jews are probably a greater Americanizing influence in Canadian life than any other ethnic group of comparable size. Other Canadians of non-British and non-French origin have, of course, also tended to acquire a primary North American identity; Canadian Jews, however, have, like their American co-religionists, become more rapidly acculturated and have been more economically mobile than other immigrants. In the city of Toronto with its staid British Victorian and

Protestant veneer—fast disappearing under the impact of heavy post-World War II immigration—middle-class second-generation Jews often seem to be the segment of the population most sensitive to the influence of New York City, the continent's one great cultural metropolis from which new styles in dress and entertainment, ideas and attitudes, radiate from coast to coast. The prominent role played by Jews in American cultural and intellectual life at all levels of taste has increased the influence of New York's "tastemakers" on Canadian Jews. With Canada as a whole becoming more Americanized in the decade of post-war prosperity,[16] Canadian Jews have been in the vanguard of the trend.

Since World War II the Toronto Jewish community has experienced a collective socio-economic ascent comparable to that undergone by American Jews somewhat earlier. It is reflected in their evacuation of the original areas of immigrant first settlement—notably the College-Spadina neighbourhood—and their movement beyond even the area of second settlement in Forest Hill Village to scattered suburbs where they constitute a small minority of the local population. Other signs of rapid acculturation and mobility are the decrease in the number of Jewish manual workers and the increase in Jewish members of the professions, the decline of Yiddish culture, and the lack of interest shown by the younger generation in the secular socialism of many of their fathers.[17] Today it is doubtful whether it could be said, as was maintained by an American sociologist in 1950, "the Canadian Jewish community . . . represents conditions as they prevailed in the United States ten or twenty years ago."[18]

III   Social and economic discrimination against Jews in Ontario began after 1910 and became widespread in the decade of prosperity following World War I. The exclusion of Jews from purely social and recreational activities probably preceded discrimination in education and employment. By the end of the 1920's Jews were barred by name from some college fraternities and prestige clubs, and less openly from others. Restrictive covenants prohibiting the sale of real estate to Jews and other minority groups in upper middle-class residential neighbourhoods also became common. Rising incomes made it possible for more Jews to spend vacations away from home in resort areas with the result that hotels and amusement parks began to refuse them accommodation and to advertise their "selected" clientele. Jews responded by establishing their own recreational facilities in the Laurentian mountains and the Muskoka–Georgian Bay district. Most of these forms of social discrimination survive today, although they are practised more covertly than formerly.

With many East European immigrants becoming sufficiently prosperous to provide their children with a professional education, quota systems limiting the number of Jewish entrants into professional schools and private universities and colleges were established in Canada and the United States in the 1920's and survive in both countries to the present day. The first generation of East Europeans were largely either manual workers, chiefly in the needle trades, or small businessmen owning and operating retail stores. Their more highly educated children aspired to enter white-collar occupations in which they would have to work for non-Jewish employers. Barriers to such employment soon were established in a number of fields.

In the inter-war period non-Jews increasingly began to think of Jews as a "racial" rather than as a religious group. Racist thinking was common in Europe throughout the last half of the nineteenth century but made little headway in North America until the first two decades of the present century. The conviction that group differences are rooted in racial heredity won its greatest triumph when the American Congress in 1924 passed legislation restricting immigration and setting up entrance quotas discriminating against the peoples of eastern and southern Europe. Belief in hidden racial differences provided a rationale for discrimination against Jews at the very time that religious, as distinct from social, tolerance was making great gains. The distinction between anti-Judaism, which has deep roots in Western history, and anti-Semitism, which is a peculiarly modern phenomenon, is often not fully recognized by Jews themselves. Recent history gives ample evidence of the greater virulence and destructiveness of the latter.

Mutual acceptance among Jews and non-Jews in Ontario advanced rapidly after World War I on the level of formal religious contacts. The rabbis of Holy Blossom played leading roles in promoting inter-faith tolerance and co-operation. Rabbi Jacobs' successor, Rabbi Brickner, frequently spoke in Protestant pulpits all over Ontario during the 1920's and his successor, Rabbi Isserman, exchanged pulpits with Reverend E. Crossley Hunter of Carlton Street United Church, the first time that such an exchange had taken place in the history of the entire British Empire. Rabbi Eisendrath was a founder of the Canadian Council of Christians and Jews in the 1930's and toured Canada in the company of a Christian minister. The present Holy Blossom Rabbi, Abraham Feinberg, has been very active in inter-faith work and has conducted institutes for Christian ministers to teach them more about Judaism.

Yet in spite of the fact that many Jews and non-Jews believe otherwise, most social scientists are doubtful that inter-faith work of this sort seriously reduces anti-Semitism, which is essentially a secular rather than a religious phenomenon and defines the Jew in racial rather than in theological terms. The most ugly manifestations of anti-Semitism in Ontario occurred in the 1930's just when interfaith activities were becoming firmly established. Signs barring Jews from beaches and amusement parks were openly displayed; newspaper advertisements for jobs and housing accommodation often read "Christians Only Need Apply." I remember seeing such signs myself on the Toronto Island and at Lake Ontario resorts east of Toronto in the late 1930's and early 1940's, some of them far more direct —simply asserting "No Jews Wanted"—than similar notices displayed in the eastern United States during the same period.

In Ontario as elsewhere the thirties were a decade of social turmoil and political extremism. Incidents of violence against Jews were not uncommon. Youths wearing swastika armbands roamed parks assaulting Jews and engaging in fights with Jewish youths in two sections of Toronto: the Kew Beach area in the East End and Christie Pits in the West End near the centre of Jewish settlement. The publicly flaunted prejudice of the signboards and the impetus given by Hitler to the more violent forms of anti-Semitism throughout the Western world made Jews appear as permissible targets of physical attack to hoodlums and bored, unemployed working-class youths.

Political anti-Semitism with its paranoid image of the Jew as world destroyer and defiler of peoples is a total ideology claiming possession of the key to the understanding of history. It became the programme of several fascist parties and groups that sprung up in Canada during the Depression decade. They were less successful in attracting followers in Ontario than in several other provinces. Nevertheless, anti-Semitic violence and political demagoguery are nearly always the outward and visible signs of milder antipathies that have deep roots in the population. Ontario Jews possessed a double vulnerability to prejudice in the 1930's: on the one hand their rapid mobility in the previous decade had elevated many of them into the middle class and enabled them to acquire status symbols previously monopolized by Anglo-Saxons, and on the other the continuation of mass immigration up to the beginning of the Depression exposed the new immigrants to traditional forms of discrimination against non-acculturated "aliens." Twenty years ago one often heard respectable middle-class non-Jews make blatantly anti-Semitic remarks that were repeated by their children at the better private schools and the élite university fraternities and sororities. The social atmosphere of upper middle-class Toronto, while genteel in tone, was thoroughly anti-Semitic, although probably no more so than in several other North American cities at the same time.

The anti-Semitic ferment of the thirties died down with the coming of World War II and in the post-war years strides have been made towards imposing legal restrictions on discrimination against Jews and other minority groups. The war, the ultimate defeat of Nazi Germany, the shock and nausea produced by subsequent revelations of the monstrous lengths to which the Nazis had gone in turning occupied Europe into a charnel house for Europe's Jews, discredited all manifestations of anti-Semitism and demands for legal action against it arose. A discriminatory incident at an ice rink in Toronto in 1946 which was protested by a delegation led by Rabbi Feinberg resulted in a decision by City Hall to make city licences dependent on no discrimination. In 1950 the Supreme Court of Canada invalidated restrictive covenants in housing. The Ontario legislature passed a Fair Employment Practices Act in 1951, the first piece of legislation of its kind in Canada. In 1952 the Lawyers Club of Toronto eliminated a discriminatory clause in its constitution. In 1953 the Canada Fair Employment Practices Act was passed by the federal Parliament. The Ontario legislature passed a Fair Accommodation Practices Act in 1954, banning discrimination by commercial establishments; it was aimed especially at restaurants and hotels. In 1954 Nathan Phillips, a Jew, was elected Mayor of Toronto, an event that would have seemed inconceivable a few years previously. He was re-elected by overwhelming majorities in 1955, 1956, and 1958. Many other recent actions and events which have chipped away part of the edifice of discrimination constructed in the twenties and thirties could be cited.

Post-war changes in Canadian life have played an even greater role in creating amicable relations between Jews and non-Jews than legislation. Legislation can reduce discriminatory *behaviour* in some areas but it does not necessarily affect *prejudice*, the state of mind underlying behaviour, nor can it influence purely social discrimination in non-commercial leisure activities, informal groups, and private associations. The renewal of mass immigration from Europe in the post-war years, however, has reduced the social visibility of Jews as objects of prejudice. The new immigration has included few Jews and, in contrast to earlier waves of immigration, the majority of the immigrants have settled in the larger cities and towns where the bulk of the Canadian Jewish population is concentrated. Awareness of the extent to which the proportion of Canadians of non-British and non-French stock has been increasing since 1945 has led national and community leaders to condemn vigorously ethnic prejudice directed against

"New Canadians."[19] Moreover, Jews now constitute a smaller proportion both of the total population and of the population of non-British and non-French origin.

IV   Little more than a decade ago the shock of Nazi anti-Semitism and its echoes abroad had led some Jews in Western countries to conclude that they faced only two alternatives as a group: complete assimilation involving their total disappearance as a distinctive ethnic-religious community or commitment to militant Zionism and possible emigration to Palestine. Probably only a small minority of North American Jews actually conceived of their situation in these polar terms, but they loomed very large in discussions of the position of Jews in the larger community. The disappearance of the more menacing forms of anti-Semitism and the creation of the State of Israel have reduced the relevance of both choices. Paradoxically, both the recent decline in anti-Semitism and the sense of kinship aroused by it during the Hitler years have encouraged North American Jews to reject assimilation while at the same time only a tiny minority have elected to migrate permanently to Israel. "Hansen's Law" of the different reactions of successive generations to the problem of ethnic identity—"what the son wishes to forget, the grandson wishes to remember"—undoubtedly also accounts in part for the recent less hesitant acceptance by Jews of their identity.[20]

Since most North American Jews now pursue a mode of life that is scarcely distinguishable from that of the rest of urban middle-class North America, their sense of group identity expresses itself chiefly through religious participation.[21] The Judaism of the 1950's, however, bears little resemblance to the pervasive ritualism and rigorous orthodoxy of the early East European immigrants. The synagogue today is almost as much a social and recreational centre as a place of worship, paralleling a similar development in most Protestant denominations. Even Orthodox synagogues have greatly modified traditional practices. North American Jews have moved in a full circle: once again they are disposed, as were the second and third generation Jews of German and English origin in the 1880's, to define themselves primarily as a separate religious grouping within a context of relatively complete acculturation to the non-Jewish society in which they remain a small minority.

In the late nineteenth century the acculturation of the children of the early immigrants from western Europe was so complete and the abandonment of traditional religious beliefs and practices advocated by many leaders of the Reform movement so far-reaching that the disappearance within several decades of Jews as a distinct group was a real prospect. The situation of North American and Canadian Jewry today is quite different. In the United States the emergence of a "triple melting-pot" in place of the prophesied single one preserves and encourages the maintenance of religious differences while destroying marked ethnic differences in several generations.[22] In Canada the post-war renewal of mass immigration has encouraged an emphasis on "cultural pluralism" which has had a similar effect in giving an aura of legitimacy to efforts to preserve religious and some ethnic differences in what has always been a bi-cultural national society. By a curious dialectic, the lessening of external pressures on Jews to abandon their identity and the persistence of covert forms of discrimination combine to maintain in existence a Jewish community with its own separate network of communal institutions.

The informal social life of both adults and adolescents is characterized by a largely self-imposed segregation of Jews and non-Jews. John Seeley and his collaborators have recently provided evidence of this in their study of *Crestwood Heights,* which—it is now an open secret—is based on Toronto's Forest Hill Village.[23] In spite of the disappearance of sharp group differences, disapproval of intermarriage remains strong—stronger probably among Jews than among non-Jews. There is no evidence that intermarriage is increasing in frequency anywhere on the North American continent. Voluntary segregation in informal social life is undoubtedly most characteristic of the big cities where there are large Jewish populations, although one very detailed study of contacts between Jews and non-Jews in a smaller city, Elmira, New York, gives a similar picture.[24] There is some evidence for Ontario, however, suggesting that Jews in smaller communities show a more active participation in general community organizations than in larger communities.[25] Cornwall, for example, had a Jewish mayor from 1930 to 1937 and from 1939 to 1956 and on one occasion no less than three of its nine aldermen were Jewish although Jews constitute less than 2 per cent of the city's population.[26]

V If the point of view that used to be labelled "assimilationism" no longer receives much open support from American Jews, concern over the problem of Jewish survival is nevertheless still widespread among Jewish leaders. It finds expression in much anxious pulse-taking through frequent community surveys designed to discover what "positive content" Jews ascribe to the fact of their Jewishness. And there is still a good deal of disagreement among sociologists and students of Jewish life as to whether the American Jewish community has achieved a stable pattern of adjustment to the larger American society.[27]

There are, I believe, minor but possibly significant differences between the American and Canadian scenes which may have a bearing on the problem of the identity of minority groups in our common North American mass industrial society.[28] The division between English-speaking and French-speaking Canadians and the probable continuation of immigration from overseas which will increase the proportion of so-called "New Canadians" in the population, necessarily commit Canada to "cultural pluralism" as an official viewpoint. The Department of Citizenship and Immigration prides itself on favouring "integration" (implying a tolerance of cultural differences), rather than "assimilation" (viewed as enforced conformity to the majority), of immigrants into Canadian life. Although this approach is undoubtedly more liberal and humane than the attitude of cultural chauvinism often adopted towards earlier immigrants, it may also encourage a certain social distance between groups which enables the subtler forms of ethnic snobbery to survive. Even French-Canadians often feel that there is a patronizing quality in the curiosity about "quaint" Old Quebec displayed by tourists from the other provinces.

Yet neither of the twin dangers to the Canadian Jewish community of loss of group identity through assimilation or, a resurgence of aggressive anti-Semitism appear at all imminent at the present. At no time in the past century have Ontario's Jews been in a more favourable position to contribute, individually and collectively, to the life of their province and of their nation.

NOTES

[1]Everett C. Hughes and Helen M. Hughes, *Where Peoples Meet* (Glencoe, Ill.: The Free Press, 1952), pp. 158–160.
[2]Some of them, however, came to Canada from the United States rather than directly from England.
[3]See Louis Wirth, *The Ghetto* (Chicago: University of Chicago Press, 1928); Albert I. Gordon, *Jews in Transition* (Minneapolis: University of Minnesota Press, 1949); Stuart Rosenberg, *The Jewish Community in Rochester, 1843–1925* (New York: Columbia University Press, 1954). The first two books describe the Chicago and Minneapolis Jewish communities.
[4]Oscar Handlin, *Adventure in Freedom: Three Hundred Years of Jewish Life in America* (New York: McGraw-Hill, 1954), pp. 74–75, 178–179.
[5]Gunnar Myrdal, *An American Dilemma* (New York: Harper, 1944), chapter 1.
[6]Isidore Goldstick, "Congress as a National Pattern," an address delivered at the Regional Conference of the Canadian Jewish Congress in Toronto, January 28–29, 1956 (mimeographed).

[7] Hershel Shanks, "Jewish-Gentile Intermarriage: Facts and Trends," *Commentary*, vol. XVI, no. 4 (October, 1953).

[8] Sociologists use the term "acculturation" to describe an ethnic group's acquisition of the language and culture of another, socially dominant, ethnic group. It does not, however, imply, as does the term "assimilation," a total loss of group identity. The latter is usually the consequence of intermarriage.

[9] Nathan Glazer, "The Jewish Revival in America: I," *Commentary*, vol. XX, no. 6 (December, 1955), pp. 493–495; Will Herberg, *Protestant-Catholic-Jew* (New York: Doubleday, 1955), pp. 197–198.

[10] Wirth, *The Ghetto*, pp. 148–149; J. Jacob Neusner, "From Many, One: A Jewish Community at the Turn of the Century," *The Reconstructionist*, vol. XXXI, no. 4 (April 1, 1955), pp. 14–20 (on Boston's Jews).

[11] Neusner, "From Many, One," p. 17.

[12] For the use of this label in the United States, see, for instance, Norman Miller, "The Jewish Leadership of Lakeport," in Alvin W. Gouldner, ed., *Studies in Leadership* (New York: Harper, 1950), pp. 209, 211.

[13] The period of greatest Jewish immigration to both Canada and the United States was 1910–14, but several thousand more Jews arrived in Canada in 1926–30 than in the two preceding five-year periods. Jewish immigration to the United States on the other hand fell by 80 per cent from 1921–5 to 1926–30, although even in the latter period the absolute numbers going to the United States were over three times as large as those going to Canada. See Jacob Lestschinsky, "Jewish Migrations, 1840–1946," in Louis Finkelstein, ed., *The Jews: Their History, Culture and Religion* (2nd ed., New York: Harper, 1955), Table 3A, p. 1214.

[14] Heinz Warschauer, "The Story of Holy Blossom Temple" (experimental ed., mimeographed; Toronto, 1956), p. 254 (the italics are Mr. Warschauer's).

[15] Marshall Sklare, *Conservative Judaism: An American Religious Movement* (Glencoe, Ill.: The Free Press, 1955), p. 249.

[16] I have discussed the growing similarities between Canada and the United States—as well as continuing differences—in *American and Canadian Viewpoints* (Washington, D.C.: American Council of Education, 1955).

[17] For a poignant account of the older generation's reaction, see Ben Lappin, "May Day in Toronto," *Commentary*, vol. XIX, no. 5 (May, 1955).

[18] Nathan Glazer, "What Sociology Knows about American Jews," *ibid.*, vol. IX, no. 3 (March, 1950), p. 284.

[19] The effects of post-war immigration on the ethnic origins of the Canadian population are often exaggerated, however. See the discussion by David C. Corbett, *Canada's Immigration Policy* (Toronto: University of Toronto Press, 1957), pp. 61–62.

[20] Marcus L. Hansen, *The Problem of the Third Generation Immigrant* (Rock Island, Ill.: Augustana Historical Society, 1938).

[21] In this paragraph and the following one I have relied heavily on Nathan Glazer's *American Judaism* (Chicago: University of Chicago Press, 1957). I am grateful to Mr. Glazer for having let me read a typed copy of his manuscript in advance of publication.

[22] American sociologists have used the phrase "triple melting-pot" to refer to the combination of high rates of intermarriage between nationality groups in American society with low rates of intermarriage between the three major religious groupings: Protestants, Catholics, and

Jews. Thus, it is held, there are three distinct melting-pots in existence rather than a single one. See Ruby Jo Reeves Kennedy, "Single or Triple Melting Pot? Intermarriage Trends in New Haven, 1870–1940," *American Journal of Sociology*, January, 1944; Herberg, *Protestant-Catholic-Jew*, pp. 45–54.

[23]John R. Seeley, R. Alexander Sim, and Elizabeth W. Loosley, *Crestwood Heights: A North American Suburb* (Toronto: University of Toronto Press, 1956), pp. 328–35.

[24]John P. Dean, "Patterns of Socialization and Association between Jews and Non-Jews," *Jewish Social Studies*, vol. XVII, no. 3 (July, 1955).

[25]Canadian Jewish Congress, Central Region, Research Committee, *The Smaller Jewish Communities of Ontario* (mimeographed; Toronto: Canadian Jewish Congress, September, 1956), pp. 22–23.

[26]*Ibid.*, pp. 10, 22.

[27]Compare, for example, Herberg, *Protestant-Catholic-Jew*, and Nathan Glazer, "The Jewish Revival in America," Parts I and II, *Commentary*, vol. XX, no. 6 (December, 1955) and vol. XXI, no. 1 (January, 1956) with Herbert J. Gans, "American Jewry: Present and Future," Parts I and II, *ibid.*, vol. XXI, nos. 5 and 6 (May and June, 1956).

[28]I have discussed these differences briefly in *American and Canadian Viewpoints*, pp. 46–51.

THE PRICE OF FREEDOM / *Albert Rose*

The extent and significance of the influence of a man or a congregation of men and women upon the lives of other men and women and upon their community are extremely difficult to measure. It is even more difficult to judge precisely the source of that authority, if any, on the one hand, and on the other the reasons why a man or a group of men choose to exert an influence upon their fellow-men. One conjecture is probably correct: that both the individual and the group utilize whatever prestige can be mustered for what is considered to be the good of the community as well as for the individual or the group. It is history which may judge this view to be incorrect and this influence to be evil.

In the past century and a half, as the means of communication have developed rapidly in a world in which lack of comprehensible communication has been and remains a serious problem, the men or groups deemed to be influential have been those who have formulated clearly a point of view on the issues considered to be most important to their well-being or future growth and development, and have promulgated this point of view strongly, firmly, and as quickly as possible with respect to the problem or situation which threatened their welfare from time to time.

There are notable examples in recent modern history of a community or nation or even a large section of the world's population looking to one man, a Roosevelt or a Churchill or a Gandhi, for an expression of hope or defiance in the face of economic or political or military or spiritual catastrophe. There are notable examples in our local or national or even in our international communities of a substantial proportion of the members of the community looking to a group, rather than to an individual, for guidance and leadership. Such groups have included local citizens' organizations concerned with civic betterment, national movements with a social or political connotation and objective, and international bodies designed by nations and their representatives to forestall, prevent, or halt war between nations, or to facilitate human well-being through international co-operation with respect to common social and economic objectives.

When a congregation of men and women, families and individuals, who have grouped together for more than a century for the practice of a religion, are considered influential in any of these senses, there can be no simple explanation. It is conceivable, of course, that a specific religious congregation might have achieved ascendancy in the course of time by virtue of the fact that its fundamental objectives extended far beyond the mere spiritual development of its members, into, for example, the preservation of fellow-communicants elsewhere in the world, or the conversion of members of other faiths. It is conceivable, even more simply, that the force of a particular congregation might be a direct consequence of or closely associated with the prestige, or wealth, or achievement of its members, both lay and spiritual. It is more probable, however, that the quality of a group which seeks reputation and effect and has reached a certain level of influence, inspires the development of leaders who place such value upon its reputed influence that their public acts are deliberately calculated. The lay leadership of such a congregation would seek spiritual leaders who would facilitate such objectives through the force of individual personality and skill in external communication, both verbal and written.

There are too many examples close at hand of groups with important external objectives, with many members who are affluent or leaders in commerce and industry, with spiritual leaders who are fluent in verbal and written expression, which are not considered of more than normal prestige in the community, to accept any of these explanations by itself. There must be some additional, perhaps subtle, consideration. Tradition, certainly, plays some part in this process. It is quite clear that in the course of a few decades or generations a group will look to a few individuals or associations for leadership or guidance; it may become a tradition to do so. Yet there is something more; indeed there is much more. There must be clarity of role for the individual or group or congregation; above all, there must be a tremendous and fundamental need for the expression of that role. Roosevelt represented for many people in many countries the hope for revival or recovery from the depths of the greatest economic depression in modern industrial society. Gandhi represented for many people in many countries the hope for a spiritual and bloodless attainment of political self-determination after centuries of external domination.

A religious congregation may represent both in its own view and in the view of those of other faiths, a minority or group point of view worthy of serious consideration. In a century of emerging democratic political institutions and of titanic struggles to retain hard-won liberties, the opportunity afforded to many small groups to express themselves on current issues—groups whose religious faith, or ethnic origin, or political affiliation is different from that of the majority—may assume considerable importance for the majority group as well as for the minority.

In all of these ways and for all of these reasons the Holy Blossom Congregation in Toronto has assumed a role of importance in the community which is understood by its members and by other members of the Jewish group, and is generally accepted by many citizens. One qualification should perhaps be made. The congregation has not had, until recently, a consistent external objective such as is evident in the preservation of the State of Israel. It was certainly deeply concerned with the preservation of its brethren in other lands but these concerns were of a sporadic nature associated with emergency situations. Israel, eighty or a hundred years later, represents in one sense a chronic emergency but its continued existence is far more than a matter of survival for some two million foreign cousins. For most Jews today Israel represents group survival; its development is the essence of self-preservation. But it must be emphasized that this was not a consideration for most Canadian Jews before 1933 nor for most members of Holy Blossom before 1947.

Nevertheless, the representation of a significant minority point of view and the playing of a role continue to have meaning only to the extent that the actors are well cast to the demands of the unfolding drama of the industrial and social revolutions of our times. In this respect the congregation has been twice blessed. For more than a century its constituency has been able to count heavily upon the quality of its lay leadership, their understanding of their position in Canadian life, their assessment of the significance of current issues, and their resolve to state their position as unequivocally as possible. And for the past sixty years this good fortune has been extended in the spiritual leadership of the congregation. The prestige of the lay leaders gained in worldly pursuits has been joined to the authority of their rabbis, whose personalities have been unusually forceful and whose skills in both preaching and writing have been recognized by members and many persons in both the Jewish and the wider communities. Thus has emerged a very real tradition in Canadian life as well as in Canadian Jewish life, a tradition in which one religious congregation emerged as the spokesman of the liberal and Jewish point of view not merely in Toronto, but at times in Canada.[1]

As more than a century has now passed and this role of spokesman has been played again and again, the essential nature of the part has become clarified. It is a role of cautious, alert watchfulness, a role of vigilance. For vigilance is the price of freedom. No concept is so meaningful to a North American Jew as this concept of freedom, for every member of the group is the child or grandchild of one who, or is himself one who, sought freedom through emigration from a society which for centuries had imposed severe restrictions upon his way of life, upon his means of livelihood, and upon his social, economic, and spiritual fulfilment.

A survey of the various enactments of this role will show that this is not an overly idealistic and benevolent assessment of the significance of the congregation for much of its first hundred years and beyond, and perhaps the best way to make evident the nature of the participation in community affairs is to give the very words of the relevant briefs, papers, letters, and sermons as they were presented. This evidence has a further significance, in that it indicates the repetitiveness or recurrent character of the issues which have been and are of concern to Jewry in Toronto, in Ontario, and in Canada. It has become entirely clear in recent years that the major problems in relations come around again and again as in a perpetual mobile to confront the members of a group concerned with the freedom of the majority as well as the freedom of a minority of our citizens recently released from centuries of social and economic bondage. These major issues have been and remain clear: religious (Christian) education in the public schools; missionaries (Christian) to the Jews; satisfactory adjustment of newcomers (immigrants) to Canadian life; the all-powerful state versus the individual (tyranny); brotherhood and mutual understanding of the members of different groups and different faiths; adequate development of the social services in the community. This brief list by no means exhausts the great variety of subjects of concern but a good many of the issues which seem less significant in retrospect were considered at the time to be tangential if not crucial to the solution of the major problems. Several of the subjects listed are the concern of other essays in this volume and for this reason are not examined thoroughly in this paper. (See particularly the essays by Messrs. Schipper, Wrong, and Seeley.)

II The privilege of an elementary and secondary school education for all children in schools constructed and maintained by a public authority at the expense of all taxpayers is an extremely important one for members of the Jewish faith. It is not generations but merely a few years since their ancestors were denied such advantages both in public and in private schools, with the result that it was with very great difficulty that the perseverent few achieved a formal education and perhaps a professional career available to a far greater proportion of non-Jews. For the Jew, the whole question of the increased availability of public education is associated very closely with the gradual separation of church and state in most Western countries. As a general rule, wherever the church and state were closely aligned the educational system was dominated by the established church and devoted substantially to the maintenance of the strength and domination of that church. Conversely, whenever the church and state were clearly separated the educational system was much less likely to be dominated by any one church. In turn, the objectives of that system were most often clearly dissociated from the objectives of any church since, in fact, there was no established religion. When the state offered freely a public education for children of all citizens the Jew was most likely to be admitted without discrimination and with equal opportunity.

Most Jewish persons, therefore, hold the view that it is the function of the public educational system to educate its pupils in secular matters and the function of the family and the church to educate their members in religious matters. The notion of separate schools for the combined secular and religious education of the members of various faiths is not supported, although there are some Jews who have always preferred—and today prefer—separate schools for their children. Most Jews, as well, are not in favour of a so-called compromise solution sometimes put forward by those who believe that religious education has *some* place in a public school system. The latter hold that the religious views of the majority group should be taught systematically to all pupils; children of other persons admitted to the public school may be exempted from this requirement if their parents so desire. It is not always recognized that when the religion of the majority group is Protestant, the nature of the religious views which should be taught is by no means clear.

During the first forty years of organized Jewish life in Toronto these problems do not appear to have been a cause for concern. In the middle of the last decade of the nineteenth century, however, the Public School Board (now Board of Education) of the City of Toronto began to give serious consideration to the teaching of religion (Christian and Protestant) as a formal subject in the public schools. On June 11, 1897, certain members of Holy Blossom Congregation led by their rabbi, Abraham Lazarus (who served from 1893 to 1898), appeared as a deputation before the Management Committee of the Board. Rabbi Lazarus read "a petition against the introducing of religion into the Public Schools."[2] This petition is reproduced in full:

> *It having been brought to our attention that you have been appointed to decide today the question of the introduction of religion into the schools, which was urged by certain Anglican clergymen before the trustees, at the last meeting of the board, we the undersigned, on behalf of and representing the Jews of Toronto, take this opportunity of stating that we view with the utmost disfavour the proposal to make any innovations in this direction. To our minds, the scheme that has been laid before you is in the last degree ill-advised, inexpedient, and ob-*

jectionable, and ought not to be entertained for a single moment. Though we feel confident that our interests are safe in your hands, and that you will not accede to a request the effect of granting which would be to encroach upon our rights and liberties, we have deemed it prudent to embody in a statement the following specific reasons, among others, why the demand ought not to be conceded:

1. If the suggested change were introduced, it would not only tend to impart a sectarian bias to the character of the teaching given in the schools (which is in itself a most undesirable thing, since the teaching afforded in them should be of such a nature as to hurt the susceptibilities of none, and admit of all children participating in it without detriment to their cherished convictions and beliefs), but it would strike a severe and perhaps an irremediable blow at the very root-principle underlying the institution of the Public School, which is that it should devote itself to the task of educating the citizen, irrespective of denomination, faith, or creed, and treat all who seek its advantages on a basis of equality, without any reference whatsoever to religion. To admit religion into the schools is to contradict the national purpose of such institutions—to make them serve private interests, and to convert them into what they were never intended to be —church annexes and State-subventioned mission-houses. For, according to modern ideas, it is the business of the State to look after the material welfare of its citizens, and not to save their souls. It is for it to further their interests and happiness in this world, and to give over into their own hands the looking after their interests and happiness in the next. Church and State must be kept apart. Politics and religion cannot run in harness together. The objects and aims of the two are dissimilar—they have entirely different spheres of action and move on different planes. A man's belief is, no doubt, a very important factor; as long, however, as it does not interfere with his morality, it is his own private affair, which the State has no right to pry into. It is a thing which rests between himself and his God. For the State to intermeddle with religion, for it to attempt to decide the spiritual destiny of its citizens, for it to endeavour to enter into a question of heart and conscience, which are for the holy of holies of a man's heart, is to trespass on a domain wherein it has no jurisdiction. All that the Government has a right to do is to see that those who live under its protection conduct themselves uprightly and honestly, and to adopt measures to this end. Upon all plans and forms of salvation, upon all shades of doctrine, it must look with impartial eye; it must, with regard to them, adopt a neutral position, identifying itself with all,

yet with none, only taking care that the peace is kept, and that the rights of all are recognized and safeguarded. As soon as the State departs from this unbiassed attitude, as soon as it recognizes one form of religion more than another, it forsakes its true functions and becomes one-sided and oppressive. We have only to read history to see what horrors have been produced through the marriage of the ill-matched couple, Church and State. Under the name of religion governments have perpetuated all sorts of crimes. They have countenanced Spanish Inquisitions, Bartholomew massacres, and Smithfield burnings. Never has any good come out of the union of Church and State.

Only when they have been divorced have men learned to live together in harmony. Religious liberty is, in fact, the most precious possession that has been acquired by us in these modern times. Oceans of blood have been shed to secure it. Upon its altar thousands upon thousands of noble men and women have willingly sacrificed themselves. To obtain this priceless boon for humanity hosts of martyrs have perished at the stake, or have been done to death on the executioner's block. To allow religion to be introduced into the schools is to undo the glorious work achieved by past efforts; it is to yield up, in one moment, all the fruits of the victory which has been purchased at the cost of so much pain and suffering. It is to set back the hand of the dial-plate of progress. It is to make a possible return to the conditions which obtained in the days of the rack and thumbscrew and the torture-chamber. Religion in the schools we consider the thin edge of the wedge. It is a retrograde step, which cannot fail to lead to trouble. It will open the door to all kinds of abuses and evils. If once the ferule of the school-master is allowed to be ousted by the cassock of the minister, there cannot fail to come again, sooner or later, those ages of bigotry, intolerance, and persecution which have left a foul stain on the fair face of civilization, and supply the darkest chapters in the annals of mankind.

2. Under the present arrangements, which seem to work very well, ministers of religion, though they have not in many cases used their privileges, have the right to give religious instruction, after school hours, to the children. If, as suggested, a half-hour for religion were to be substituted in place of something in the morning or afternoon session, this would involve injustice on both sides.

If those who did not wish to participate were sent away, they would be deprived of a half-hour of secular instruction which they have a claim to, and if they were given other lessons during the half hour, they would be having an undue advantage over those whose time was being taken by the minister.

3. Jewish children who attend the Public Schools do not wish to be differentiated from their fellow-pupils. They have no wish to draw upon themselves unnecessary attention, nor do they like to be looked upon, or to be singled out from the general body as if they were inferior to the rest. There is no doubt, whatsoever, that the proposed change will be just the very thing that would tend to produce this extremely disagreeable state of affairs. It would result in splitting up the children of every school into sects, it would breed within them clannish feelings instead of fostering in their hearts a spirit of unity, brotherhood, a common patriotism, and public spirit. Instead of helping to blow and smooth over all differences it would tend to emphasize them. In the schools we would have reproduced on a small scale the sectarian bickerings and strife which characterize religionists in the great school of the world outside. In all probability we should have the Anglican children playing in one corner of the playground, the Presbyterian lads in another, the Methodist in another, and the Baptist pupils in another, whilst the Jewish children, like their forefathers, driven from all society with their fellows, would have to wander around from post to post with no corner of the playground to amuse themselves in at all.

4. If religious instruction were to be introduced into the Public Schools, the effect of the innovation would be to defeat the very object which it was intended to serve, for it would result in depleting the Sabbath schools. Parents would argue that if the Government looks after spiritual welfare of the children they need not. Having had the benefits of religious training during the week, the children would have an additional excuse for staying away from the churches and the Sabbath school on Sunday.

5. In the city there are over 180 churches, to each of which there is attached one Sabbath school. If, with all these institutions, the children of a city cannot be made religious enough, the reason can only be that the ministers are not doing their work properly. They are neglecting to duly utilize their opportunities, in which case they have themselves to blame.

Unlike the Roman Catholic minority we Jews do not maintain, demand, or wish for Separate schools. As far as possible we try to unite in harmony and in hand with our fellow-citizens in the interests of education, enlightenment, and culture, and endeavour to obliterate any superfluous distinctions between ourselves and those amongst whom we live. If religion were to be introduced into the Public Schools, however, we should be forced in self-defence, and in order to save our children the inconvenience which would be caused them by the proposed legislation, to petition the Government to give us the same privileges as our Roman Catholic fellow-citizens, who have ever so much less reason than we for their action, since they represent only a varient form of Christianity, whilst we are professors of a totally different faith. This would mean the erection of Separate schools for us; also it would necessitate immense outlay on the part of the School Board, and make it impossible for its trustees to keep down expenses. After a time it would probably lead to Separate schools for each denomination. The Manitoba difficulty would be transplanted to Toronto. If the churches would put more work into the Sabbath schools, the cause of religion, which is as dear to us as it is to them would be upheld.

We Jews open our Sabbath schools on Wednesday afternoons from 4:30 to 5:30, in addition to Saturdays and Sundays, because we recognize the necessity of religious instruction for our children. Why cannot the church follow the example of the synagogue in this respect, considering that it has better facilities than we have?

In conclusion we beg to say that whilst we cordially agree with the clergymen who spoke before the trustees last Thursday as to the overwhelming importance of religious instruction as a factor of education, we join issue with them on the means they propose to adopt toward securing the better attention being paid to it. We consider that the churches if they made good use of their present opportunities are quite equal to the occasion.

Signed:—

A. LAZARUS, *Minister, Toronto Hebrew Congregation Holy Blossom*

ALFRED W. BENJAMIN, *President, Toronto Hebrew Congregation Holy Blossom*

EDMUND SCHEUER, *Superintendent, Holy Blossom Sunday School*

The School Board of 1897 were apparently impressed by the force and logic of this petition expressed in the much stronger parliamentary language of the nineteenth century, and with the support of the members of certain Christian denominations these views prevailed. Religious education in the public schools did not again become a strong issue in the Province of Ontario for more than forty years. Nevertheless, it was always an issue, with those who favoured religious instruction constantly alert to expand or enlarge such arrangements as were permitted and Jews and certain Protestant denominations constantly alert to maintain the status quo. It is worth noting, for example, that Rabbi Ferdinand M. Isserman of Holy Blossom preached on March 5, 1926, during the first year of his ministry, on the subject "The Bible in the Public School." In the course of this sermon he developed a concept of the public school as a unifying force in which differences of race, religion, and social grouping should be eliminated or, at the very least, ignored.

The bible is not mere literature, like Shakespeare's plays. It is the authoritative source of many great religions. Its reading is a religious exercise, and hence it ought to have no place in a public school. The public school in a democracy is the great unifier. It is the melting pot in which religion and racial differences are obliterated. It should draw no lines of caste or class or creed. It should ignore religious as well as social differences. It should and can teach through its curricula the lessons of love, and virtue and human fellowship, and leave to religious institutions the task of specific religious teachings. Having the bible read in it has no religious value. Many parts of it are unintelligible to the child mind and even to the adult mind. What men need today is not more loyalty to the bible or a divine book, but more loyalty to the ideals of tolerance, love and human brotherhood which the bible teaches. The bible must be interpreted if it is to be of any value, and shall a presbyterian teacher, interpret it to anglicans, and a baptist of Jarvis Street to a baptist of McMaster? The public schools, the citadels of democracy, the training ground for citizenship, should be kept clean from religious controversy and religious discussion. They cannot afford to become appendages of religion. They must reaffirm the historic principle that church and state should be separate. Religious teachings are indispensable, and the duty for their dissemination rests not on the state but on the parents and their religious organizations. The reading of the bible in the public school is but the first step in the direction of religious teachings in the schools and their sectarianization, and against it I must utter my warning.[3]

In the midst of the Second World War the Conservative party was returned to power in Ontario for the first time since the early years of the 1930's. Among its most publicized campaign promises was a proposal for a thorough examination of the educational system of the Province. The new Government of Ontario acted upon this undertaking in 1945 by appointing a Royal Commission on Education (the Hope Commission, after Mr. Justice Hope, its Chairman). In the meantime the Premier, the Hon. Mr. George Drew, indicated publicly that he would consider the introduction of a "non-sectarian" form of Christian education into the public schools. The Canadian Jewish Congress, by this time generally recognized as the national and regional spokesman for Canadian Jewry, submitted a brief to the Royal Commission stating the unequivocal opposition of Jews in Ontario to this proposal. In an address to the Central Region of the Congress on January 15, 1945, Rabbi Abraham L. Feinberg of Holy Blossom insisted, as had his predecessor twenty years before, that the introduction of Christian education in the public schools would be a retrograde, if not anti-democratic, step. *We do not resist the efforts of the Department of Education to institute genuine Christianity in schools but we do resist the assumption that a dogmatic Christianity will advance the unity and welfare of this Province. One of the fundamental objectives of a public school system should be not only to prepare young people for a career, but to develop in them the technique for getting along with each other, one of the most vital things on which democracy depends. Failing in this constitutes a weakness by which democracy can be attacked and destroyed.*[4]

It is now well known that the representations of the Canadian Jewish Congress, and of non-Jewish groups as well, did not succeed at that time. In the Province of Ontario for more than a decade religious instruction in the public schools has been obligatory although any parent may seek exemption for his child, and a Board of Education may seek exemption in any of its classrooms or schools. These exemptions are rarely requested. With the formal introduction of religious education in Ontario the Congress has reiterated its stand frequently and continuously in the press, at its Regional Conferences and in its publications. Thus on the occasion of the presentation of a formal brief on this subject to the Premier of Ontario, the Hon. Mr. Leslie Frost, on January 16, 1957, the Congress, still standing firm for its point of view, used again the words of the first submission and thus demonstrated the continuity of resolution within the Jewish community. *In June 1897 a brief was submitted to the Toronto Board of Education in the name of the Jews of the city of Toronto and signed by three distinguished citizens of Toronto of that day, Messrs. Alfred Benjamin, Edmund Scheuer and the Reverend A. Lazarus, Rabbi of the Toronto Hebrew Congregation (Holy Blossom). The effective opening words of this submission were:*
"To our minds, the scheme that has been laid before you is in the last degree ill-advised, inexpedient, and objectionable, and ought not to be entertained for a single moment."[5]

This, the representatives of the Congress affirmed, remains the view sixty years after its original expression.

Debate and discussion have continued without respite on the question of the propriety of religious education in the public schools. In a sermon delivered on Friday, February 13, 1959, Rabbi Feinberg presented a manifesto in which he attempted to summarize the case against the present programme within the educational system in the Province of Ontario. His statement consisted of ten points in which every aspect of this crucial matter as he saw it was explored.

1. Public school religious instruction endangers the health of our democratic system, by enabling a majority to propagate a manufactured brand of religion through the sheer force of numbers, thus replacing the power of right with the rights of power—as though matters of faith could be decided by ballot.

2. It imperils the sacred freedom of the church by shifting to the state the central function of the church: guidance of children in the way of God.

3. It contradicts what Christianity upholds as the spirit of true humility, by tempting dominant Protestantism to reach into public schools against the interests and wishes of weaker denominations who are taxed to support them—although Protestant leaders vigorously oppose similar action against themselves in Latin countries where they are a minority.

4. It aggravates the disease of dependence on the state which plagues our society by seeking from the government a cure for the inadequacy of church Sunday schools.

5. It violates the basic law of child psychology by compelling minority children to choose between participating in religious exercises that offend and shame the spiritual training given by their own parents, church and synagogue—or accepting the uncomfortable role of being "different" from the classroom community to which they want to belong.

6. It imperils the development of a unified Canadianism, by breaking up the horizontal fellowship of equal faiths studying and sharing together, into vertical congeries of separate segments, one of them superior and the rest "inferior"— and by thus persuading some members of minority groups that they must create their own parochial schools.

7. It impedes the effort to foster mutual respect and good will among religions, as symbolized in Brotherhood Week, by encouraging self-righteous arrogance in the majority and self-pitying resentment in the minority.

8. It wastes the precious hours and energy of our schools at a time when education in the West is being confronted with the threat of Soviet scientific supremacy, by duplicating a course of study which is the prime obligation of church and home.

9. It imposes a confusing emotional and moral burden on teachers, especially the ill-trained and inexperienced, by demanding that they teach theological "opinion" and "dogma" based on one specific interpretation of Scripture, instead of "fact"—with textbooks that propound either less or more than they believe, and with enough latitude for an occasional "missionary complex".

10. It ultimately reduces the prestige of religion in the child's mind, by converting the quest of God into a classroom chore instead of exalting it as a life of spiritual adventure—and by abusing the universal term "religion" to define a course of study which is a diluted form of one religion: Protestant Christianity.

III   Immigration to North America was at its height during the years following the opening of the Bond Street Synagogue and until the onset of World War I in 1914 interrupted the steady flow of newcomers from Europe and particularly from eastern Europe. Although the great majority of emigrants went directly to the United States and many who came in the first instance to Canada later moved across the border, a sufficient number settled in Canada to help boost its population from 4,833,239 in 1891 to 5,371,315 in 1901 and 7,206,643 in 1911. As has been noted frequently in these pages, the ethnic origins of these later nineteenth-century and early twentieth-century immigrants were quite different from those of the first three-quarters of the nineteenth century. The newest arrivals were migrants from Russia, Poland, the Balkan countries, Hungary and Italy for the most part, and among their number was a larger proportion of Jews than had been the case with the earlier movements from Germany, Great Britain and Ireland, and the Scandinavian countries.

In Toronto, as Warschauer has noted, the newspapers began to take notice of the Italians, Jews and other groups of recent settlers as the Anglo-Saxon character of the city began to change in the 1890's.[6]

In 1897, the *Mail and Empire* published a series of articles on various ethnic groups including the Jews. The series was entitled "Foreigners in Toronto by a Reporter" and appeared in the Saturday issues of September–October, 1897. These articles were written by the former Prime Minister of Canada, William Lyon Mackenzie King, when he was a young social scientist embarked upon graduate studies in the problems of labour and labour organization of that day.[7] In part the article on the Jews read:

As is generally known, the Jews of this generation come from almost every quarter of the earth save Jerusalem, and there are accordingly Jews of many nationalities represented in Toronto. Of these the Russian and Polish are the most numerous; then there are many from Galicia (Austria), a number of German Jews, and a small minority of English. The total Jewish population is in the neighbourhood of 2,500 of which the Polish and Russian Jews constitute about three-fifths. There are from four to five hundred German Jews and from two to three hundred English. Forty years ago there was in Toronto a mere handful all told. Recent accessions have come mainly from Russia, Poland, and Galicia, in consequence of the persecutions to which the Jews were subjected in those countries. In many cases they were denied the right to possess property, the right of education, and even of residence itself outside of restricted areas. . . .

Education could have no more practical example of its unparalleled service to mankind than is to be found in a comparison of the Russian and Polish Jews with the English and German Jews of this city. It is not in any inferiority of the intellect of the one class compared with that of the other, nor in the habits of thrift and economy which are characteristic of both, that the difference in their present position lies; it is rather almost entirely the lack of any proper educational training in the case of the former and a fairly good education in the case of the latter, that their relative positions are defined. It is surely not an unfair inference to draw that, taking advantage as they are of the schools of this city, the younger generation of Jews will prove to be better than their fathers before them.[8]

Many of the Jewish and large numbers of other newcomers of the years after 1890 settled first of all in "The Ward," roughly the district bounded by Queen, University, Dundas and Yonge streets.[9] Because of the poverty and poor housing this area rapidly assumed many of the characteristics of a severely blighted or slum area, notably great overcrowding and high rates of communicable disease. By 1910, "The Ward" was considered to be a major problem of social degradation for the city of Toronto. In the midst of this area flourished the evangelical sects and mission houses of various Christian denominations, dedicated to the "saving of souls" and, if possible, by the conversion of non-Christians from the errors of their inheritance. Through the provision of various social services, some financial assistance, and midwifery all neatly packaged with the Gospel, a number of conversions of Jews did occur. By 1911, the members of Holy Blossom Congregation were seriously concerned.

Holy Blossom had been led for more than a decade by Rabbi Solomon Jacobs, an Englishman first, in his own view, and a Jew by religion, a preacher in "the Cathedral tradition" whose sermons were attended for the force and beauty of their eloquence by many prominent non-Jews. On June 4, 1911, Rabbi Jacobs lashed out at the efforts of the self-appointed missionaries to the Jews. The story in the *Globe* for June 5, 1911, was given prominence with the headline "RESENTS EFFORTS TO CONVERT JEWS" and the report featured also Rabbi Jacobs' stern recommendation "That Money be Used to Reclaim Drunkards, Wife-beaters, Fallen Women and Loafers—Jew is Happy in His Faith." The text of this sermon was printed in full in the newspaper and read in part:

A strong protest against the establishment of the new Presbyterian Mission to the Jews and against the efforts made to convert the Jews to Christianity was delivered by Rabbi Jacobs at the Pentecost service held in the Holy Blossom Synagogue. Rabbi Jacobs preached from the text, "All that the Lord has spoken we will do," Exodus xix., 8.

"These were the words that the Israelites of old uttered as they stood at the foot of Mount Sinai to receive the law," said the rabbi. "That was the reply they made that day to those who sought to wean them from their religion.

"It was announced the other day that the Presbyterian Church was about to erect a building at the cost of $35,000 to be used as a centre of an aggressive campaign for the social, moral and spiritual uplift of the Jews in this city.

"How long will the Presbyterian Church delude itself with the thought that it is possible to convert the Jews? How long will it continue to collect funds from narrow-minded men and women under the pretext that their hirelings are doing such a wonderful work in winning souls for Christianity?

"The truth is that the entire movement is now, as it has been in the past, a huge mistake and failure. The enormous funds raised for this object go most towards providing a comfortable income for salaried officials or superintendents —generally apostates—who give the most roseate reports so as not to lose an easy living. Contributors to this fund might well take a hint from the reply of Theodore Hook, who, when he was asked to subscribe to the funds of a society for the conversion of the Jews, replied:—'I regret being unable to let you have any money, but if you will send me a few Jews I will try to convert them.'

"The Jews in 'The Ward' do not need any assistance from the Presbyterian Church. They think that the money could be better applied for the improvement of the sick, the lame, and the blind, morally and physically, of the Christian community. If it were used to reclaim drunkards, wife-beaters, fallen women, idle loafers, street roughs, and the Godless element who walk about the city using vile and blasphemous language, and who are themselves led and lead others into temptation, and if funds are still left, let the Presbyterian Church form a society for the conversion of so-called Christians to the true teachings of Christianity as it was taught by the Founder of their faith."

The question of Christian missionaries to the Jews was considered a dead issue for more than forty-five years after this event although a careful examination of the newspaper files reveals that there were sporadic, if brief, controversies from time to time. One such incident occurred in the spring of 1929 when Rabbi Isserman of Holy Blossom severely criticized the maintenance of interest in the conversion of Jews and in particular, the preaching in one of the Presbyterian churches.[10]

Nearly three decades later, in the early days of 1957, there were few among Toronto's 75,000 Jews who believed that the vision of the conversion of Jews in Canada to Christianity had remained in the minds of any but the most fanatical evangelistic sects. It was a considerable shock, therefore, for members of the Jewish community to read in the *Globe and Mail* of January 5, 1957, that the Canadian Council of Churches had received a report prepared by an interdenominational commission urging Protestant denominations in Canada "to tackle seriously the problem of Christianizing the Jews." The report went on to list the main stumbling blocks "in the evangelization of the Jewish people" from the church's point of view, namely, the Jewish emphasis on nation and race, the crudity with which Christian theology is often presented, the persecution of the Jews by so-called Christians and Christian nations, the tendency to ignore the Jew in the community, the price to be paid by the converted Jew and the adoption by the Jew of the Canadian way of life. The report indicated that it saw the main inlet for Christian principles and ideas to the Jews as lying in children and through friendliness in the homes. "There are Jewish people who will not enter a mission or a church but may be reached through the home approach. When an atmosphere of friendliness is created it lends itself to becoming a centre to which other Jewish friends can be invited." The report concluded:

We must look upon the Jewish people as individuals. They carry their burden of sin and suffering and frustration even as the rest of us. The Jew is a person. We must treat him as such. Wherever we find him, consider him, as all others, as a potential child of God.[11]

There is little question that a significant proportion of the members of Toronto's Jewish community looked to the present rabbi of Holy Blossom, Abraham L. Feinberg, to reply to the invitation in this report. In his fifteen years at Holy Blossom, Rabbi Feinberg had carried on its tradition of fearless and forceful expression of concern with respect to public and private actions infringing upon the dignity, worth, and liberty of the individual and the group. Many persons, both members and non-members of his congregation, phoned and urged that he comment publicly. There were numerous expressions akin to personal relief when Rabbi Feinberg did issue on January 16, 1957, a "Statement in Reply to Canadian Council of Churches" entitled *Christian Missionaries to the Jews!* In his statement the Rabbi dealt particularly with the assertion that the Jew is a potential son of God and deplored the suggestion that the friendship of Jewish and Christian children should be cultivated as a means to the end of the conversion of the former. The most pertinent passages of this statement are the following extracts.

A recent report to the Canadian Council of Churches urges Protestant denominations to tackle seriously the Christianizing of Jews. This intensified program to convert Jews is tactless, unrealistic and misguided—however well-meaning and sincere. It widens the gap between church and synagogue and greatly disturbs a relationship which had become increasingly harmonious during these past years. No one denies the church's right to propagate what seems to them the ultimate and absolute truth.

Yet we Jews find it difficult to regard with equanimity the published assumption that we dwell in spiritual darkness, stubbornly adhere to an inferior and superseded faith, and are therefore a prime target for missionary endeavour.

Surely our entire democracy is based on the assurance that every person, whatever his creed or caste, is actually created in God's image and endowed with God's spirit. No modern, cultured Canadian can lightly overlook the implication that he is only potentially a son of God, and bereft of the Divine birthright! Jewish history for almost twenty centuries has been shadowed by the attempts of zealous Christian churchmen and potentates to force acceptance of the Christian creed. From the days of Constantine in the Fourth Century, when Christianity was adopted as the official religion of the Roman Empire, to the baptized but still-barbaric Visigoths of Spain, to the Inquisition, Crusaders, seventeenth-century Poland, the Russian Czars, throughout many generations, literally millions of Jews were confronted by the choice of baptismal font—or loss of all earthly goods, exile, and frequently death. And even in modern, civilized Europe, conversion to Christianity was often the only "ticket of admission," as the great German-Jewish poet Heine described it, whereby Jews could obtain access to a university education, a trade, a career, or a desirable place of residence.

The gentle, persuasive method outlined by the Council of Churches report is a far cry indeed from the flaming pyres of the Inquisition. Regrettably, however, Protestant churches were advised to use "the home approach," and engender "an atmosphere of friendliness" through the children. Are we to conclude that the friendship of fine, warm-hearted, profoundly generous and brotherly Protestant ministers for Jews is calculated as a means to an end—and that they would sow discord in Jewish homes by a kind of benign bribery of innocent children? I cannot believe this was the deliberate advice of the report, or that the Protestant clergy will follow it!

One of modern Christendom's most eminent thinkers, Paul Tillich, has conceded that "by historic providence Jews have an everlasting function in history." . . . That declaration of Judaism's role in God's eternal Purpose clashes favourably, and I trust triumphantly, with the goal set forth in the Council report. Our grim, hate-ridden world needs true Judaism no less than it needs true Christianity.

Judaism is my religion, the best I have ever known, the source and secret of strength, the basis of belonging and well-being; Christianity is best for others. Loyalty to one's own faith, whatever it be, is a foundation-stone of character and citizenship. Instead of weakening a child's trust in the faith of his fathers, and endangering spiritual stability, we might better strive to fortify it.

The challenge of this hour is for men and women of all faiths to translate into every-day practice their own lofty teachings.

More urgent than Christian missions to Jews, are Jewish missions to Jews, and Christian missions to Christians. True religion begins at home! By their fruits, and example, shall ye know them![12]

IV   It would be foolish to suggest that the few Jews remaining in this world are substantially alone or without powerful allies in their concern for the preservation of freedom. It would be even more foolish to fail to remind one's friends and enemies alike that in this age of chaos no group has been as exposed to and as deeply involved in the cataclysms affecting mankind as that body of people known as Jews. The end of the feudal system in eastern Europe, the political upheavals in central and western Europe, the First World War, the Russian Revolution, the inflation and disillusionment of the years between the wars, the rise of dictatorships in Italy, Germany, Russia, and Japan,[13] the Second World War, the expansion of Russian hegemony in Europe after the war—every one of these major social, economic, and political revolutions has affected drastically or taken its toll of Jewish lives. The destruction has been in far greater proportions than that suffered by any nation, any ethnic group, any religious grouping. Seven million Russian losses from 1941 to 1945; 100,000 Japanese dead in the first atomic explosion; thousands of Polish, Dutch, Belgian, and French casualties at the hands of German military and occupation forces: yet each of these catastrophes involved a small proportion of the total population, a mere 4 to 5 per cent at most in the first example, often quoted by postwar Russian leaders.

Jewish concern with the social, economic, and political instability of mankind and its institutions may be better understood in the simple facts of Jewish population. In 1938 it was estimated that there were approximately 16,700,000 Jews in the world, nearly 60 per cent of whom were in Europe, 32 per cent in North America. At least 6,000,000 lost their lives during the next eight years. In 1954 the total Jewish population was estimated at a mere 11,600,000, although this did represent some recovery from the little more than 10,000,000 considered alive when the Second World War closed. Yet approximately 2,500,000 of those remaining live in the Soviet Union and are considered by many Jews as lost. Only 29 per cent of the recent estimate resided in Europe (including the United Kingdom) and slightly more than half resided in North America.

It is not simply a matter of post-mortem concern which motivates most Jews to fear, despise, and combat fiercely the threat to freedom wherever and howsoever posed, and, in particular, the threat raised by the increasing powers of the state and the declining significance of the individual over the past century. Judaism rests upon a fundamental belief in the dignity and worth of the individual. Judaism must widen its concern to include the freedom of all mankind. Conversely, it has been said that the political and economic freedoms of the peoples of many nations have varied directly with the political and economic freedoms accorded to the members of this small minority of their population. Thus Jews, in Germany, Poland, and Russia, were always a convenient scapegoat to explain away the loss of freedom. The convenience of potential tyrants has always been assisted by the disingenuous exposure of Jews: by segregation of residence, by limitation of occupation, by nature and place of worship, even by name.

In Canada, which was one of the principal beneficiaries of the flight and export of bodies and brains, of hewers of wood and masters of talent, the number of Jews rose from 6,414 in 1891 to 16,401 in 1901 and 74,564 in 1911. At the outbreak of the First World War, therefore, the Canadian Jewish community constituted a shade more than 1 per cent of all Canadians. (In Toronto, the Jewish population of 1,425 in 1891 reached 3,090 in 1901 and 18,300 in 1911.) The first major test of this minor facet of Canadian life came with the war. With Great Britain at war in August, 1914, Canada was at war, and all its people, whatever their length of residence or ethnic or national origin, were expected as a simple matter of course to respond, if not as soldiers, then as workers and loyal citizens.

Canadian and Toronto Jewry today, in the light of the changed status of Canada in international and Commonwealth affairs, would find it difficult to understand the crucial position of Rabbi Solomon Jacobs of Holy Blossom in 1914. He was the spiritual leader of the oldest Jewish congregation in Ontario, the most Anglo-Saxon portion of the British possessions and dominions in North America. It is on record that Rabbi Jacobs had warned in his sermons of the German threat to Britain long before 1914. Once Canada was at war he threw his substantial prestige behind the Canadian war effort on behalf of Great Britain. His emphasis on the importance of the British connection and the need for an Allied victory may now be seen as a two-edged sword. On one hand Rabbi Jacobs sincerely believed that vast numbers of men were promised freedom through the spread of democratic British parliamentary institutions; on the other, he knew from personal experience that members of his faith were more secure, and likely to remain free to live and to grow within the lands of the present British Commonwealth of Nations and in the United States of America than anywhere else in the world of his day.

Within fifteen years of the end of war, however, the Jews of Germany and Europe faced the most serious threat to freedom and to life itself since their forerunners faced the exigencies of Biblical times. Even the Russian pogroms of the late nineteenth century paled into insignificance before the threats of mass extermination put forth by Adolf Hitler and ultimately carried out between 1938 and 1945 by the most insensate killers in recorded history. At Holy Blossom, Rabbi Maurice N. Eisendrath, who had come from the United States in 1930, lashed out at the incipient totalitarian movements long before most Canadians were even aware of the fact that what happened in Europe and what might happen to the 600,000 Jews in Germany were of the slightest concern to them. Throughout the decade of depression, war, and preparation for total war, Jewish leaders raised the alarm because they knew instinctively that the threat of mass extermination to a small minority could no more be contained than the weapons of mass destruction which were being developed. Within a matter of five or six years they had the wry satisfaction of dying in the knowledge that Catholics, Protestants, Poles, Frenchmen, Dutch, and Englishmen, not to mention Americans, were all in mortal danger of slavery "for the next thousand years," as Hitler proclaimed.

By 1938 Rabbi Eisendrath apparently was sufficiently depressed to preach on the subject "World without Jews." He was not the first or last to pose the question, "What would it avail the world to be rid of its Jews?" What social problems would the mass extermination of six million or even sixteen million solve? What economic or political problems? What hungry children in India or China would be fed if not one Jew remained? What boundary disputes would vanish, what national sovereignty would be bolstered, what charges of imperialism or colonialism dispelled?

... it is the Nazis' proudest boast that people and government are in perfect accord; that the masses and the men at the helm of the state are at one in believing that the plundering of innocent men and women, the desecration of synagogues, the starvation of whole communities of Jews, the marching off to concentration camps of individuals whose only sin consists in the carelessness with which they have chosen their grandmothers, that the murder of harmless youths and maidens, as they are being murdered to-day and will be murdered in increasing numbers in the days immediately ahead; that all of this barbarism and savagery are justified as long as they are the means to that sublimest Nazi end—the elimination of the last lingering Jew from the German realm.

... it is not my purpose ... to indulge any further in such denunciation of this unparalleled brutality. ... It is with an altogether different theme ... that I would deal ... the theme which would consider, as frankly as possible, whether humanity would be the worse or the better off if we were suddenly confronted with the realization of the Nazis' fondest dream: a world without Jews.

... if only we recognize how manifold and precious have been Israel's gifts to the whole of humankind! If only we perceive how inescapable would be our reversion to the right of might and the rule of brute force if we purge from our life our Judeo-Christian morality; if only we understood how dismal and dark, how impoverished would be any future without Jews, without a people from whose loins have sprung a Moses, a Jeremiah, a Jesus, a Paul, a Spinoza ... without that Jewish spirit which has given mankind its God, its Scriptures, its Religious Liturgy, its Moral Code, which loyal, faithful Jews have kept ablaze through three thousand tragedy-ridden years, and which a stubborn, stiffnecked people do not propose to relinquish now, no matter how strait the gate nor how charged with punishment and terror may be their scroll. ... .[14]

In the light of history, then, it is surely not difficult to understand the uneasiness and the dismay with which the American and Canadian Jewish communities generally have viewed the revivification of the power and significance of Germany in world affairs, even though that country is divided between East and West.

Thus in the early years after the Second World War, Rabbi Feinberg, who had come to Canada from the United States late in 1943, urged Canadian and Western leaders to avoid the trap of building up a new Germany as a feeble defence against Russia and at the same time urged Canadians not to reject out-of-hand any and all Russian pleas and notes and letters urging conference, discussion and debate. This point of view, that talking and listening—forever if necessary—may be the only thing that will save us, is now, years later, in some favour in Canada. In the course of a number of warnings, the Rabbi has reminded Canadians of the threats he has seen to be inherent in the revival of German, and Nazi, power. In November, 1951, he emphasized that ex-Nazis were back on the scene and preached need for vigilance.

Jews must forgive the German people, and leave them to the verdict of history and the judgment of God, Who alone may condemn his children. The teaching of Judaism bids us forgive; the tradition of the Jewish folk demands it. Despite untold suffering from man's inhumanity, the Jewish mind has never fashioned a hell of torment, even for Hitlers. Vengeance is reserved for the Lord, but we Jews cannot forget. It is our duty to warn the world of the potential capacity of the German nation for barbarism. We are the signal station of danger.[15]

In the past few years such warnings have become a regular clarion call.[16]

V The price of freedom is eternal vigilance, and also courage. This is the essence of the voice of Holy Blossom as heard for more than a century. At the time of Passover 1957, Rabbi Feinberg summed up the theme of this historical account in an essay entitled "To Be Free, Be Brave," reproduced here in full; in it he drew attention to the meaning of the Passover story for the freedom of all peoples.

Tomorrow evening, Jews throughout the world, in home and synagogue, will sit down to the ritualistic Seder meal (which according to New Testament scholars, was the occasion of the Last Supper), to commemorate the deliverance of the Children of Israel from Egypt 3,500 years ago—the first mass revolt against oppression in human history.

Although the story of that ancient Exodus revolves about the Israelites, its meaning has been for all time and space and peoples. In fact, as the climactic expression of Passover, the 250 persons at the Seder "family" in Holy Blossom Temple will read from the prayer-book: "Soon may God cause the glad tidings of redemption to be heard in all lands, so that all mankind, freed from violence and from wrong, may celebrate the universal Passover in the name of our God of freedom." "God of freedom!" ... *The Passover prayers again and again name God as the author of the redemption from Egypt; even Moses, the titanic leader and legislator, is deliberately ignored—so that the passion for, and pursuit of, freedom shall be identified as divine. The first of the Ten Commandments established the entire basis for the Moral Law in the categorical statement that God "brought you forth from the house of bondage!"*

FREEDOM GOD-GIVEN   *Freedom, then, is a right guaranteed by Deity. Canadians are free and equal not because the British North America Act protects them through a Supreme Court in Ottawa, citizens of the United States are free and equal not because the Constitution is upheld by a Supreme Court in Washington—but because both, like all people everywhere, are so regarded by the Supreme Will of the Universe! Words or acts of political governments cannot grant liberty in a creature already free from birth by his inherent nature, as the child of a God of freedom—and they may not take liberty away. It is the word: "in the image of God created He him." The first verses of the Bible of Western civilization are the Declaration of the Rights of Man; all else is footnote and commentary.*

That is why church and synagogue must not look the other way when people are herded into concentration camps, hounded by witch-hunters, handled like an inanimate commodity and humiliated by race discrimination. ... And that is why the fight for freedom is an act of religion—the fulfilment of God's mandate for man and His spirit within man.

IT'S HUMAN STRUGGLE   *The struggle for freedom must be waged by moral and spiritual forces within the human being himself—those powers which link him in partnership with God. It cannot be delegated to a United Nations, such bodies, as we now realize, degenerate into loud gongs for self-righteous oratory, instruments of intrigue for power blocs, gymnasia for legalistic acrobats like Dag Hammarskjold, and an opportunity for recently liberated nations to get revenge on "imperialists." ...*

Freedom cannot be assured by inquisitorial blood-hounds tracking down "Communist spies" to their idealistic adolescent indiscretions on a college campus twenty years ago. The strategy of slander generates fear, not freedom, and disillusionment with, not zeal for, democracy. And it certainly does not derive from God, in whose sight the murder of a man's good name is little less than the destruction of his life.

Freedom is not to be won by war. The method of war is rigid regimentation, man as a means, not an end—and the effect of war must be the widespread ruin that converts everything but sheer physical survival into an expendable luxury.

Freedom can be secured only by the vigilance and valor of ourselves—the courage and consecration of the individual who knows that rebellion against tyrants is obedience to God. Freedom cannot be inherited from our forefathers or bequeathed to our children. In every generation men will arise who thirst for personal power through the subjection of others—and in every generation the aroused will of common people must stop them. As Byron said, "who would be free himself must strike the blow!"

We shall plan and pay—by hard thinking that disdains the siren voice of propaganda, by scorning to accept Munich-style appeasement of international brigands as a convenient escape from crisis, by sharing our plenty with the ill-fed, ill-clothed and ill-led two-thirds of mankind—and by remembering that we can't resign from the human race.

These may, I humbly suggest, be the outline of a work sheet for fighters for freedom in a world which requires that we be brave, to be free![17]

NOTES

[1]It is not intended in this essay to suggest that Holy Blossom Congregation and its lay and spiritual leaders were the only and most influential spokesmen for the Jewish community, although in the first half-century this was probably true. The influence of later congregations and other members of the Jewish community is clearly recognized. Nevertheless, it is the intention to delineate and clarify the very significant contribution of the members of Holy Blossom.

[2]*Daily Mail and Empire* (Toronto), June 12, 1897.

[3]Holy Blossom Congregation, *Weekly Bulletin*, vol. I, no. 23, March 12, 1926.

[4]*Toronto Daily Star*, January 16, 1945.

[5]Submission to the Honourable Leslie M. Frost, Prime Minister of Ontario, by the Canadian Jewish Congress, Central Region, January 16, 1957, mimeographed, p. 1.

[6]Heinz Warschauer, *The Story of Holy Blossom Temple* (experimental ed., mimeographed; Toronto, 1956), p. 195.

[7]R. MacGregor Dawson, *William Lyon Mackenzie King: A Political Biography*, vol. I, *1874–1923* (University of Toronto Press, 1958), p. 65.

[8]As quoted in Warschauer, *Holy Blossom Temple*, pp. 195–200.

[9]Cf. Bureau of Municipal Research, "What is the Ward Going to do with Toronto?" Toronto, December, 1918.

[10]See, for instance, the *Globe* (Toronto), April 1, 1929.

[11]*Globe and Mail* (Toronto), January 5, 1957, p. 11.

[12] Holy Blossom Temple, *Christian Missionaries to the Jews*, a Statement in Reply to Canadian Council of Churches, Jan. 16, 1957, mimeographed.

[13] The events of those years recall Maurice Samuel's well-known apocryphal story of the Japanese dictator cabling to Hitler, "Please send us some Jews so that we may have a pogrom."

[14] Maurice N. Eisendrath, *Holy Blossom Pulpit*, volume VIII, pp. 3, 4, 15–16.

[15] *Globe and Mail* (Toronto), November 10, 1951.

[16] See, for instance, the *Telegram* (Toronto), July 31, 1957.

[17] *Ibid.*, April 14, 1957.

SOME RADICAL PROBLEMS OF INTERGROUP RELATIONS /

John R. Seeley

Two outstanding follies beset the human adventure: the setting forth on enterprises inherently impossible of accomplishment, and the failure for fear of failure to embark on those that could hardly fail to succeed. These are the analogues in action to the statistician's "errors of the first and second kinds," and it is the business of science, wisdom, and sensibly expended sweat to help us minimize the risks that attend any action or any inaction of any sort or kind at all.

Errors of the first kind are the peculiar, though not exclusive, risk in North America. It is here that a quite incredible fall of luck—a vast and rich continent needing only to be seized from a small and defenceless indigenous population—together with some good management in the adaptation of European ideas to American circumstances, has resulted in a peculiar bent of thought that either is or is a large part of "the American way," common at least to Canada and the United States. This bent lies so markedly in the direction of unwarranted optimism together with some understandable predilection for avoiding examination of the ground upon which the optimism rests, that the ascription by Europeans to Americans of a "juvenile" or "adolescent" view of life is no more unjust than the converse ascription by Americans to Europeans of a "tired" or "old world" outlook.[1] In any case, if one danger rather than another needs attention here, it is the danger of unwarranted optimism on unexamined premises.

In nothing does this optimism manifest itself more blatantly perhaps than in the North American view of man and his possibilities, whether men be considered jointly in their interaction—as a society—or severally in their isolation—as individuals. The key term in the optimism is "management" just as "management," more particularly "man management" (or, more honestly, man-manipulation), is the key function in the society. With rare exceptions, Americans—at least those of the audible and decision-making classes—seem to believe that the major problems that confront man can by suitable management be managed into solution. The attitude suggests, if it does not rest upon, the "oceanic feeling" that is said to characterize the infant ego: the conviction—if one may use that word for something so nearly unexamined—that there are no restraints upon human action, that there is in effect no such thing as "the human condition."

It is difficult to doubt that experience has confirmed North America in its chosen view: the forests have indeed been felled, the plains laid waste, the natives virtually exterminated, the rivers harnessed, the cities birthed—and, on that basis, the most fabulous outpouring of goods the world has ever seen, initiated, multiplied, elaborated, and perhaps made so secure that an ever-more-abundant economy, like an ever-expanding universe, is a more reasonable assumption than any likely competitor. Indeed, as theoreticians have pointed out long since, and as the businessmen of the present generation have with some astonishment learned, the economic problem is no longer the problem of production, but the problem of consumption: no longer whether the food can be brought to the children's mouths, but rather whether the children can be brought to stomach what there is to be embouched. Even though this super-abundance poses problems which are as yet unsolved, it is, taken by itself, no inconsiderable accomplishment. And this outcome is, moreover, in large part a product of the genius for organization, that talent for management, that exuberant optimism on which doubt is, in this paper, seriously to be directed.

It is all too natural to assume that what can be done with goods—has been done with goods, rather—can be done with men. Men, like metals, are resistant, it is true, refractory, rough in their more original stages, but surely also elastic, malleable, formable, and capable of utilization. There were difficulties at times with materials (and a few remain), but by and large the secrets were extracted, the refractorinesses forced, and the resistances overborne. Who is to say that the same view as was taken towards materials, may, if taken towards men, with the same ingenuity and determination, not make possible the "reconstruction of man and society," and open up for immediate exploitation in time (rather than contemplation for eternity) a species of paradise in which individual and society, desire and satisfaction, need and satiation would coexist in unbroken harmony? The possibility of such a paradise, or any reasonable facsimile thereof, is not lightly to be foreclosed—if indeed it is a possibility.

At this historic instant it is not only *possible* to hold such views, it is almost necessary—necessary, that is, unless the goal of an ever-expanding economy is to be abandoned just as it is first, now, within human grasp. For, as already pointed out, the economy now rests on ever increasing consumption; and it seems, on the basis of experience so far, that men's acquisitive propensities are not "naturally" unlimited, that accordingly desire must be "stimulated" not to say created, that this requires a science of man-management and a Madison Avenue soldiery to serve it, and indeed that the planned reconstruction of man and society is not only upon us but well under way.[2] This "science" of man-management, whether turned to immediately good ends or to bad—the selling of goods; the vending of a "father figure" President; the bestowal on donors to charitable funds of "an opportunity to give"; the "reduction of intergroup tensions"; teaching parents, themselves under suitable management by experts, to manage their children—is one in its assumptions, one in its methods, confusion and probably ultimate fateful impact.

The particular species of man-management to be examined in the rest of this paper is the field marked out by "intergroup relations." It has its own peculiarities, and it has interest and importance in its own right. But the examination may also serve, we hope, to raise questions in the mind of the reader about the whole set of methods that embrace present-day orientations and procedures in everything from selling soap to winning elections. Let us now turn to "intergroup relations" as such.

Unless discussion is to be merely a sort of patter under cover of which we propose to do what we propose to do anyway[3]—and much, if not most, discussion does serve this no doubt "useful" purpose—we require, even more than we need "factual information," some clarity as to what it is that is being talked about, and some clearness about the possible or supposed relationships from which the discussion proceeds. It cannot be said that the field of intergroup relations has been notorious for such clarity, and without wishing to underestimate the part played by "cussedness" or ignorance in the refractory human material, it might still safely be asked whether want of clarity has not contributed as much as anything to the lack of any sensible progress in these matters since the Age of Enlightenment—or, indeed, perhaps since the age of Greece or Rome. Such clarity undoubtedly requires the exercise of a procedure alien to the short-run pragmatism[4] which is the dominant American thoughtway and the only distinctive American contribution to the Philosophic Conversation; but surely, on the basis of the pragmatic assumptions themselves, if pragmatism does not "work," we should abandon it!

At a most elementary level, it does not seem clear from the vast volume of literature on the subject nor the still more clamorous spate of speech, whether the intergroup relations programme, whatever it is to be, is to address itself to thought, feeling, or action, to any two of them, or to all three. If to thought and feeling, to conscious or unconscious levels or both? If to action, to essentially private acts, to those acts which are only public in the sense that we cannot conceal them, or to those acts that are most fully public in the sense that they are, are intended to be, and clearly embody public policy? And within each of these categories of possibility, are we aiming at "positive" or merely "counter negative" goals: the cessation or diminution, for instance, of mutual openly warlike acts or the initiation or augmentation of a system of designed mutual gratification or benefit?

While there are a few among the philosophers and operators in the field who will explicitly elect for one or other of these possibilities, a more common reply to the question "Which?" is the reply of the child before Santa Claus: "Why, all of course." And even among those prepared to return a decently limited answer to "Which?" most rest their narrowed choice on an equally unexamined set of premises as to the wisdom of "one step at a time,"[5] unexamined both as to whether their total agenda can be at all accomplished a step at a time, and, even assuming so, as to what is the order (and minimal magnitude) of steps required to accomplish the purpose.

Those who blithely elect for "all" take as an underlying implicit assumption a universe in which one might say, in the language of the statistician, that all goods (or all "spiritual" or moral goals) are "positively correlated," that is, that any increase in the supply of one will most commonly be attended by an increase in the supply of all others. This is a happy thought, indeed a possible source of boundless comfort. But is this correlation, in fact, generally the case, and if so with reference to what phenomena? And if it is not true, to what incredible wastes and follies may we not be committing ourselves upon the basis of assuming its verity?

Is the assumption, indeed, credible—most especially with reference to human relationships? We all know, surely, instances to the contrary. In reference to all matters material, we know from economics that every good has its price, and from mechanics that every output requires its proportioned input, that is, there are no "free" goods, no happy "bonuses," no organization without disorganization, no creation without destruction, no having of anything except at the cost of something else, no "positive correlations." In matters less material, in psychology for instance, for any given individual at any given time, if we are happily able by some method (e.g., hypnosis or other suggestion) to secure the abolition of some symptom of psychological distress (e.g., hysterical blindness), we are likely, as often as not, to be able to observe shortly the appearance of a new symptom (e.g., headaches or paralysis) such that "the last state of that man is worse than the first"—for him or for us. More broadly, anthropologically and from a cross-cultural viewpoint, it is said that every culture encourages and develops some human potentialities *at the expense* of others. Even in the highest "spiritual" matters we are all conscious, out of experience as well as discussion, of conflicts between such mandates as those to "justice" and those to "mercy."[6] Within history, we are for the most part confronted, it would seem, by either-or choice rather than by a both-and system in which one good on the whole tends to imply or bring with it another.

In any case, for the short run, at least, it would be safer, one would think, to generalize from the "hard" view[7] that spiritual goods, like other goods, are in limited supply, are "competitive" in employment, and confront us with the problems of competitive uses—and that this is true for love, insight, intimacy, just dealing, humility, mercy, just as for time or money.

Obviously, the choice *between* these views has a bearing on an intergroup relations programme that assumes that if we have this A (e.g., more polite evasion of discussing issues like Christmas carols in public schools) this B and C and D (e.g., more love and understanding and peace) will be added unto us.

Not only are assumptions of this order not usually made explicit for examination, but it is difficult, at times, to discover just what aspects of human life the intergroup relations programme is supposed to deal with. Just what *are* people talking about when they use this term? Whatever else may be implied, it seems clear from usage that what is being pointed to is the problem of "semi-intimate" (or "semi-distant") relations, relationships in which the two parties are socially both "near" and "far"[8] and destined to remain so with relative permanence. There is no problem of intergroup relations with the relatively intimate, those felt to be members in some sense of the "in-group." One does not, for instance, hear of an intergroup relations programme for "management" and "labour," even though both interact, are partially united and partially divided against one another with reference to interest, share some symbols and not others, and indeed have all the formal differentiating characteristics of "Jew" versus "Gentile," "Negro" versus "White," or "Catholics" versus "Protestants," except that in some transcendent sense they are held to be members in common of a more inclusive group, so that relations of at least that degree of potential intimacy are held to subsist between them. Neither, *per contra,* does one hear of intergroup relations programmes for, say, Canadians (taken together) in Canada and Nigerians (taken together) in Nigeria or even South Africans in South Africa. We have with these people "external relations"—good or bad—but they are too "far," socially (as long as they stay in "their" country), to pose the problems that intergroup relations programmes are meant to address. It is thus not within the realm of the truly "domestic" relations nor within the realm of the thoroughly "external" that the problems of intergroup relations lie, but somewhere in between, in a cloudy zone of ambiguity, in the realm of the "semi-domestic" or "semi-external."

More than this analysis is required, however, even to pose the problem. A *handful* of Javanese, Hottentots, Quakers, Mormons, Hungarians, or British, residing permanently in, but scattered over Canada, pose problems for a few people, of hospitality, propriety, or decency, but do not require an apparatus of intergroup relaters to mediate their individual relationships. There must be "enough" of one of these categories—not to form a "group," for "Jews" and "Negroes" and "Catholics" are no more, or hardly more a group, than are red-headed-women-born-in-January—to arouse feeling somewhere, in the "majority" or in another "minority," that what characterizes them as a category is a distinction of sufficient importance to make necessary the recognition of that category as a primary consideration in dealing with them individually or collectively at all. So number and concentration are necessary, as well as semi-externality, before any problems of intergroup relations (really inter-category dealings) can arise.

But at least one more aspect is essential—the temporal. No programme of intergroup relations (in the usual sense) is needed where the programme accepted on both sides is that of rapid one-way (or, for that matter, two-way) assimilation. As long as the melting-pot view of American society and culture was eagerly entertained as a good, and as long as, in practice, interaction did, by and large, move towards cultural amalgam, just so long did we have programmes of "education" and "Americanization" (the period, most appropriately, of the "Settlements") and not programmes of intergroup relations. The problems of the latter arise only when time has to enter into calculation on a large scale, that is, when in no foreseeable run of time is one-way or mutual assimilation likely to occur, and hence when long-run destiny, as well as present circumstance, is held to maintain (if not constitute) a significant difference, a difference that makes a difference, and therefore a matter that matters.[9]

So the so-called problems of intergroup relations subsist between categories of persons who can neither approach one another in intimacy to the point where whatever is meant by "assimilation" is felt to have taken place nor remain sufficiently distant from each other for the problems to be defined as those of external relations—and who, moreover, are believed to be bound to this mutually tantalizing near-far status for an indefinitely long run, if not "for ever." It should be particularly noted, perhaps, that in most cases the non-separation-but-non-assimilation definition is common to "both sides," though this may be the only programmatic point of agreement. Moreover, each "side" will blame the other, explicitly or implicitly, for the fact of non-assimilability: "clannishness" (an irrational preference for small-group exclusiveness) will be alleged of one side, philistinism (mass insensitivity to the finer, softer, subtler, small-group values) of the other. It should also be noted in passing that whether there is any or no warrant, or much or little warrant for any such allegations, the belief in their warrantability can hardly be given up without breaching the very wall of non-assimilation that makes the beliefs necessary; that is, the separation exists because of the alleged difference, belief in which must be maintained in order to perpetuate the separation, . . . which preserves the difference that is "valued." We even have the spectacle of a deliberate and conscious recreation of a difference (via the revival of such a dead language as Erse, for example) in order to increase the sense of separateness which is thought to be needed to give members of a "minority" the inner strength to face their separateness as a consequence of the value of their difference.

In these situations, ringed about by ambiguities and irrationalities—if not constituted by, then certainly compounded by them—human beings are to interact; and the supposition of an intergroup relations programme is commonly that they shall in some sense interact "better"—but without disturbing the constituting definitions of irreconcilable difference. We might at least expect reasonable and clear answers to what is meant by "better" and what is, in fact, in the defined direction, possible.

What is meant by "better" is often indicated by some such phrase as "the reduction of intergroup tensions,"[10] although this is a probably quite unusually modest demand. Now, of course, nothing so simple and direct is intended. One way of "reducing intergroup tensions" is, as the fashion is in the territory of our late, great wartime ally, to eliminate or "liquidate" (as their phrase has it) one or other of the counterposed groups. For people really committed to the democratic ideology, the direct method of liquidating opposition is not open; for others, democracy serves as a shield covering their present minority status, and what they would do once they had effective control of the organs of state can only be guessed at from their utterances. Another way to reduce intergroup tensions, however, far short of liquidation of its members, would be to destroy the group *qua* group, that is, by warmth of sun or cold of wind to cause members of the one group or the other to shed their out-group mantle or adopt the in-group mantle, as the case may be. An assault of friendliness, a raid of warmth upon a minority by a majority has hardly ever been tried, though the reverse (upon a majority by a minority) has been practised by Communists, Quakers, and followers of Gandhi, with notable, if not always the calculated or desired results. But this procedure is also barred by the unspoken rules of the game.

A third procedure, of course, would be deliberately so to act that the very ground that was supposed to differentiate between the two groups became defined as trivial, or eagerly to await this reducation to triviality by time. We no longer need "intergroup relations programmes" between Methodists and Anglicans, or Baptists and Presbyterians, because by and large the laymen who so call themselves regard the distinctions as nearly trivial. (Indeed, the clerics of the "respectable" Protestant denominations have at one and the same time to maintain a ecumenical movement to bring their organizations back together and an educational movement to prevent their laymen demanding "premature" union because they, the laymen, can no longer see any meaningful ground for disjuncture.) But this procedure is also barred by the ground rules since (*a*) neither party may call the value of the other's distinction into question without being thought hostile by the questioned party, (*b*) neither party may question the value of his own group's distinctiveness, without being thought disloyal, and (*c*) under the system of forced dichotomies imposed by the parties—*everyone* is Jew or non-Jew, Negro or non-Negro, Catholic or non-Catholic, native-white-Protestant or not—there can be no legitimate third party.

What is meant then by the "reduction of intergroup tensions" is a strictly non-radical programme (non-radical in the sense that it may not be permitted at all to touch the roots of the problem) which aims at best to reduce the extrinsic tensions, that is, the tensions which are thought to have nothing to do with the basic or differentiating difference. This sounds like good common sense. From a humane viewpoint, or from the viewpoint of maximizing social order or integration, it would seem desirable that where there are irreconcilable differences, these should not be further complicated by beliefs in non-existent differences or the actualities of irrelevant differences.[11] If, for instance, the difference between Protestant and Catholic is a transcendent and irreconcilable difference (to the protagonists), then it seems better that Protestants not erroneously believe, in addition, that Catholics-can-do-as-they-like-as-long-as-they-go-to-confession, and that Catholics not believe that Protestants-can-do-as-they-like-because-there-is-no-authority-and-every-man-is-his-own-priest. It would also seem better that each not visit upon the other the expressions of hostility which have their sources elsewhere, for example in dissatisfaction with one's marital, financial, or social achievements or the place of man in an indifferent universe.

This is all very humane, very liberal, very rational—and, to a very large degree, very silly.

It has been well said that "War is the pursuit of diplomacy by other means," though the point might have been clearer if it had been stated plainly that diplomacy, trade, and politics are the pursuit of war by other means. This is not to "take a pessimistic view of human nature"; it simply means, what is surely obvious, that, given the conflicts of important interest that diplomacy, trade, and politics imply, lacking these orderly means of settlement we should be driven back upon violence, and if enough social organization remained to manufacture them, bullets would have to re-replace ballots. Now such orderly procedures can arise in, broadly speaking, one of two ways: by imposition from above or supposition from below. In the first case, a powerful authority may put overt peace, but very real order and good government, above the values at issue between the contending parties; in the second case, men may come to see that the values implicit in or growing out of overt peace, and real order and good government, are much to be preferred to the values actually at issue between various "sub-groups." The first solution is again barred to us by the unspoken "rules of the game": we do not want a dictator to knock our heads together to make us forget our "important" differences, partly because we abhor the method and also because we have no guarantee that he will not find himself driven to exploit these differences (now suddenly revealed as our weaknesses) for the sake of maintaining his own power. But, as to the second way, the general adoption by men, emotionally as well as intellectually, of the view that these sub-group differences are relatively quite unimportant (relative to the uniting values), this amounts to nothing less than the "trivializing" of differences, or, at least, their reduction from the level of morals or "ultimates" to the level of "taste" and preference, which was referred to before as barred by the rules of the game. (It is barred from the rules of the game, trivially, for tact or diplomatic reasons; but it is barred from the rules, vitally, because some of the groups who are to be "related" regard their difference as itself of ultimate importance.)

The difficulty may be more apparent than real. It may be that claims of difference founded on ultimate values, are, like demands in military warfare for "unconditional surrender," merely a basis for negotiation,[12] that is, an element in war itself. If it is true that such claims are made by the representatives of the contending groups out of the formal necessities of their positions and are well understood to be *pro forma* only, while, denied in words but never to be denied in practice, a whole set of other ultimates is operative and paramount, then we are condemned merely to a situation of permanent stress and danger, but not, of necessity, defeat. The hesitance, to take an example from another sphere, of the communist-noncommunist protagonists to commit themselves to the test of nuclear arms, suggests that the survival of humanity may be more of an ultimate than either of the contending sets of ultimates to which the sides appeal.

But the stress and danger so engendered are themselves sources of hostility and potentially of war. Indeed, in the presence of any claim to universal ultimacy, unless methods of force and fraud and similar tactics[13] have been renounced beforehand, naked war is already in preparation—or the taking over of the universe by one group at the expense of the other. So that even if the statements are *pro forma*, they must be abjured, or certain methods precluded or the risks of overt war made certain. The middle ground—the illegitimation of extreme methods—may seem preferable, but what it implies, of course, is that the stated values are not as ultimate as the mandate against force and fraud, and this leaves only then the possibility of (moderately) pacific relations among groups, none of whom claims universality and ultimacy for the values in respect to which they differ.[14] But just as soon as the claims to ultimacy and universality of value *are* renounced, group bonds are weakened, the necessity for organization is diminished, the need for "spokesmen," "leaders," and other functionaries of vested interest is lessened —and the whole matter threatens to become one of "individual taste," of permissible and interesting variation, a matter, at most, for inter-individual tolerance (or appreciation, perhaps) rather than intergroup relations. But this catastrophe of good sense, the leadership on both sides is commonly concerned to avoid, with the connivance, if not the sympathy and support, of the intergroup operators.

So we must probably accept as a datum a situation in which the importance of the *definiendum* of the various groups is exaggerated to the point of ultimacy, that is, to the point of denial of a whole set of transcendent values, while at the same time the same members of the same groups are called variously (or manipulated or socially engineered) to maintain with one another relations of amical intimacy. One might put the situation another way. One might say that men are to be brought to regard their group-defined differences as of transcendent importance in a moral sense, and simultaneously to act as nearly as possible in that intimate amity which presupposes something close to mutual identification at least as far as ultimate values are concerned. This is indeed difficult doctrine.

It is perhaps time to return from attempts to describe the goals as defined to a re-examination of possibilities.

There would seem to be, broadly speaking, three major ways to "reduce intergroup tensions," neglecting now the only obvious way which is barred by common consent. We might hope to reduce the general or average level of hostility or hate in people. We might hope to leave the level where it is but erect stronger barriers to its expression, or to its expression in particular (e.g., naked and effective) forms. We might, alternately, hope neither to affect level of feeling nor to alter modality of expression, but to divert the expression on targets other than those now customary.

The problem of lowering the general level of hate, which seemed so easy of solution (at least abstractly) when, less than a generation ago, social science seemed to promise that if you knew the cause of some human distress you could likely do something to remedy it, now seems either insoluble or needing to be restated in terms so long-run as to be virtually visionary or utopian. It is no longer possible to believe, as it was, perhaps, as late as twenty years ago, that a radical alteration of the social structure at one extreme or of the child-raising and sex practices at the other, will sensibly diminish characterological hostility. We have had our social and political revolutions, we have had our toilet-training difficulties and sex frustrations removed (or altered in form) and we have not notably altered the problem at this fundamental level. It is not even clear that we have altered the basic direction of hate—from extrapunitive, say, to intrapunitive—though there are faint suggestions from the nature of the new juvenile delinquency that this may be the case, and the gain is certainly equivocal if not pyrrhic. So we must renounce, I think, any proximate hope for any real attrition of the reservoir of hate.

But where we cannot have destruction, we may—as with other diseases, such as tuberculosis—settle for latency. For those who can believe, moreover, that it is precisely the expression of hate, its becoming manifest, that provokes new hate into existence or awareness in its object, the maintenance of latency may be no small good. If it is true that the hate of X is largely a function of the expressed hate of Y and Z (and all other persons "significant" to him) then the case for dissembling or dissimulation or "control" is indeed weighty. But, sad to say, the common-sense belief is no longer credible. When we see the hate-and-rage-filled children of calm and loving parents, children whose teachers and relatives and "significant figures" have *shown* them virtually nothing but love, we are somewhat shaken in the earlier and naive view that the *externa* of behaviour affect significantly the *interna*, in terms of the relative proportions or dispositions of love and hate in the character. What seems to be more nearly true is that love and hate, like murder, will out, and that the matter of latency versus manifestation (in the everyday sense) is not of first-order importance, though perhaps—we do not know—not to be discounted altogether. Programmes of suppression—whether initiated or directed by the self or by others—have, therefore, little to recommend them.

This leaves us with the question of target. It may be put thus: given a certain level of hate, and a certain necessity for the expression thereof, what, in terms of objects, is the morally optimum distribution of that hate and its expressions.

Struggle how we may, I do not see how we can avoid answering that question, and in practice, of course, we answer it in action in terms of some calculus or target preference system never made explicit. Diversionary attempts may be and are made to deflect feeling upon abstractions such as "evil" or poverty or disease, but they are little more than evasion: evil will speedily be seen to be embodied in men or groups or institutions, and the hate that hates the sin and not the sinner is so rare a bird in the emotional aviary that the upshot is a choice of human target by indirection anyway. In purely moral terms, moreover, it is difficult to doubt given the fact of hate, that men should be as wise in their choices for the object of it as they are mandated to be for the receipt of their loves.

If it is possible to ask then, "Whom should we hate?"—or, more exactly, "Given our hate, whom may we hate," insofar as we have choice, "with least illegitimacy"—I think we may return a rational answer: those at the root, if such there be, of the hate-engendering system. It is not wise or good to hate at all, but it is better to hate an oppressive and authoritarian institution than a supportive and liberative one, and, among particular men, a radically evil man than a good one. (It is idle to say—although it is true, of course—that we cannot make the distinction between good and evil men; it is idle to say so, because while we cannot distinguish reliably, securely, or well, we cannot live without attempting to do so, and, moreover, lending credence to our own incredible performance.) Among the wittingly guilty, in this sense, must be those who add on a grand scale to human defeat and frustration, and among the perhaps unwittingly guilty, those who do so wittingly for the sake of comfort and vested interest.

Falling into both of these groups must be those who cry "brotherhood" where there is no brotherhood, and "otherhood" where there might be. It is hard to say which leads to the greater catastrophe: the Baldwins[15] who falsely persuaded many that they could live in brotherhood with the Nazis, or the Faubuses who are attempting to persuade many that they cannot do so with the Negro. The one attempts to define as secondary or trivial a distinction of primary or ultimate importance; the other attempts to define as ultimate or primary a distinction of no consequence at all, or none beyond the level of personal choice or private taste.

The world is not, of course, made up of Baldwins or Faubuses. But it is made up of those who, out of delusion, want of perspective, or naked self-interest exaggerate the distinctive importance of their group—or, what amounts to the same thing, its culture, ideology, or religion—and by that much attenuate the perceived importance of all other groups and by that much abridge human brotherhood, and of those who, in some sentimental fog or out of some intelligence-free enthusiasm, tell us that no group (even a group that would subvert it[16]) is outside the human brotherhood and thereby render the bond and concept meaningless.

This view leads towards the hard doctrine that the best way to serve amity, at least in the sense of least unfavourably distributing our hostilities and hates, is to return from the blurry amiabilities of the smooth-relations and peace-at-every-instant and love-everybody-all-the-time school or persuasion to the hard, discriminating pursuit of an inquiry as to what values or virtues are really ultimate, given the nature of the universe and the nature of human nature.[17] Beside these, then, all subsidiary values fall into the altogether tolerable categories of taste and preference, and hardly need a super-organization to prevent disruptive tensions from arising among followers of this wing of preference or that, any more than we need an organization to make the lovers of James Joyce lovable to the lovers of Gertrude Stein, or both to the lovers of Eddie Guest—or Ed Sullivan.

But it is not only the fuzziness of the aims of the intergroup relations people, or the footlessness of those aims where they are clear, that is bedevilling: there is, in addition, the problem of method. (By a curious but common enough paradox, the question of method or means may turn out to be central to the problem of goals or aims as well.) The problem of method is, as stated at the outset, not peculiar to the field of intergroup relations; it emerges at every attempted conjuncture of social science knowledge with any plan of action, "good" or "bad."

For what makes a programme of "intergroup relations" hopeful is the cumulating social scientific knowledge upon which it depends for its effectiveness. At the moment, to be more precise, it, and the programmes like it, rest upon differential social scientific knowledge, the advantage resting, momentarily, chiefly —but remember also Hitler and Himmler, Stalin and Beria—with the "good" people, those who intend at least to better human relations in one way or another. What social science can do, to an extent probably sufficient to make a difference, is to provide the meliorists and improvers with superior knowledge, or quite literally, cunning. It is, perhaps, particularly to be noted that this is not a static matter. The social scientist must not merely now place superior tools of "man-management" in the hands of the good operator; he must continue to keep him ahead of the game. When, for instance, the meaning of a Szondi or Rorschach test is described in detail in *Life* magazine, it is no longer possible to count upon it in the same way to screen out of positions of group leadership those with particular destructive needs. So a new weapon must be forged.

The alliance between knowledge and power has always been an uneasy one, the more problematic the more ethically sensitive the man of knowledge on one side and the less equivocally and certainly good the institution he served on the other. What loads it, in this century, with new uncertainty and guilt, what gives it much of the haunting quality of "The Sorcerer's Apprentice," is the quite decisive shift of authority it seems capable of effecting, not merely in the *externa* and *res publica* of conduct (the old province of government) but in the *interna* and *res privatissima* of feeling, concept of self, belief, and personality structure. This is the century of psychoanalysis, but it is also the century of brain-washing —both relatively crude as yet; it is the age of "pastoral counselling," but also of "thought control"; of effective advertising, and mass propaganda. It is the day of what Vance Packard calls the "Hidden Persuaders."

To some, more easily comforted than I, it will seem that the problem is simply to keep the new weapons in the "right" hands, instead of the wrong ones. Perhaps successful brainwashing in the hands of the trustees for utopia is not to be feared so much as welcomed. This is too easy. Too easy, because in practice the weapons cannot be so monopolized unless (*a*) the utopia already exists, and (*b*) a virtual dictatorship, of the "good," exists to retain them there. Too easy, because no one who wants the weapons ever believes other than that he is already a trustee for utopia. Too easy because the very nature and conception of the tool makes possible, if it does not ensure, the outcome Lord Acton so pithily put: that power corrupts; and absolute power, absolutely.

The problem is the problem of whether good manipulated is any better than good coerced—that is to say, no good at all. Who will regard seduction into virtue as better, vitally better than enslavement to it? If there is no freedom, there is no freedom; and if there is no freedom there is no good in any sense that has continuity with what men have hitherto weakly, intermittently, but indefeasibly served and loved.

But freedom, in this finite world, is a function not only of the undying hunger for it subjectively, but of the (relative) distribution of power objectively. Any radical concentration of power—via force, via technology, whether gunpowder or H-bomb, via knowledge—is of necessity the prelude to a dark night, freedomless and sterile, in which the highest good is order, and all others almost nugatory. That social science—yes, well-intentioned social science—could contribute to such a radical concentration is as hard to doubt as it is that the atomic scientists have done so, and, with varying degrees of guilt, know it. Indeed one should not say that social science "could" do so; it is doing so already.

The atomic scientist is in many ways fortunate: the problem of assessing, coping with, or providing against the results of his work is a problem for social science and not for physics. He must keep his guilt, but he may, indeed must, pass on his problem. The social scientist is not so lucky. The problems arising out of his work are themselves social problems, and hence problems for him. He has not only his guilt, but his perplexity.

The social scientist's problem, to come back to the question of bettering intergroup relations, is not one-fold but at least three-fold. His first question must surely be whether or not to make the problem his at all. If a murderer wants to know how to live in amity with his supply of future victims, I doubt if his problem is worth my acceptance, both because I doubt if it can long be done, or, if so, if it is worth the doing. Similarly, if groups want to cling to definitions of themselves that define all others into some secondary limbo, and want to know how at the same time to sustain relations of fraternity with these others, I have the same two grave doubts. The second question is the relatively trivial technical one: how, indeed *can* they be improved? The third is the really difficult one: how can intergroup relations be improved *by methods that do not render powerful and so debase their users*—the "good manipulators"—or render impotent, and so debase, those upon whom the proposed methods are used or tried out.

To this third question, I do not know any answers that hold out any hope or prospect of quick relief. By an agonizingly slow, a nearly geologically moving process we may be able over generations, by methods now known, to reform ourselves and one another sufficiently that the going balance between love and hate is sensibly affected—provided no major catastrophe,[18] of man or nature, that would permanently impoverish life, intervenes.

Outside of that process, I see no short-cuts—or, at least, no short-cuts that do not involve the simultaneous and mutual renunciation by the groups in question of those comforting illusions, those monstrous claims, that, were they present in an individual, would be the very diagnostic criteria for the pronouncement "psychosis." Securing such renunciation would have about the same prospects of success, the same rate of progress, the same formal problems as the negotiation of genuine and major disarmament pacts. No one should underrate the mountainous difficulty of such a procedure, with reference to either international disarmament or our problem. But neither may we indulge that ultimate and self-confirming pessimism that would label it patent folly to try.

NOTES

[1] What frightens the Europeans, of course, and lends edge and bite to their characterizations, is that they see themselves in impotent wisdom, their great allies in witless power, and the enemy in possession of enough of both quite probably to divide and in due course to destroy the ill-assorted mates.

[2] See, for illustrative purposes, Vance Packard, *The Hidden Persuaders* (New York: David McKay, 1957); William H. Whyte, *The Organization Man* (New York: Simon and Schuster, 1956); Seeley, Sim and Loosley, *Crestwood Heights* (Toronto: University of Toronto Press; New York: Basic Books, 1956) and Seeley, Junker, Jones et al., *Community Chest* (Toronto: University of Toronto Press, 1957).

[3] For a discussion of discussion, see John R. Seeley, "Guidance: A Plea for Abandonment," *Personnel and Guidance Journal* (American Personnel and Guidance Association, Inc., Washington D.C.), May, 1956.

[4] What a "long-run pragmatism" would be, and how it would differ from "idealism," or how it would give us better guide to conduct in the here and now, is hard to say. If the test of "truth" were its outworking in the full sense and the long run—*sub specie aeternitatis*—few philosophers would reject the test, except that the criterion is impossible of foreknowledge.

[5] Commonsense suggests too readily that all enterprises are like a journey, capable of being taken a mile at a time. But equally common experience might suggest that in many cases they are more like the atom bomb in their structure: before the assembly of a critical mass nothing happens, equal steps do not add continuously to effect, and the rate of action may be decisive for the looked-for effect occurring at all. "Nagging" is a common instance of the dissipation of effect consequent upon a slow rate of assembly of subcritical units of exhortation or anger. Similarly, a single lethal dose of some poisons—e.g., alcohol—may have sensibly different effects compared with the same dosage ingested in small steps.

[6] If we reconcile these antinomies at all, we do so ideologically at some point in infinity, like the meeting-point of parallel lines, which we call "God." Such reconciliations may be intellectually satisfying and emotionally consoling for some, but for all or nearly all their immediate practical bearing is remote.

[7] Right or wrong, it was on the latter, or "hard," view that Freud came to his psychoanalytic formulations. Not only was it largely his observation of the uselessness of curing hysterics by suggestion that rendered him sufficiently dissatisfied with the psychiatry of his day to face obloquy in seeking new methods, but throughout the development of his models of human nature, his most basic assumption was that of a "closed system," a system in which energy (emotional energy or "libido") is distributed, but neither created or destroyed. This implies that libido or energy "invested" in one object, or in the holding firm of one set of defences, cannot be used for other objects or other defences, and the process of psychoanalytic psychotherapy is largely, like the up-dating of a neglected investment portfolio, the liberation of energy from its unproductive or counterproductive uses at one point

for more rational (i.e., better chosen) investment at another. If Freud's model does not correspond to the facts, if indeed human nature is more nearly caught by Erich Fromm's model, in which the very liberation of a given amount of energy *ipso facto* implies the return of more than was used up, we stand before a first-order necessity of change in all our thinking, a change so vast that it is one on which we ought sensibly to require a body of evidence equally vast before we can be won over to it. Most men—perhaps "sick" in relation to Fromm's "norm"—feel themselves to be limited on Freud's analogy, and observation of their behaviour would seem to confirm the more pessimistic view, not only now but *per saecula saeculorum*.

[8]See, for example, Georg Simmel's seminal essay on "The Stranger," in translation by Kurt H. Wolff, *The Sociology of Georg Simmel* (Glencoe: The Free Press, 1950), pp. 402–408.

[9]It should perhaps be added that, even given all these characteristics, intergroup relations would not pose quite the problems they do for us except in context with other notable characteristics of North American culture: a general intolerance for ambiguity, a very much abbreviated time perspective, and a burning faith, already referred to, in the "solubility" (almost immediately) of all problems. The first, the hyper-Aristotelian bias, emerges in the preference for dichotomies rather than continua—"they" or "us," "black" or "white," "Negro" or "White," with nothing in between, despite the known facts as to the distribution of African genes in the American plasm pool! The second characteristic, the foreshortening of time perspective, effectually bars the leaving of solutions to relatively long-term (e.g., five or six hundred years) processes that might work out solutions or realignments necessarily now unforeseeable and, perhaps, even if foreseeable, not to be hastened. The third, the "management" attitude, derives partly from the other two, and very often implies that we must needs nag and tinker, where a more ripened wisdom might suggest we had better rest and let lie. The "fallow acre" finds scant hospitality in the North American scheme of things.

[10]See, for example, by this title, Bulletin 57 of the Social Science Research Council, by Robin M. Williams, Jr. (New York, 1947).

[11]The corollary, that all vital differences ought to be plainly exposed, is rarely noted by the intergroup operator. Attention is rarely directed to the claims of groups to moral (and later to legal) hegemony. Those who focus attention on such claims—or, worse, on acts based upon them—are usually thought to "worsen" group relations and heighten intergroup tensions.

[12]If this is not so, the problem is evidently irresoluble and the defeat is total.

[13]For example, a policy of "outbreeding" (in quantity) the rival group, so that the merits of the case are resolved in terms of gynaecological athleticism.

[14]If this view is accepted it seems probable that the organizations for better intergroup relations would lose a great part of their membership and, more particularly, their leadership. A great part of the latter consists of "spokesmen" for the contending groups: men who, believe what they may personally, cannot in their public pronouncements diminish by one whit the attribution of inflated value to what distinguishes the group of each from that of the other.

[15]It was the Baldwin-sown field that Chamberlain, willy-nilly, reaped at Munich. What made Chamberlain seem, perhaps, the more pathetic figure was the difficulty of believing (if he really did) such folly *so late*: the same thing that makes a Koestler a figure of tragedy and a Howard Fast a figure of fun.

[16] Any group, for instance, that believes in suppressing by force (when it has power) the expression of competitive or contending opinion, sustains with the rest of mankind relations that are something less—or other—than fraternal.

[17] It must surely be clear, in virtue of the countless clamorous claims of the contending parties, that such a programme must, by mutual cancellation, exclude the pretensions to universality and ultimacy of numberless over-cherished values, since no common and consistent scheme could sustain their incompatibilities.

[18] Of course it is on the very edge of such catastrophe, both of war direct or of war rendered likely by population explosion (in China and India, more particularly), that we are now living. If the worst comes to the worst, as well it may, talking about improving intergroup relations may well seem a luxury, and doing anything, a superfluity.

Existence

Fackenheim /

Kamerling / Silberman

JEWISH EXISTENCE AND THE LIVING GOD / *Emil L. Fackenheim*

The modern Jew is an enigma to himself. When he reflects on his existence as a Jew, he cannot but be filled with wonder. Other individuals and peoples may wonder how they have come to be what they are; the Jew must wonder why he should exist at all. For if there are laws of historical change, the Jew should, according to these laws, have disappeared long ago. Was there ever another people which continued to exist, under like circumstances, through the centuries? The answer is that there was not. Other peoples require the bond of a common land, or a common language, or a common culture in order to continue in existence. The Jew, for long centuries, has had none of these. Consequently, self-appointed experts in the laws of historical change have been forever quick to predict his impending disappearance. But thus far at least these prophecies have always been confounded. The Jew still exists—a source of wonder both to others and to himself.

How is one to account for the continued existence of the Jew? Certainly not in terms of persecution or discrimination. It is true that such forms of hostility may unite their victims, creating in them a group-will to survive. They may cling defiantly to the very trait which singles them out for penalty. But they may also do the very opposite, that is, try to get rid of the fatal trait. In the case of the Jew, unlike that of the Negro, this is not impossible. Furthermore, persecution, while frequent, has by no means been constant in Jewish history. There were long periods in which the Jew was invited to participate in the life that surrounded him; and he never showed lack of eagerness to accept this invitation. The conclusion, then, is clear: to account for Jewish survival in such negative terms as persecution or discrimination is impossible.

Nor do we fare much better with such positive terms as "love of tradition" or "loyalty to the group." To be sure, tradition had a strong hold on the Western Jew until the beginning of the nineteenth century, and on his East European brother until the beginning of the twentieth. But this tradition was, for the most part, not static, fossilized, inert; it was fluid. Also, it was frequently exposed to the threat of disintegration. Yet it did not disintegrate; rather, it preserved itself. Why should Jewish tradition have preserved itself rather than disintegrated? To ask this question is to ask the question of Jewish survival all over again. In short, "love of tradition" does not explain Jewish survival; it is an aspect of the very thing in question.

Precisely the same is true of feelings of loyalty to the group. No doubt such feelings are, in some periods of history, a powerful force for cohesion and survival. But in the case of the Jew the question is why there should have been such feelings at all among a people which had not, for long centuries, shared a common land, or a common language, or a common external destiny. In the case of Jewish survival, then, "national feeling" or "group-loyalty" is not an explanation, but part of the very thing to be explained.

But perhaps collective feelings can exist and survive independently of the experiences which nourish them? Perhaps there are entities such as a "racial will" which are passed on through the blood? We need not waste our time on such fictitious entities. For they exist only in the minds of the demagogues and charlatans of our century.

It becomes abundantly clear, then, that to account for Jewish survival is possible only in terms of the Jewish faith. All the other supposed causes of Jewish survival, such as tradition or feelings of group-loyalty, can themselves be explained only in terms of the Jewish faith. It is because of the Jewish faith that the Jew still exists, as we have said, a source of wonder both to others and to himself.

This fact places the Jew of our time in a unique position so far as the relation to his ancestral faith is concerned. Like everyone else, in the world of today, he is prey to religious doubt. Like everyone else, he is unsure whether he can, and if so to what extent, accept the faith which was handed down to him. But unlike everyone else, he must admit that it is because of that faith that he exists at all.

II In current usage, the term "faith" all too often signifies a mere milk-and-water assent to abstract "tenets" and "principles," and the tenets and principles are, as a rule, nice, innocuous, and "uncontroversial." This is not the kind of faith which can move mountains, or which could be responsible for Jewish survival. The term "faith," when applied to the Jewish past, signifies total commitment. And the commitment was either to an all-consuming experience in the present, or else to memories of such experiences which had taken place in the past.

Whatever one may think of the Biblical account of Jewish origins—whether one takes it to be literally true or merely mythological—two facts are beyond doubt: the first is that even if the Biblical account is merely mythological there is an element in it which is true; the second is that countless generations of Jews accepted it as true. The first fact concerns the faith of the Biblical, the second that of the post-Biblical Jew. The first fact serves to explain how the Jewish people was born; the second, why it survived. The Jew of today must contemplate both these facts: if not in order to learn what, as a Jew, he ought to be, then at least in order to understand what, as a Jew, he is.

III It is possible to doubt that Abraham, or even Moses, ever existed. One may advance the hypothesis that Israel never stood at Mount Sinai, and that, consequently, the unique divine revelation by which Israel supposedly was constituted never took place. But it is not possible to doubt that the Biblical account of Jewish origins, however mythological, reflects something which did take place. What took place was a succession of overwhelming religious experiences. The presence of the Nameless was felt in experiences which were themselves nameless.

As such, these experiences were not specifically Jewish. To experience namelessly the presence of the Nameless is the core, not merely of Jewish, but of all religious life. What distinguishes forms of religious life is the way in which the Nameless, and the nameless experiences, are interpreted.

There are, to be sure, some varieties of mysticism in which all interpretation is rejected. The Nameless, and the nameless experience, both remain nameless. They remain, consequently, utterly divorced from all that is familiar and named. And all existence becomes a striving for an end which, if achieved, transcends all understanding and all utterances.

This, however, is the exception rather than the rule in the religious life of man. The rule is that the Nameless, and the nameless experience, at once relate themselves to something familiar and nameable. In virtue of this relation, they are themselves given names. Thus a religion comes into being.

In the primeval Hebrew experience, there was such an immediate relating of the Nameless to something familiar. But the familiar in this case was not, as it was so often, a part of nature or nature as a whole; nor did the nameless experience utter itself, in this case, in nature-symbols and thus give rise to a form of life which consists in ritualistic imitation of the rhythms of nature. In the primeval Hebrew experience, any attempt at a direct relating of the Nameless to nature was explicitly repudiated. The familiar and nameable which here received religious significance was not nature but human action.

But the nameless experience was not action. It had to interpret itself as a *call* to action. And this call could not be a call unless it was "heard." Nor could there be a "hearing" unless there was a "speaking." The Nameless interpreted itself as "speaking," and the nameless experience as "hearing." What was heard was a commandment and a promise: the call to action, and the consequences which followed if the call were heeded. Thus in the primeval Hebrew experience, the presence of the Nameless manifested itself in the form of a divine-human covenant.

It must be noted, however, that this experience was not, or at least not primarily, an individual experience. It was a collective experience. It therefore manifested itself in a covenant, not between the Nameless and individuals, but between the Nameless and a people. Indeed, only in this experience did this people *become* a people. This is the secret of the birth of Israel.

It is sometimes said that the Jewish faith has been, since its inception, one of "ethical monotheism." This assertion is true in one sense, but not in another. If by "monotheism" is meant the belief in one universal God, the One God of the universe and mankind, it is more than doubtful whether the early Hebrews were monotheists. And if "ethical" refers to codes of conduct universally human in application, it is more than doubtful whether their beliefs were ethical. Its God was One, not in being the only God there was, but in demanding a commitment so total as to dwarf all else. And He was ethical in that He challenged to action, and in that this challenge was absolute. Compared to the absoluteness of this challenge its content was, for the time being, secondary in importance; and distinctions such as that between "ethical" and "ritualistic" were not made until a later age.

These facts ought to occasion no surprise. Religions begin with committing experiences, not with universal ideas; and where there is no commitment, religions do not begin at all. But if the commitment is radical, it is only a question of time before it becomes universalized. In the Hebrew experience, the only important God became, in due course, the only existing God; and His all-important commandments, commandments addressed and applicable to all men. This development completed itself in the Hebrew prophets.

The prophets universalized the primeval Hebrew experience, but they did not dissipate it into un-committing generalities. The primeval experience persisted. The Nameless had become the God of all men: but He was still immediately challenging, here and now. His commandments had become, at least in part, universally valid, but they had not become abstract "principles." They were addressed by the Nameless, not to "mankind," but to each man. This is why the prophetic God, while universal, could nevertheless remain in covenant with the people of Israel. He was the God, not of the abstraction "mankind," but of every nation.

There are those in the modern world to whom a religion is the "higher" and "more enlightened" the more it expresses itself in abstractions. The prophets would have been in vigorous disagreement. To them, the use of such terms as "mankind" and "deity" would have indicated, not enlightenment, but a flight from commitment and the divine challenge. The prophetic God, in becoming universal, had not ceased to challenge; nor did He challenge abstractions such as "mankind" which not even a God can challenge. Rather, He now challenged Ethiopians and Philistines as well as Israelites. But the business of a prophet in Israel could hardly be to fathom the challenge to Ethiopians and Philistines.

It was in the experience of the Nameless, then, that the people of Israel was born. This was possible because of three factors: first, because it interpreted itself as challenge to action; secondly, because, being a collective experience, it challenged the group; thirdly, because it was an experience so profound as to persist even after its universal implications had become manifest.

IV But primeval experiences do not last forever. Presumably they take place, even in primeval times, only intermittently, although this fact is easily concealed from later observers by the clouds of myth. In Jewish history, as in the history of most religions, "revelation" came to be a term referring mainly to events lying in the past. The question therefore arises as to why the Jewish people was preserved, when the collective experience of the Nameless had become what, at first sight, was a dead past recorded in dead documents.

The answer is that neither the past nor the documents were dead. The past lived on, legislating to present and future; and the document which recorded it became the Bible, that is, the Book *par excellence*. Jewish thinking centred on its exegesis; Jewish living geared itself to its commandments and promises; Jewish experience interpreted itself as derived from the primeval experiences recorded in the Book. From the Biblical to the modern era, the Jews remained a people by virtue of the Book.

But is such a survival of the past, and of its record, proof that both are alive? It may well seem that, if the Book ruled the Jewish spirit for almost two thousand years, it was not because the former was alive, but because the latter was dead; and that Jewish life, during these long centuries, was composed of the monotonous practice of sterile commandments, and of a forlorn hope in a long-lost promise. How can a religious life be anything but barren which springs, not from the immediate experience of the Nameless, but from slavish submission to the authority of a codified book? But except for rare periods of religious decline, the Jew's loyalty to the Book was not one of slavish obedience. Rather, the Book without kindled the soul within. In re-thinking its thoughts, the Jew thought his own. In imagining its experiences, he re-lived them. In obeying its commandments, he made them into a way of life. The past did not kill the present; instead, reviving itself in the present, it gave life to the present.

How was such an extraordinary relation to the past possible? Why was the present, during these long centuries, so rarely at odds with the past? Why did it not claim its own autonomous rights against the past? How could religious experience forever regard itself as subordinate to the great religious experiences of the past? There are many partial answers to these crucial questions, but the decisive answer lies in one element of the Jewish faith—the Messianic element.

The Messianic faith is, of course, Biblical in origin. It was the prophets who first spoke of an End of Days in which God alone would rule and all would be fulfilled. Moreover, this faith was implicit in the primeval experience itself. For once the experience of the Nameless had interpreted itself as challenge and promise, it was only a question of time, and religious profundity, until a new religious dimension had to come into view: that of a future in which all that was to be done by either God or man would be fulfilled.

But so long as the primeval experience persisted in Jewish life, an explicit Messianic faith was, so to speak, not needed. Religious immediacy could have lived without it. It was when the past, and its record, took the place of the primeval experience that the Messianic faith moved into the very centre of Jewish religious life. Had it not done so, no mere hankering after the past could have saved Jewish life from spiritual—and physical—extinction. The past could live on in the present only because both present and past were for the sake of the future. And the Jewish people could live on, when He who is nameless was not present, only because the memory of His presence transfigured itself into the hope of his ultimate and all-consuming return.

This account of Jewish life during these centuries is thus subject to emendation. Jewish thinking was a re-thinking of past thought, but it was *thinking* only because it was directed on a future consummation. Jewish imagination was a re-living, but it was *living* only because it anticipated the End. Finally, and perhaps most significantly, Jewish obedience to past commandments constituted a way of life, which was possible only because it regarded itself as preparing, and waiting, for Messianic fulfilment. In short, Jewish existence experienced itself as being between Revelation and Redemption. Revelation had been the call for human, and the promise for divine, action: Redemption would be the consummation of all action.

Still, it may seem that the Messianic hope leaves the fact of Jewish survival unexplained. Did this hope not concern the future of a united mankind? Should it not have led those who held it, instead of to group-survival, to voluntary self-dissolution—thus anticipating the End? The mystery deepens if one considers that the Jews were, at that time, dispersed among other nations—nations which, for the most part, shared their monotheistic beliefs. Could it be that the hope of the post-Biblical Jew was, after all, not the universal prophetic hope; could it be that, having lost all universalistic fervour, it had become nothing more than a national hope? This, however, is to confuse empty abstractions with religious realities. The truth is the reverse. Had their hope been nothing more than a national hope, the Jews of the Diaspora would have been forced many times to abandon it. It was precisely because it was more than national that they could retain it. Hence, it may seem paradoxical but it is nevertheless true that it was precisely because of their Messianic sense of kinship with all the nations that the Jews did not lose their identity among the nations; had they lost that sense of kinship, they would have disappeared among the nations.

Not much reflection is needed to remove the paradox from these assertions. How could a small people live, for any length of time, amid mighty nations and rich cultures without abandoning a merely national hope as both immoral and absurd? Immoral because a moral God could hardly confine His attention to one small and insignificant people; absurd because all the evidence seemed to point, instead, to the fact that this people had been overlooked by history. Clearly, in the centuries of the dispersion, only the most narrow and unthinking could have insisted on Jewish survival on the basis of a solely national hope. But it was the most thinking and broad-minded who did, in fact, insist on Jewish survival. And this was possible only because their insistence sprang from a hope for something more than national survival. Their hope concerned the relations between the Nameless and all men.

Why, then, did this hope on behalf of mankind not lead to voluntary self-dissolution in mankind? Simply because "mankind" did not exist. There were only actual nations, and some of these did not regard the world as in need of redemption, whereas others believed that it had already arrived. For the Jew to dissolve into either would have meant to him, not to hasten the End, but to betray his post.

One must conclude that the Jew of the Diaspora survived because he was able to rise to prayers such as this, uttered by a Chassidic rabbi in an age of fear and hate: "O Lord, send speedily the Messiah, to redeem Thy people Israel! Or, if this be against Thy will, send him to redeem the nations!"

V   The question now arises as to whether the Jew of today can share the faith of his ancestors, or whether he must consider himself merely its unwilling product. Can being a Jew today mean an acceptance of a religious commitment similar to, if not identical with, the commitment of his ancestors? Or is being a Jew today a mere accident of birth?

No doubt, individual Jews have asked this question throughout the ages. It became universal, however, only when the Jew entered into the modern world. Then it became inescapable. This was because the modern world cast increasing doubt on the central part both of the Biblical and of the post-Biblical Jewish faith—that is, on the living God. The Biblical Jew had experienced His presence, and the post-Biblical Jew had hoped for it; but man in the modern world had come to suspect that all supposed experiences of divine presence were just so many illusions.

This attitude sprang from the modern ideal of scientific and moral enlightenment. Did not a rational universe preclude the possibility of irrational divine incursions into it? And did not a rational way of life consist in reliance, not on revelations and promises of divine aid, but on the unaided power of human reason? Ever since the Age of Enlightenment, it has seemed to the modern-minded—and who is not modern-minded, at least to a degree?—that the denial of the living God was an essential aspect of man's scientific and moral self-emancipation. If a man was to be fully free in his world, God had to be expelled from it.

The word "expelled" is used advisedly. The ideal of enlightenment did not compel one to deny that a God existed, but it did seem to compel one to deny that He could be present here and now. The living God had to become a mere "Deity," a "Cosmic Principle"—remote, indifferent and mute. Time was when the prophet Elijah contrasted the idols which could not speak with the living God who could. Ever since the Age of Enlightenment, it has seemed to the modern-minded that God could speak as little as the idols.

The religion of the modern-minded came to reflect this conviction. Far from centring on the experience or expectation of a present God, it on the contrary presupposed His necessary absence. It became the mere subscription to "ideals," "principles," "tenets," and, in North America, "platforms." Would anyone think of God as a mere ideal who was prepared, so to speak, to meet Him in Person?

On entering the modern world, the Jew had no reason to be suspicious of the ideal of enlightenment which ruled it. On the contrary, he had every reason to embrace it with enthusiasm. Who was to be enthusiastic about it if not the Jew, who had just emerged from the confines of the mediaeval ghetto? Who was to approve of the ideal of universal emancipation if not the Jew, who stood in special need of emancipation? But despite this whole-hearted approval which the Jew very naturally manifested, he soon discovered something of which he was not sure he could approve. The modern expulsion of God from the human world made Jewish existence problematic. The "Jewish problem" appeared on the scene. And it was a problem without solution.

For the pre-modern Jew this problem did not exist. He was faced with no serious difficulties of self-interpretation. He believed himself to have once met the living God, and to be committed to this meeting until the Messianic hope would be fulfilled. But what if God did not live, that is, relate Himself to persons and peoples? What if He was a mere cosmic entity dwelling in infinite and impartial remoteness? Or perhaps did not exist at all? What if all the supposed experiences of divine presence had been so many illusions? The moment the living God became questionable Jewish existence became questionable. The Jew had to embark on the weary business of self-definition. This business was weary because no definition would fit.

Was Jewishness a matter of "religion"? Was one a Jew because one subscribed to the "tenets" of ethical monotheism? But while Judaism consisted of ethical monotheism, it could not with impunity be regarded as consisting of mere tenets; and Jewishness could not consist of subscription to them. For there were those who subscribed to ethical monotheism without being Jews, and those who were Jews without subscribing to ethical monotheism. The inescapable fact was that one was born a Jew, and that one was not born subscribing to tenets and principles. The definition omitted the fact that the Jews were a people.

This omission was by no means an accident. A living God could address Himself to a people, but an abstract and lifeless "Deity" could not, for it could not address itself at all. In the case of such a Deity, the best one could do was somehow affirm it. But such affirmations could have no connection with the origin of those who made it. In short, if the living God had to give way to an abstract Deity, the "tenets" of Judaism and the Jewish people fell apart.

But perhaps an alternative definition could heal this defect. Was Judaism not the "culture" of the Jewish people, the product of its "religious genius"? Could Jewishness not be defined in terms of the people which had produced the culture?

Yet this definition too had a fatal flaw. Perhaps this flaw was not apparent, or did not even exist, for the detached observer. But the Jew was not a detached observer; he was a participant. As such, he had to ask himself a crucial question which the definition could not answer. The question was: why ought he remain a Jew?

So long as the Jew believed in a living God the question answered itself. To remain a Jew was his duty under the divine-Jewish covenant. But what if God did not live? What if He could not enter into covenants? What if Judaism was not a divine-human encounter, but merely the product of "Jewish genius"? Had Jewish survival then to be either an end in itself, or else a means to presumed future "contributions" of "Jewish genius" to the "world"? But either view smacked of a chauvinism which no morally sensitive Jew was ever able to swallow. Hence the less forthright accepted the duty to Jewish survival as a mere pious fiction, while the more forthright frankly abandoned it. Jewish survival was merely a right, not a duty; whether or not one chose to remain a Jew was a matter of taste. But if this latter view found general acceptance how long would the Jews of the Diaspora continue to be? And how long would the Jews of the State of Israel continue to be Jews? On the other hand, how many Jews are really prepared to advocate, and work towards, Jewish self-dissolution and to dismiss three thousand years of Jewish existence as a tragi-comic mistake? If a single generalization may safely be made about the contemporary Jew, it is that he still regards Jewish survival as a duty, to be performed whether he likes it or not. He may not have the slightest idea why it should be a duty; he may even consciously reject this duty. Still, he feels it in his bones.

After two hundred years of fruitless probing, the conclusion ought to be obvious. The "Jewish problem," as a problem of self-definition, is insoluble. Jewish existence cannot be understood without reference to a living God. And the Jew of today who persists in regarding Jewish survival as a duty either persists in something unintelligible or else postulates, however unconsciously, the possibility of a return to faith in a living God.

VI   But the possibility of such a return must surely be dismissed by the modern-minded without a moment's thought! Can one believe, in this day and age, in a self-revealing God? Has this belief not been refuted, once and for all? And must not those who persist in it be dismissed as mere victims of wishful, or fearful, thinking? In the twentieth century, faith in a living God may well appear to be a mere relic of bygone ages, and Jewish self-dedication to Jewish survival, a mere part of it.

But the modern world never did refute the belief in a living God. It merely rejected it. One cannot refute the irrefutable; although—if the irrefutable is also unprovable—one is always free to decide that it does not exist.

To be sure, modern thought refuted many traditional beliefs; and some of these were once associated with the belief in a living God. In an age of natural science and critical history, it is hardly possible to believe in miraculously split seas or documents dictated by God. But to reject revealed documents is not necessarily to reject revelation. And to be suspicious of miracles is not necessarily to reduce all religious experience to projections of the unconscious mind. One does well indeed to suspect that much that passes for religious experience is unauthentic, and that it is, not a meeting with the Nameless, but the mere solitary disport of the mind with its own conceits. But to regard all religious experience as such—and hence to dismiss it as merely pseudo-religious—is a procedure dictated, not by scientific evidence, but by intellectual prejudice. Or rather, it is to make, under the guise of a scientific judgment, a religious choice. And the choice is against the living God.

Time was when those who made this choice were imbued with the spirit of Prometheus. Like that figure of ancient myth, they wanted total control of their world for the sake of spreading liberty and light. In the world of today, there are still some left who are imbued with the Promethean spirit, but their number is no longer large. Some of those who have decided against the living God are engaged in spreading, not liberty and light, but terror and utter darkness. Others have made that choice only to shiver in loneliness and despair. And others again —and these are the vast majority, at least in the Western world—have lost the assurance of their choice. They are no longer sure whether they have really made the Promethean choice; they are unsure even of what it is. Religiously, they are in a state of turmoil.

But perhaps this turmoil is contemporary man's most authentic religious expression. It would appear to be, at any rate, something unique in the entire religious history of man. The contemporary kind of religious turmoil may have existed, in previous ages, among individuals. But never before did it shake a whole age.

All ages prior to the modern were religious ages. They may have disagreed as to the interpretation to be given to the presence of the Nameless, but they agreed that the Nameless *could* be present. In sharp contrast, the modern age—at least in its most typically modern expressions—has been anti-religious in spirit. Either by denying its existence or by expelling it into the distance of irrelevance, it denies that the Nameless can be present. What both the pre-modern and the modern ages have in common is that they make their respective religious choices without giving serious attention to the alternative. They make their choice without full awareness that it is a choice. Man in the mid-twentieth century is bereft of such dogmatic certainties. Possibly for the first time in human history, he is brought face to face with the most radical of all religious questions. Like man at all times, he must face up to this question. But unlike men at other times, he is compelled to recognize that it *is* a question. Unlike the former, he cannot fail to recognize that the question can be answered only by a decision, and that the decision *is* a decision. And he suffers the turmoil of this recognition. The question is: is human existence closed or open to the Divine? Can the Nameless be present, or are all supposed experiences of such a presence mere illusions? Does God live, or is man inexorably alone?

It is all too human to shrink from great choices. One is tempted to pretend that there is no choice to be made, and to drift in indecision. Or perhaps one will escape from the choice by making it glibly, only to discover later that one has not made it at all. Such flights from choice are readily understandable because to face up to the choice is to endure turmoil—the turmoil of the conflicting possibilities. One cannot make a genuine choice without first enduring this turmoil, and one must endure it until the time is ripe for decision, for choice and for action.

If this is true of all great decisions, it is true, above all, of the great religious decision placed before contemporary man. Is choosing for or against the living God a mere matter of scientific hypotheses? Or is it a matter of choosing the path of least resistance? Or of discovering, with the help of reputable psychologists, the most comfortable road to peace of mind? Is it not a choice in which one either commits his whole being or else does not commit himself at all? If this is the case, it is no wonder, then, that man in the present age seems bent on shrinking from this choice. Instead he pretends that there is no decision to be made; and he reinforces this pretence by all kinds of activity, inside and outside church and synagogue, which distract his attention from it. Or, assuming an air of glib resolution, he issues manifestos which announce that the decision is made, and he reinforces these by repeating them at regular intervals. But the great religious choice placed before contemporary man cannot be evaded indefinitely;

nor can its turmoil be circumvented by the proclamation of manifestos, no matter how often this ritual takes place. The restless flight from the decision must yield to the quiet endurance of its turmoil. Only he who endures the tension of the conflicting possibilities can really know what the decision is about; only he can know when the time is ripe for it to be made. But what will the decision be? And when will the time be ripe for it to be made? This cannot be known in advance.

VII The Jew of today is a man of today; he is confronted with the religious question of today; the question is whether or not the Nameless can be present to us. But he is also confronted with the Jewish question of today: whether— and if so why—Jewish survival is a duty. The remarkable thing is that he cannot authentically face up to the religious question without at the same time facing up to the Jewish question.

The Jew of today cannot authentically face up to the religious choice simply as an individual. To do so is, in effect, to evade, if not his Jewishness, then at least the question posed by his Jewishness. And the question demands a religious answer. Hence to evade it is, for the Jew, to evade part of the religious question itself, and thus to fall into unauthenticity. The Jew cannot face up to the religious question "simply as an individual." Whether he likes it or not, he must face up to it as a Jew. To do so is to recognize that the duty to Jewish survival is, for the Jew, part of what is at stake in the religious choice. Man of today must endure the ancient question of whether or not the Nameless can be present. As part and parcel of that question for him, the Jew of today must endure the hardly less ancient question of whether or not Jewish survival is a duty. The religious turmoil is, for him, at the same time a Jewish turmoil. And Jewish religious life today consists in the endurance of this double turmoil.

When the time is ripe for decision, the Jew may well decide that the ancient duty to Jewish survival must be abandoned. Should this be the eventual choice, then the Jewish people, as it has existed for three thousand years, will cease to be. Jewishness will become a mere right, to be made use of only by those with a taste for it. Jews of the State of Israel will become Israelis, and Jews elsewhere will either become members of a denomination like other denominations, or else a minority doomed to eventual extinction.

But the Jew may also, in the end, decide to reaffirm the ancient duty of Jewish survival. This will be possible only if the Jew has remembered, and accepted as authentic, the ancient encounter of his people with the living God. He will then accept himself as part of a people constituted by an encounter with the Nameless, and still extant as a people only because it continues to be committed to that encounter. He will have accepted himself as a Jew because he will have accepted the time-honoured Jewish obligation: to prepare and wait for the End in which all that is to be done by either man or God will be fulfilled.

THE RELIGIOUS ROOTS OF THE STATE OF ISRAEL /

Aaron M. Kamerling

On the fourteenth day of May, 1948, the Provisional State Council in the city of Tel Aviv signed the Israel Proclamation of Independence. The sentiments expressed in the opening lines of the Proclamation are stirring and breathtaking: the unity of land, people, and faith is established; the hope for a return to this land is reiterated and the more recent and direct association of Jews with the country is stressed. In exalted language, an ancient people proclaims its rebirth.

The land of Israel was the birthplace of the Jewish people. Here their spiritual, religious and national identity was formed. Here they achieved independence and created a culture of national and universal significance. Here they wrote and gave the Bible to the world.

Exiled from Palestine, the Jewish people remained faithful to it in all the countries of their dispersion never ceasing to pray and hope for their return and restoration of their national freedom.

Impelled by this historic association, Jews strove throughout the centuries to go back to the land of their fathers and regain statehood. In recent decades, they returned in their masses. They reclaimed a wilderness, revived their language, built cities and villages, and established a vigorous and evergrowing community, with its own economic and cultural life. They sought peace, yet were ever prepared to defend themselves. They brought blessings of progress to all inhabitants of the country and looked forward to sovereign independence.

The State of Israel thus began its career of independence and sovereignty.

Ten years have elapsed since that fateful day. The threats to the survival of this fledgling state were many: war, economic boycott, border sniping and killing, infiltration and blockade, political pressures to cede territory and to readmit thousands of Arab refugees. All these were gradually overcome by a tenacity of will and an extraordinary discipline of its citizens which won the respect of all free peoples of the world.

These external threats did not deter the leadership of the state from proceeding with the tasks of "Ingathering of the Exiles." This was indeed the deeper reason for the founding of the State. The end of homelessness was one of the cardinal principles of the Zionist movement. The fact that the immigrants came from so many countries, especially in Asia and in Africa, gave substance to the claim that a return to Zion was not just an expression of Jewish nationalism, artificially stimulated and made possible by political manoeuvering in the chancelleries of Europe and in the halls of Congress of the United States. The Jews of Yemen knew nothing of the nationalist slogans and cared less about the theoretical hair-splitting of Zionist ideology, when they were transported to Israel on "eagles' wings." The prayer "and may our eyes behold Thy return to Zion in mercy" was of greater significance to them than the massive volumes on the history of Zionism.[1] This was true also of the immigrants from other Asiatic countries.

The religious roots of the Jews of Oriental lands are clearly evident in their attitude to and in their comprehension of the meaning of the State of Israel. The policy of "Ingathering of the Exiles" from all countries of the Diaspora was to them the implementation of the religious commandment of "the Return to Zion." Upon their arrival in Israel, the Jews of the Orient were granted equal citizenship —a status they were deprived of for many centuries. However, in eastern and western Europe the secular aspects of Jewish nationalism are no less a part of a great and unbroken tradition of religious hope and expression. It is true that many of the classical Zionist utterances were in response to the challenge of the environment. Anti-Semitism hastened a re-examination of the precarious position of Jews in many countries of oppression. The literature of the Zionist movement reveals a soul-searching quest for honest solutions. The techniques employed at the very inception were those found desirable and effective in other nationalist movements in the nineteenth century. The instrumentalities of the movement— the organization, the Congress, the Shekel, the educational devices—all these were tried and tested methods, but they were novel experiences in the two thousand years of dispersion of the Jewish people.[2] The men responsible for this reorientation were trained in the disciplines of modern science and thought. Yet they sensed intuitively the depth of the Jewish tragedy and the strong and abiding attachment of the masses of Jewry to Zion. This love was, indeed, a mystique, incomprehensible and strange when subjected to the tests of empirical inquiry and the canons of rationalism. The very word "redemption" (geulah) was enough to stir the hearts and minds of millions. It was upon such foundations that the Zionist ideal flourished, and for this reason it is incorrect to speak of Zionism as an exclusively secular nationalist movement.

The State of Israel, to be sure, is a secular state. But, in the view of many of its leaders, the State itself is only an instrument in the realization of the higher aspirations of the Jewish people: the creation of a society which will embody the vision of prophets and sages of yesteryear, the vision of man's ceaseless striving towards ethical and moral perfection in every sphere of human activity. There are those who see in the State an historic opportunity to weld the diverse groups of Jews into a nation "like all the nations," without an imperative to build something unique and different in the scale of human values. The Jew whose loyalty to the group is expressed in cultural rather than religious terms, would place an emphasis upon Hebrew life and culture. Still others would experiment with a variety of social forms of organization from collective ownership to free enterprise, depending upon their particular economic philosophy, with the sole view of making the State a powerful vehicle for progress.

The throb and pulse of contemporary Israel have caused disappointment in certain quarters where it is felt that it has been deflected from its traditional course, prescribed for it in half a century of debate and discussion in classical Zionist literature. Hence, voices are heard that Israel is not a Zionist State. Eliezer Livneh expressed this doubt succinctly: "As a result of complicated spiritual, social and economic developments, Israel has reached the point where we can no longer say readily and unequivocally to what extent it is fulfilling the Zionist mission for the sake of which it was established."[3]

What is this Zionist mission? It is exactly in this area that tempers rise and interpretations differ. Religious and non-religious Jews would clash violently on the meaning and the goal of this mission. Yet, in a period of crisis, as during the Sinai campaign of 1956, the supreme goal of the nation was the defence of the land of Israel. A unity of purpose was engendered which transcended all debates concerning a Zionist mission. This consciousness of unity and solidarity in moments of danger justified the conviction that the restoration of the State was in itself the fulfilment of the Zionist mission. Yet statehood is not an end in itself. For the Zionist mission, if viewed from the perspective of defence of independence and sovereignty of the State, is but a surrender to the exigencies of the political realities of the Middle East. War is frowned upon in the Jewish tradition, and no responsible leader of Israel's government would receive a hearing in the market-places of the teeming cities of Tel Aviv, Haifa, or Jerusalem, if his message were to envision a permanent state of belligerency. It is not necessary to point out at this stage that the foreign policy of the State of Israel from the very beginning has been seeking incessantly a direct confrontation with the Arab statesmen in order to achieve a peaceful settlement of all disputes.

It is now imperative to deal with the problem of the genesis of the idea of interdependence of people, land, and faith, since it is crucial for our determination of the religious roots of a modern secular state.

The attempt to isolate faith from the context of ancient Israel and to describe Israel in purely secular and political terms, has been the aim of the Alt and Noth school of Bible history and Bible criticism.[4] To Noth, there are only two entities —people and land. Faith is incidental. He, therefore, begins his monumental volume *The History of Israel* (1958) with the settlement of the twelve tribes in Palestine. The covenant of Abraham, the leadership of Moses, the Exodus, Sinai, the sojourn in the wilderness: these constitute "pre-history." Is there a kernel of truth in this "pre-history"? We do not know. What we do know, Noth reminds us, is the recollection of these events which was written down in Palestine many years, perhaps centuries, after the consolidation of the Twelve-Clan League in that land. He writes (p. 5): "It must be stated emphatically that the Old Testament tradition does not recognize any earlier form of 'Israel' than this union of the twelve tribes domiciled in Palestine." Shall we then completely dismiss the authenticity of the Pentateuch (the Five Books of Moses), the traditions of which are hallowed in the religion of the Jewish people? Higher Biblical Criticism has, for a time, succeeded in demolishing the unity and authenticity of the Pentateuch, only to see it restored again by latest archaeological discoveries to its position of pre-eminence amongs the books of the Bible. Noth agrees that the Pentateuch "sets out to relate events that have happened," but he goes on to say (pp. 42 f.) that "it is certain that it did not originate and was not planned, at any rate from the outset, as a historical work at all, but has its source in the successive coalescences of sacred traditions which are based on particular historical events."

The most trenchant criticism of Noth's theory on the origin and early history of Israel is offered by John Bright. This scholar maintains that Noth has not succeeded in his attempt to reconstruct the events of that history, because "the origin of Israel and its faith is left without adequate explanation" and that it is beyond belief that "Moses was only some Transjordanian *sheikh* whose memory was enshrined in a grave tradition."[5] He chides Noth for his assumption "that Israel's faith grew, as it were out of the ground, without founder, but then straightway felt so keenly the need for a founder that it was obliged to blow up the figure of the colorless Moses to gigantic proportions in order to accord him status."

In short, we have here another example of the uncertain and devious paths of Biblical scholarship. Noth earnestly tries to discover the truth concerning the political and institutional history of early Isreal, but when he stumbles upon extraordinary phenomena he suddenly retreats and confesses that "this self-testimony [Old Testament] makes the history of Israel not merely unique, as every national history on earth is unique and unrepeatable, but *utterly unique* in character among the historians of the nations (p. 48)."

The union of people, land, and faith in the Covenant, in God's revelation or in His self-disclosure, in the Divine constitution of the Torah, in the Promised Land, taught and propounded by Moses and the prophets, was the premise upon which the foundations of Judaism were built. Objective scholarly research cannot erase subjective facts of history, especially when these facts are recorded in the literature of a people. Subjective facts, such as faith or voluntary acceptance of instruction in ritual, prayer, law, and ethics, are powerful incentives to national unity and cohesiveness. These elements prevail at the very cradle of Israel's life and culture. Of greatest importance, therefore, is the position on early Israel of one of the eminent Jewish Biblical scholars of our time, Yehezkel Kaufmann.[6] He establishes the link between people and faith and between faith and land. With regard to the former, he declares (p. 43) that "it seems certain that this monotheistic view of human history is rooted in the historic sense of the Israelite nation, in its consciousness of itself as unique, elected—a feeling that it had from the time of the religious revolution in the days of Moses." As regards the latter, i.e. the link between faith and land, he states (p. 76) that "although Israelite religion was universal in essence, it had evolved in national forms. The land of Israel was its territorial sphere, the life of Israel was the sphere of its historic expression; its *Holy Land* was Palestine, its festivals, temples, priests and prophets were exclusively Israelite." Kaufmann does not hesitate to consider the subjective facts of the history of a people as a guide to its development. His reference to the concept of election as a psychological phenomenon (feeling) is evidence of his intuitive grasp of the events as they unfolded not in "pre-history" but in the history of ancient Israel, as recorded in the Pentateuch. For these singular and unique events constitute the religious roots of the First, Second, and Third Commonwealth of the Jewish people.[7]

What transpired after the consolidation of the monarchy under Saul, David, Solomon, and the subsequent rulers of the Divided Kingdom is not only of great moment for the Jewish people and Judaism, but of significance for the spiritual progress of mankind. The prophets, from Amos to Jeremiah, faced the problem of corruption of secular power, although they accepted the state as a necessary institution in the life of the nation. Like every human institution, the state can be used to advance or to negate social values. It can further the interests of its citizens through just legislation, or it can be deflected from its path of social righteousness. Thus we find that politics and ethics, law and justice become intertwined in Israel's national life. This conception dominates later Jewish jurisprudence; indeed it was the foundation of Mosaic law.

Those who tried to establish the claim that universalism in Judaism emerged triumphant, failed to note the tension that always existed between the two motifs in ancient Israel: universalism and particularism. There is no contradiction between these two aspects of the Jewish religion. The prophets taught that Jews may sojourn in foreign lands, and they may build houses and vineyards. They may worship the God of their fathers and recall the glory that was once Israel. Yet a conception of Israel forever detached from its soil is contrary to the plain record of the Bible. Moses has already regarded dispersion as a curse.[8] Just as laws, ceremonies, and festivals are completely dependent upon the Covenant with God, so are the people of Israel and the land of Israel inseparable. This idea permeates the teachings of the Bible.

Thus the ideal of national restoration is ever present in Biblical prophecy. Its message of return to Zion, of rebuilding the waste places, of ingathering and settlement is based upon this mystique of interdependence of people, land, and faith. The holiness of the land of Israel becomes enshrined in Jewish consciousness.[9] In days to come, Israel will be restored and "Zion shall be redeemed with justice" and Jerusalem shall again "be called the city of righteousness."[10]

But the prophets went further than to exhort a return to Zion. They projected the issue of purpose. Just as communion with God is the deeper reason for the performance of the commandments, so has the state necessary functions to perform in the Divine government of the world. One of the functions of a state is the furtherance of the social and ethical ideals of the Jewish faith. This is true of all the prophets in ancient Israel.[11]

It is against the background of Scripture that the Holy Land begins to loom large in the imagination of the Jew in the period of the Talmud and in later Rabbinic Judaism. As the Land of Promise, it was now sanctified because God's Providence (Shechinah) dwells in it. Morover, many commandments connected with the sacrificial cult and with agricultural activities could not be fulfilled beyond the borders of its sacred soil. Only in Palestine can one truly live in accordance with the laws of the Torah.

The Rabbis of the Talmud never for one moment doubted the central position Palestine occupied in the faith of Israel. They asserted that "the Land of Israel is holier than all lands," and that "the Schechinah reveals itself there exclusively." Furthermore, "the land was created in the beginning, while the whole world at the end of Creation." Israel was indeed worthy of supreme gifts, and as a recompense for vicissitudes, struggles, and suffering, God gave the Jewish people "the Torah, the Land of Israel and the World to Come."[12]

A return to this land was to be regarded as a religious duty.[13] But the Rabbis insisted that the restoration of the land was not to be sought by means of violence, nor must Jews rebel against the nations among whom they dwell. The Rabbis spoke of these obligations as "oaths" which God imposes upon Israel.[14]

If the land of Israel was holy, the city of Jerusalem was envisioned by the prophets as the City of God. Beauty and goodness were hers. Jerusalem illumined the path of the righteous and inspired faith and hope in the darkest periods of Jewish history. "The earthly Jerusalem" (Yerushalayim shel mattah) was believed to be paralleled by "the Jerusalem above" (Yerushalayim shel ma'alah) which had been prepared before the creation of the world. The extravagant praise of the city in rabbinic lore was due in no small measure to the tender consideration given her by prophets and psalmists in Scripture.[15]

The ancient yearning for restoration was linked throughout the weary centuries of dispersion with the coming of Messiah and with the ethical perfectibility of mankind. The idea of redemption from exile was extended to include the entire human race in the true spirit of Biblical prophecy. All nations will hail Messiah, but the Jews will now be gathered from all the corners of the earth and they will converge on the Holy City of Jerusalem. A resurrection of the dead will take place and the Temple in all its glory will be dedicated to the Service of God.[16]

Pilgrimages to the Holy Land by Jews were undertaken even in Graeco-Roman Diaspora. In addition to making contributions to the Temple, pilgrims streamed into Jerusalem for the three festivals: Tabernacles, Passover, and Pentecost. Loyalty to the spiritual homeland is attested by many ancient writers. Zion remained a reality in the lives of Jews wherever they sojourned. Daily prayer had been orientated towards Jerusalem. Exile and Zion thus became symbols which stirred their conscience and imagination, and which alternately created moments of sadness and joy, despair and exhilaration.

Jewish history is replete with records of journeys of Rabbis, scholars, and men of piety to the Holy Land. Those steeped in talmudic and mystic lore felt intuitively the spiritual significance of a personal attachment to this land. Others cherished a handful of sacred soil from Mount Moriah to be placed in the coffin and thus be symbolic of internment in Palestine. Still others believed "that they would be spared the underground migration which awaited all bodies buried elsewhere before they could arise from the dead in the Messianic age."[17]

Yehudah Halevi was one of the most celebrated pilgrims to the Holy Land (about 1140). Physician, philosopher, poet, he composed beautiful Zionide elegies describing his inner call to make the journey.

My heart is in the East, and I in the uttermost West

Zion! Wilt thou not ask if peace be with thy captives
That seek thy peace—that are the remnant of thy flocks?

In his recent *History of the Jews*, Professor S. W. Baron has an illuminating comment on Yehudah Halevi. He states:

When he composed the moving poem Siyyon ha-lo Tish'ali *(Zion, Doest Thou Not Ask for the Peace of Thy Captives?), Halevi conceived it as a personal confession of himself as the "Captive of Hope," longing to shed his tears on the desolate hills of Judea. Little did he dream that before very long almost all Jewish congregations in the world would incorporate this elegy, alongside the biblical Lamentations, in their ritual for the Ninth of Ab. Nor could he anticipate that the cries of anguish of his perceptive soul responding to the Jewish and universal crisis in a deeply divided world would evoke their greatest response in the era of a resuscitated modern Jewish nationalism, long after that particular separation between the Christian West and Islamic East had given way to other imperial and ideological divisions.*[18]

Not only poets but rationalist thinkers taught the centrality of Palestine in the Jewish faith and in their systematic treatments on Judaism they gave prominence to this doctrine. Thus the great philosopher Moses Maimonides (d. 1204) devotes several sections of his code, the Mishneh Torah, to the question of a Jew's obligation to live in the Holy Land.[19] His own visit to Palestine was brief, and although he chose to live in exile, his loyalties and ties to the land were strong and abiding. Interpreting the verse in Ps. 102:15, "for Thy servants take pleasure in her stones and love her dust," he said: "The greatest of our sages used to kiss [the rocks] on the borders of Palestine. They used to kiss the stones of the land and rolled themselves in its dust."[20]

The sources—rabbinic, kabbalistic, and philosophical—reveal an intensity of inquiry concerning the problem of the return to Zion. Geography, history, laws, and ethical commandments are woven into a pattern in consonance with the exalted role of Palestine as the Holy Land. In numerous treatments, the debate centres on the question of a return to Zion as a positive commandment. Scripture always is the basis for discussion and speculation. The precarious position of the Jews in the dispersion plays a prominent part, yet it is in a religious context that solutions are sought for and the authorities unanimously upheld the doctrine of holiness of the land, implicitly and explicitly inferred from Scripture.

The strong religious interest of Jews in Palestine gave rise to a host of Messianic pretenders, who offered to redeem Israel from bondage and lead it back to the Promised Land. Abraham Abulafia, David Reubeni, Solomon Molcho, Shabbetai Zevi, and many others, out of sincere belief in their own vocation or from opportunistic motives, presented themselves as Messiahs to the Jewish people. Historical events, whether the Crusades or the oppressive policies of governments of Moslem and Christian Spain, Europe, or Asia Minor, hastened the reception of the message of imminent deliverance in the countries of dispersion. In Turkey, Messianic excitement swelled to a climax in 1666 when Shabbetai Zevi began his ill-fated activities, and his influence did not diminish even when he embraced Mohammedanism.[21] It should be added that while the activities and the preachments of many Messianic pretenders had a negative effect on the Jewish historical condition, there was a positive element in their message: they expressed a yearning for "moral perfection" (sh'lemut ha-midot) and "human freedom" (v'ha-cherut ha-enushi).[22]

In eighteenth-century Poland there was a religious movement which intensified the love for Zion and paved the way for East European Jewry to participate in the colonizing effort in Palestine; this was Hassidism.[23] Nurtured on the soil of the esoteric doctrines of Kabbalah, Hassidism continued to weave the web of mystical speculation concerning God, Messianism, the land of Israel, in much popularized form. In homilies and parables, the Hassidic Rabbis of Galicia and Poland now gave full expression to this love for Zion. Though barren and desolate, this land was still "the very essence of the world and the lifeblood of the universe."

The mystical lore of the Zohar (the Book of Splendour) and the practical implications developed by "the Ari ha-Kodosh," Isaac Luria of Safed, served as a basis for Hassidic teachings. Emotionalism replaced the high spheres of thought. The "mysterium tremendum" of which Rudolf Otto speaks[24] as surrounding God's majesty is presented in Jewish mysticism not by mere flight of the imagination, but by powerful delineation of God's will and His commandments to man. It was in this context that the Safed mystics, cognizant of the terrible consequences of the expulsion of Jews from Spain in the year 1492, concentrated on "the End" and on "Exile and Redemption." G. G. Scholem, writing of the catastrophe of 1492, states: "The last age became as important as the first; instead of reverting to the dawn of history, or rather to its metaphysical antecedents, the new doctrines laid the emphasis on the final stages of the cosmological process."[25]

The reason for the acceptance of Hassidic teachings by the masses of Poland was precisely the Messianic element bequeathed to them by the Safed mystics. Its concept of "deliverance" satisfied their hunger for redemption. "Deliverance" takes on in Hassidism a more pragmatic meaning. Instead of "pressing the end," as Buber puts it, Hassidim makes periodic pilgrimages to the Holy Land. No wonder, then, that on the eve of Passover in 1798, Rabbi Nachman of Bratslav, at the age of twenty-six, announced to his disciples that after the holiday he would undertake the hazardous journey to Palestine. When his wife inquired how he proposed to support her and his daughters, he replied: "You will become a cook and your daughters will be servants."[26]

The Jews entered the modern world in the eighteenth century. Until that time, they had lived in many lands, often separated from their neighbours by ghetto walls. They fulfilled economic functions, but lived apart from the general community. In these enclaves of Europe they created a Jewish environment which enabled them to survive persecution and hostility. Tradition regulated their mode of thinking and believing; ceremonial and ritual law was decisive in all matters pertaining to the cycle of their individual lives, as well as to the customs and mores of the community. New winds of doctrine, new stirrings in Europe, now changed the character of their tradition-bound existence. In Germany, the spirit of Enlightenment with its emphasis upon the idea of universal brotherhood of man, reason, science, and progress triumphed. In Poland, Hassidism, as has been pointed out, engulfed the impoverished and oppressed Jewish communities with its tremendous emotional appeal and its protest against the narrow spiritual confines of their ghettos and touched a responsive chord in their hearts. These movements were the living streams which fructified Judaism in the nineteenth century. Both contributed to the rise of Zionism.

The Enlightenment brought about a serious re-examination of the idea of a return to Zion. Mendelssohn, in his attempt to hasten the process of integration of Jewry in Germany, did not incorporate in his conception of Judaism as "revealed legislation" such traditional beliefs as a personal Messiah, Zion, and resurrection of the dead. The triumphs of reason in his day, the drive towards full emancipation and civil rights, were responsible not only for Mendelssohn's neutrality on these issues, but for the attitude of the early Reform leaders, who, under the spell of Enlightenment, began the elimination of references to these beliefs from their prayerbooks and theology.

The debate continued throughout the nineteenth century, as the centre shifted from Germany to Hungary and the United States. It is generally admitted that Reform Judaism in that century, in espousing liberalization of ritual practices, halted the exodus of Jews from the Jewish community. At the same time indifference to the Jewish faith, baptism and intermarriage, presented serious threats to Jewish group survival. The vitality of the traditionalist group, however, was not seriously impaired. Those who yearned for ethnic as well as religious identification with the Jewish people were antagonized by the radicalism of the extremist Reform leaders, and were all the more hospitable to the message of Zion. They looked askance at the reform of the liturgy, the relegation of Hebrew to a place of secondary importance, and the apologetic "reinterpretation" of those Biblical and talmudic passages which speak of Israel's restoration to its historic land.

It is necessary to point out here that while the Enlightenment had brought about the revision of traditional religious concepts in Reform Judaism, it also contributed towards a secularization of the Messianic idea of a return to Zion, a fact which was clearly evident in the subsequent history of Zionism. Thus Jewish socialists, labour groups, and agnostics shared in this nation-building process, together with all the religious groups in the community.

In America, under the spell of Enlightenment, reason, optimism, and democracy, Reform Rabbis issued creedal statements which challenged the doctrine of interdependence of people, land, and faith. The American environment did not require such reorientation and the consequence was a reduction of Judaism to a nebulous "Mosaic persuasion." The particularistic elements were purged and eliminated altogether under the blows of the precise formulations of the "Pittsburgh Platform" of 1885. We must not, however, attribute to the leaders of Reform both in Germany and in the United States any motives of self-rejection when they revealed shortsightedness in their espousal of Judaism solely as a faith or religious community. Many Reform Rabbis took an anti-nationalist position because they truly believed that universalism was the proper course and direction for Judaism in a world which believed in progress and the perfectibility of man under God. Second Isaiah supplied the necessary rationale for this religious philosophy and "the mission of Israel" amongst the nations was exalted above the immediate issues of survival under pressure. The debate concerning a recovery of traditionalism for American Reform lasted for half a century, and the "Columbus Platform" of 1937 saw a reconciliation of Reform Judaism and Zionism. In fact, leading American Reform Rabbis in the twentieth century became the greatest spokesmen for Zionism.[27]

It is often asserted that political Zionism was solely a reaction to anti-Semitism and a child of rampant secular nationalism. This charge is untrue, as it is a falsification of the plain historical record. The religious roots of Zionism are completely ignored by those who reject the ethnic ties of the Jewish people. It is true that anti-Semitism hastened a reappraisal of the precarious Jewish position in the dispersion, and this led to a consolidation of forces within the Jewish community. The reason for the success of political Zionism, however, was its recourse to the secular instrumentalities of the modern world with which to achieve recognition as a national movement. The revival of Hebrew was a miraculous achievement, and its importance lies in the fact that the language of the Bible is today a vehicle of expression in a modern secular state. Language was just another link in the chain of Jewish tradition, and the use of Hebrew fortifies the conviction that the chain has not been broken in the millennial experiences of Israel.

Having surveyed the relationship of land, people, and faith in Jewish historical context, it is now imperative to consider the treatment of the question in the idiom of contemporary religious philosophy. Two eminent teachers of religion have addressed themselves to the problem of the association of the Jewish people and the land of Israel: Martin Buber and the late Chief Rabbi of Palestine, Abraham Isaac Kook.

In 1944, Buber's Hebrew work *Israel and Palestine: The History of an Idea*, made its appearance. In May, 1948, the State of Israel was proclaimed. Buber states in his preface to the English edition of this book, published in 1950, that "it has not proved necessary to alter anything in the text of the present work, which is intended to shed light not on the history of a political enterprise but on that of a religious idea or rather on the spiritual history of a faith."

This book is one of the most important treatises on the religious roots of the State of Israel. "Zion," to Buber, "has retained this sacred character (Ps. 48:3, 'the city of the great King,' that is, of God as the King of Israel) ever since. In their prayers and songs the mourning and yearning of the people in exile were bound up with it, the holiness of the land was concentrated in it and in the Cabbala Zion was equated with an emanation of God Himself. When the Jewish people adopted this name for their national concept all these associations were contained in it."[28] In profoundly moving language, Buber traces "the history of an idea" from Biblical times to the great personalities of the Zionist movement: Moses Hess, Leo Pinsker, Theodor Herzl, Ahad Ha'am, Rav Kook, and A. D. Gordon. Recalling the testimony of the Bible, he explains anew the meaning of Promise and Redemption—terms charged with spiritual significance in the entire history of Jewry. "The Promise means that within history an absolute relationship between a people and a land has been taken into the Covenant between God and the people." Redemption, to Buber, signifies that "the renewal of the world and the renewal of Zion are one and the same thing, for Zion is the heart of the renewed world."[29]

Rabbi Kook settled in Palestine in 1904. A mystic of rare depth and perception, he advanced the doctrine of "holiness" in the life of the Jewish individual and society. The Promised Land was preordained for Israel. A bond was created from the days of Abraham and it will never be severed. The Jew, in returning to this land, will again be distinguished for his creative powers, even though this creativity will assume new forms. The new values will be holy. In Zion, the creative gifts are renewed as of old. "In the land of Israel, the spiritual fountain of the inwardness of holiness, which is the light of the life of the soul of the congregation of Israel, flows continuously."[30]

A return to the land, according to Buber, means also a return to "the holiness of nature [which] remained hidden when Israel took the holiness of spirit into exile." A regeneration of the body follows. "We have forgotten the holiness of the body. We have a holy flesh, we have it no less than we have a holy spirit."[31]

Rabbi Kook had high regard for the youth of Palestine, though some young pioneers were known to desecrate the sacred soil by their irreligiosity. A story is told that "when the late Chief Rabbi Kook was once asked to take action against some young workers who had infringed the religious law, he replied by recalling the immunity enjoyed by the workers in the Holy City in olden times. The High Priest could enter the Holy of Holies in the Temple only on the Day of Atonement and after making the most elaborate preparations, but the builders and masons could enter it at any time to carry out repairs to the fabric. The workers of to-day were repairing breaches in the House of Israel, and even though they departed from the law they must not be treated as transgressors."[32]

The religious roots of the secular State of Israel are abundantly clear, and the long historical record only substantiates the persistence of the idea of "Holiness of the Land" which began to impress itself upon Jewish consciousness at the very dawn of Jewish history, when God commanded Abraham to go "unto the land that I will show thee" (Gen. 12:1). Yet it is imperative to answer the question whether or not this State will develop into a theocracy—a fear which has been expressed by liberal Jews, and especially those who are truly dedicated to the concept of separation of the provinces of "religion and state." Such a fear is unwarranted. While the influence of the Jewish religious tradition upon the secular framework of the State may be observed in many areas of Israel's national existence, one can hardly call it "a theocratic State." As Sir Leon Simon rightly declared: "The mere fact that the normal day of rest is the Jewish Sabbath, and that the festivals are statutory holidays, links current practice with Torah even for those who are not meticulous in their fulfilment of the observances traditionally associated with those days. And the fact that Hebrew is the normal language of Jewish life in Israel is of capital significance in this connection.[33]

The greatest challenge facing Israel's leaders in so many domains of its national life is to build into the fabric of a secular enterprise the spiritual verities of a hallowed religious tradition. In spite of the recurrent crises in foreign relations, Israel's citizens are ever ready to examine the goals of statehood. This soul-searching is Israel's nobility.

NOTES

[1]D. Ben Gurion, "Words and Values," in *Forum*, vol. III (August, 1957), pp. 9–10.
[2]A. Bohm, *Die Zionistische Bewegung*, I (Tel Aviv, 1935), 211–229; A. Bein, *Theodor Herzl: A Biography*, chapter VII, "The First Zionist Congress," pp. 226–242.
[3]E. Livneh, "Is Israel a Zionist State?" in *Midstream*, Summer, 1956, p. 27.
[4]See A. Alt, *Das System der Stammesgrenzen im Buche Josua* (Sellin Festschrift, 1927); *Die Ursprünge des Israelitischen Rechts* (Leipzig: S. Hirzel, 1934); *Kleine Schriften zur Geschichte des Volkes Israel* I, II (1953). Also M. Noth, *The History of Israel* (New York, 1958): see review by H. H. Ginsberg, "Light on the Dim Past," in *Midstream*, vol. IV:4 (August, 1958), pp. 94–98; *Das System der zwölf Stämme Israels* (Stuttgart: W. Kohlhammer, 1930); *Ueberlieferungsgeschichtliche Studien*, I (Halle: M. Niemeyer, 1943).
[5]John Bright, "Early Israel in Recent History Writing," in *Studies in Biblical Theology*, no. 19 (1956), p. 84f.
[6]Yehezkel Kaufmann, "The Biblical Age," in *Great Ages and Ideas of the Jewish People*, ed. by L. W. Schwartz (New York, 1956).
[7]The reference here is to the First Commonwealth which closed in 586 B.C., during the reign of King Zedekiah; the Second Commonwealth which closed in 70 A.D. with the destruction of Jerusalem by the Romans; and the Third Commonwealth which is the present State of Israel.
[8]Lev. 26:32; 26:33; 26:44; 26:45. Gen. 13:14–15.
[9]Deut. 11:12. Zech. 2:14.
[10]Relevant passages in the Bible are: Isa. 1:21; 1:26–27; 60:4; 60:8–9. Amos 9:14–15. Hosea 3:4–5. Joel 2:18–19; 4:1; 4:17; 4:20. Micah 2:12; 4:6–7. Zeph. 3:20. Jer. 3:18; 23:6; 46:27. Ez. Chap. 36–39. Obad. 1:17; 1:20. Zech. 8:13; 10:10. Mal. 3:12. Daniel 7:27; 12:1.
[11]Isa. 28:16–17; 2:2–3. Jer. 5:1. Ez. 17:11ff.

[12] For these quotations see, respectively, Mishnah Kaylim 1:6, "Esser kedushot hen—Eretz Yisrael mikudeshet mikol ha-aratzot"; Moed Katan 25:1; b. Taanith 10, "Eretz Yisrael nivreth t'chilah v'chol ha-olam kulo livsoph"; Mechilta to Yithro, 23, "Torah, v'Eretz Yisrael v'ha-olam ha-ba."

[13] The most notable talmudic and rabbinic passages referring to the future of the Jewish people are: b. Berachot 28b, 34b; b. Shabbat 118a; b. Menahot 45a; b. Baba Mezia 3a; b. Erubin 43b; b. Baba Bathra 76a; Gen Rabba LXXXV, 2; Shir ha-Shirim Rabba, VII, 10; Sifri on Dt. 1:1.

[14] b. Ketubot IIIa.

[15] Isa. 2:2f; 62:1–5; b. Sukkah 51a; b. Kiddushin 49b; Midrash Tehilim on Ps. XLVIII; Ab. R.N. 28; Midrash ha-Ne'elam, in *Zohar Hadash*, section, "Noah."

[16] Saadia Gaon, *The Book of Beliefs and Opinions*, trans. by S. Rosenblatt (New Haven, 1948), chapter 6, "Redemption," pp. 304–312. Also J. Guttman, *Die Religionsphilosophie des Saadia* (Göttingen, 1882), p. 236.

[17] See *Great Ages and Ideas of the Jewish People*, ed. Schwartz (New York, 1956), p. 423.

[18] S. W. Baron, *A Social and Religious History of the Jews*, VII (New York, 1958), 168.

[19] On the question of Zion and the perfectibility of man, see Maimonides, *Mishneh Torah*, Hilchot M'lachim, 12–5 and 4–10.

[20] Quoted in J. S. Minkin, *The World of Moses Maimonides* (New York, 1957), p. 380.

[21] S. Dubnow, *Weltgeschichte des jüdischen Volkes*, VII (Berlin, 1930), 64–83.

[22] G. G. Scholem, *Shabbetai Zevi B'ymei Chayav*, I (Tel Aviv, 1957), 8.

[23] Hans Kohn, "Zur Geschichte der Zionistischen Ideologie," in *Der Jude*, VII (Berlin, 1923), 321f.

[24] Rudolf Otto, *The Idea of the Holy* (London, 1923).

[25] G. G. Scholem, *Major Trends in Jewish Mysticism* (Jerusalem, 1941), p. 240f.

[26] Sh. A. Horodetsky, *He-Hasiduth v'ha'Hasidim*, III (Jerusalem, 1923), 24.

[27] See A. H. Silver, "Israel," in *The World Crisis and Jewish Survival* (New York, 1941), p. 134: "National restoration was the very heart of the messianic ideal which was a political-spiritual concept from its very inception. To substitute for this national ideal an anti-national, purely transcendental, nebulous Messianic Age, on the plea of religious evolution, is to be guilty not of revision but of distortion. It is both new and counterfeit."

[28] Martin Buber, *Israel and Palestine: The History of an Idea* (London, 1942), Introduction, p. lx.

[29] *Ibid.*, pp. 18, 35.

[30] Quoted in J. B. Agus, *Banner of Jerusalem: The Life, Times and Thoughts of Abraham Isaac Kuk* (New York, 1946), p. 215.

[31] M. Buber, *Israel and Palestine*, pp. 150f.

[32] I. Cohen, *The Zionist Movement* (New York, 1946), pp. 268–269.

[33] Sir Leon Simon, "The Land of Israel," in *The Jewish Heritage*, ed. E. Levine (London, 1955) pp. 219–220.

THE SEARCH FOR RELEVANCE / *Lou H. Silberman*

The end of the eighteenth century saw the Jews of western Europe begin their encounter with a culture that, no matter how deeply it had been rooted in the modes and forms of mediaeval thought, now stood in radical opposition to an age believed left behind. Renaissance and Reformation had, of course, not broken the ties with yesterday. Indeed, the situation of the Jews exhibited the tenacity with which the hand of the old held on; nonetheless the world of the revolutions, American and French, was different from and other than its predecessors on the stage of history. But revolutions do not just happen. Their foreshadowings and anticipatory rumblings are discernible, if not to those involved in them, at least to those who look back at them. Thus a Solomon Maimon escaping from his hated Polish ghetto and a Moses Mendelssohn snatching himself out of the Dessau Judengasse were brought face to face with a world jarred from its accustomed tracks and not yet settled in new ways.

Nine hundred years earlier, the similarly out-of-joint world confronting Saadya Gaon had been described by a contemporary Islamic scholar, "Muslims, Jews, Christians and Magians, they all are walking in error and darkness. There are only two kinds of people left in the world. The one group is intelligent, but lacking in faith. The other has faith but is lacking in intelligence."[1] It had been to the reunion of faith and reason that Saadya and most of his successors had applied themselves, to produce the architectonic religious-philosophic structures that were the glory of the high Middle Ages.

If the world Maimon and Mendelssohn faced was as chaotic as was Saadya's, nonetheless its chaos was such that the older answers no longer served. Even more, those very answers had themselves been undermined during the intervening centuries. In Christian Europe it had not been the newly minted coin of Thomas Aquinas' *Summa* that Luther threw aside, but the battered, clipped, devalued coinage of later scholasticism. So too in Jewry, it was not the *Moreh Nebukhim* still shining from its creator's glowing thought that failed, but the foundering hulk of Jewish Aristotelianism subjected to Crescas' philosophical criticism on the one hand and the contempt of the Lurianic mystics on the other.

The old, no matter how precious, could not merely be reaffirmed in the face of the challenge of the new. It had to subject itself to the rigorous scrutiny of

European philosophy and discipline itself to the demands of contemporary thought, if it were to have relevance for those who like Mendelssohn were coming out of the Jew-streets of Europe. Before this had happened, before an affirmation of the new synthesis was made, many—and these by no means the worst—were, even as in the days of Saadya, lost to Israel. The synthesis was made, however, in the nineteenth century. The dominant post-Kantian idealism of the German universities became the basis of a series of Jewish religious philosophies representing the struggle of individual thinkers on the one hand and on the other, a series of "practical" formulations that resulted in varying institutional expressions of Judaism. Whatever then the varieties of Jewish thought in western Europe, they reflected in large measure, although with notable exceptions, aspects of idealistic philosophy as it dominated the European intellectual scene.

II Julius Guttmann, in his history of Jewish philosophy (1933), summed up both the result and the problem arising from this situation. "The promise-filled beginnings of a modern philosophy of Judaism were too closely tied to the presuppositions of German idealism to be effective after the latter's collapse. Thus the end of the nineteenth century saw the establishment of a new philosophical trend independent of the earlier tendency, within the framework of an all-inclusive movement toward a systematic comprehension of Judaism." Guttmann pointed out that the first task this new trend faced was to provide "a correct and convincing portrait of the real facts of the teachings of Judaism. Thus in general the presentation of a philosophic analysis of Judaism trailed after the historical description which sought to permit the teachings of Judaism to speak, as it were, for themselves." The result was that Jewish religious thought as a synthesizing process came to a limping halt as it awaited the results of historical analysis. In its place, thinkers, apparently less timid, offered political, economic and social syntheses as affirmative and committing philosophies of Jewish existence.[2]

Only Hermann Cohen, the leader of the Marburg school of neo-Kantian philosophy, dared a new statement of Jewish religious philosophy rooted in the neo-Kantian revival that burgeoned at the end of the nineteenth century. Here too, and this seems to some students implicit in Cohen's own later writings, the relevance of the statement was compromised by a growing dissatisfaction with the philosophic structure with which Judaism was to come to terms. Yet as Guttmann insisted, Cohen's influence was by no means peripheral. Indeed, it is clear that he renewed the process of Jewish philosophy in modern times and in this sense he was not so much the end of an old as the beginning of a new era. Those who followed after him moved far from "his critical philosophy to follow the metaphysical and irrationalist tendencies that in general dominate contemporary thought," but their debt to him is no less real and his creative synthesis in *Die Religion der Vernunft aus den Quellen des Judentums* remains a towering peak on the topography of Jewish religious thought.[3]

Guttmann concluded his work with the discussion of Cohen for, writing at the beginning of the thirties, he held that it was too soon properly to evaluate the new tendencies. Albert Lewkowitz, writing at the same time about the spiritual influences that touched Judaism in the nineteenth century, went beyond this cursory glance to describe the newer philosophical positions and to suggest that while they made their influence felt on Jewry in many ways, Jewish religious thought was for a long time untouched. It is clear that the institutional expressions of Judaism were content by and large to reiterate the older formulae or to adjust piecemeal to the philosophical exigencies of the times. This was particularly so in America where the influences were far more practical than systematic, and, when the latter did make themselves felt, they were largely academic derivatives from the fading official European systems.[4]

Yet, as suggested above, Cohen's renewal of the philosophical enterprise within Judaism was not barren of results. When, at the end of the first decade of the twentieth century, the mordant voice of the resurrected Danish Protestant theologian Soren Kierkegaard was heard proclaiming the ultimate seriousness of the religious situation of man, even though his language was quite foreign to Cohen's apprehension of the matter, there were those who were prepared to respond to the challenge and who undertook to formulate personal statements of Judaism that would render in relevant fashion the meaning and sweep of the tradition. The twenties and thirties in Germany, far from being a wasteland, produced centres of creative Jewish thought not yet duplicated in America. The tragic exile and destruction of European Jewry, while it paradoxically brought to fruition some aspects of this process, brought to an end the particular situation and circumstances in and from which the process emerged. Thus there are torsos strewing the spiritual landscape; there are names whose works are destined to slumber silently unread, until the future shall have awakened the past. In America both a prevailing anti-intellectualism, or at least an anti-philosophical atmosphere, and the desperate need for action in the face of compounded tragedy inhibited, while at the same time it made imperative, the search for relevance.

To be fair, however, it must be conceded that in many ways the total situation was uncongenial to the religious enterprise. The voices commanding the attention of thoughtful men spoke with increasing hostility of this direction of man's existence. Religion was "the opiate of the masses," or an "illusion" to be removed therapeutically in the future. Its creative defenders were concerned less with its intellectual structure and more with their desire to re-fashion it as an instrument of social reconstruction. Its traditional defenders shook their heads in ever increasing dismay.

This, then, is the soil and seedbed of contemporary Jewish theological thought. The plant, flower, fruit, and seed it produced remain yet to be examined. Although description might be thought in order, there are easily accessible statements that render such a procedure unprofitable. But more than that, it entails reducing to the "historically viewed" that which might well engage us on the level of personal concern and commitment. In so far as contemporary Jewish religious thought is relevant it is not ready for the historian's mounting pin; in so far as it is irrelevant, it is of no concern to us at the moment. In this regard perhaps it is well to enter a *caveat* concerning the meaning of relevance. It is not here to be understood in an absolute sense, although this is not precluded. On the other hand, it is not to be taken in such a relative sense as to transform it into mere subjectivism. Rather is it to be used existentially as having its particular meaning and impact grounded in the situation in which we exist. That its meaning may be more ultimate than such a procedure suggests is not only not denied but is indeed affirmed without at the moment the responsibility of demonstrating it being accepted.

III   At the critical centre of any theological undertaking lies man's attempt to comprehend and understand God. Thus it is from this point that the search for relevance begins. The problem of the nineteenth century may well be characterized by the comment of Guttmann as he brought his sympathetic discussion of Cohen to a conclusion. "In Judaism the cleansing of man from sin requires God's forgiving grace, but for Cohen it is only the idea of a forgiving God which as the goal engaging man's belief gives him the strength to renew himself ethically. Cohen was himself continually concerned with this attenuation. His work breathes a truly living religious spirit which he sought with all of his power of conceptualization to seize hold of and embody in the structure of his system. Yet in all his various formulations he was unable to escape the problem. There always remained in the midst of his wonderful construction of religion a last unreconciled tension between its content and its concept." Martin Buber summed up this tension, which was the nineteenth century's legacy, in these words, "Cohen did not consciously choose between the God of the philosophers and the God of Abraham, rather believing to the last that he could succeed in identifying the two. Yet his inmost heart, that force from which, too, thought derives its vitality, had chosen and decided for him. The identification had failed, and of necessity had to fail. For the idea of God, that masterpiece of man's construction, is only the image of images, the most lofty of all the images by which man imagines the imageless God. It is essentially repugnant to man to recognize this fact, and remain satisfied. For when man learns to love God, he senses an actuality which rises above the idea. Even if he makes the philosopher's great effort to sustain the object of his love as an object of his philosophic thought, the love itself bears witness to the existence of the Beloved."[5]

These words, although written as late as 1943, not only point to the failure, glorious though it was, of the nineteenth-century endeavour, but indicate as well what the direction away from it had been. It was Buber himself who, at the focus of European thought and under the impact of "the metaphysical and irrational tendencies that in general dominate contemporary thought," sought a statement of man's apprehension of God in terms meaningful to a world that was determined not to know God.

His seminal work *I and Thou*, first sketched in 1916, written in 1919, and published in 1922, has had and continues to have an influence far beyond the sphere of theology, for it is concerned to hold up before man's eyes the true nature of his existence. Its basic distinction between the two modes of existence, relation (the encounter of persons, I–Thou) and connection (the manipulation of objects, I–It), has provided categories whose meanings are relevant to the whole sweep of man's life. They are fruitful in examining what happens in a classroom; they are involved in the psychiatrist's therapy; they are to be found "at the level where thought and imagination are fused . . . in the works of poets and dramatists."[6]

It is from the reality of this relation—I–Thou, and through its tragic though necessary fading into mere connection, I–It—that man comes to encounter God, to stand in the unfading relation with the eternal Thou, for all relation, all love finds its ultimate focus in Him. For Buber this is not a conceptual system, foreign to and imposed upon Judaism, but is in very truth the universalized description of what he had seen as the heart of the Hassidic community when he lived as a child with his grandfather in Lemberg and what he came to understand as he studied the tales of the teachers of that movement. Thus, when one recognizes or, perhaps better, when one experiences these modes of human existence, the ultimate encounter belongs in all naturalness to man's life. There is no tension between "content and concept." Every relation provides that openness which leads away from argumentation about God to the immediacy of relation with Him.

Buber has provided for the possibility in general of personal religion not at odds with but in very truth the flowering of the total stance of the individual towards existence. Yet that is not all. From the very beginning of his creative career, he has been concerned with community. But community is not an abstraction; it is something real and exists not only in the present but in history as well. If the philosophic thought of the nineteenth century had isolated God in a concept, it had as well either fragmentized man in the crowd or collectivized him into class or mass. Thus the recognition of relation was the rediscovery of community; and the paradigm of community was the "holy community," the community of the covenant. Here again the idea was seen not as an intruder but rooted in the historical experience of Israel. "To what is called in the song of Deborah and in other ancient passages of Scripture 'people of YHWH' a secular concept can approximate, namely that of a 'true people,' that is a people that realizes in this life the basic meaning of the concept *am*, 'people,' of living one *im* 'with,' another . . . The 'social' element in the apodictic laws is to be understood not on the basis of the task of bettering the living conditions of society but on the basis of establishing a true people, as the covenant partner of the *melekh* . . . the *melekh* YHWH does not want to rule a crowd but a community."[7]

If then Buber's category of relation, I-Thou, provides the possibility of a human–divine encounter relevant to and not isolated from man's common existence, so too does it provide the basis for an understanding of Israel relevant to God thus met. Although Israel as a nation has been shattered on the rock of history, it has ever and again sought for modes of existence in which the reality of community shall be renewed. The true Israel is the people of the Covenant standing over against, being addressed by, and addressing the eternal Thou, the people whose only real existence is in relation which always transcends the forms and means expressing it.

It is at this point that, paradoxically, Buber comes in full circle face to face with some of the practical formulations of the nineteenth century. These practical results had varied widely, running from a denial that any external expression of a philosophical-theological position was required essentially (although on a non-essential aesthetic, moralistic basis some form of expression was allowed) through an insistence that some expressions were essential without too deep an inquiry into the ground of that insistence, to the acceptance of two basically unrelated areas of existence, homiletically joined. For Buber the problem and the questions are posed on quite other grounds. Although one cannot commit the unconditioned encounter to any mode of expression, certainly not to one external to it, one cannot at the same time reject before the fact any mode of expression. Buber's position is clearly put in these words of one of his leading interpreters: ". . . the law too, to be meaningful, must be part of the dialogue between God and man and cannot legitimately be upheld as a separate objective reality. Religious truth is obstructed, writes Buber, by those who demand obedience to all the *mitzvot* without actually believing the law to be directly revealed by God." Buber himself spoke of his point of view in this matter as "not a-nomistic, but neither is it entirely nomistic." The tension between history expressed as law and the present moment expressed as command is not resolved but affirmed.[8]

IV This answer has a lonely grandeur and a fearsome challenge and was at the centre of a dramatic confrontation involving Buber and his collaborator and co-worker, Franz Rosenzweig. The exchange of opinion between these two men "might have become," writes a contemporary commentator, "one of the major religious debates in modern Judaism." It did not, suggests the same writer curiously, for Buber was "wise to exercise self-restraint in not accepting Rosenzweig's challenge." Yet in the encounter, even in its truncated form, the issue of the Law, not necessarily of the two attitudes towards it debated here, is made awesomely clear.[9]

Rosenzweig's essay "The Builders: Concerning the Law," was written as an open letter to Buber on the occasion of the republication in 1923 of eight addresses under the title *Reden über das Judentum* (Lectures on Judaism) and was directed most particularly to the last lecture "Herut" (Freedom), delivered in 1919. Rosenzweig's essay contrasts what he understands to be Buber's tremendous gift to his generation, the recognition of the true dimension of Jewish learning, with his failure "to come to terms" with Jewish law. For Rosenzweig, Buber had rejected all attempts to limit Jewish learning to a predefined "essential." He had restored the entire sweep of Jewish experience as the subject-matter of learning (*Lernstoff*) and had then sought out the principle of selection through which the latter becomes "the teaching" (*Lehre*). Writing to Buber he said: ". . . you made explicit a new principle of choice . . . a principle more to be trusted than any other offered, for it is not a part of the subject-matter. Indeed it is not a principle at all but is a dynamic. You demand of him who learns that he make himself the stake of learning, that he rivet himself to the chain of tradition as the latest link, thus becoming one who chooses because he is able to rather than one who merely wishes to choose." In other words, "Teaching comes into being at the point where subject-matter ceases to be matter and transforms itself into dynamic." But having done this, Buber, so Rosenzweig pointed out, turned his back on the Law. Torah as "the Teaching" can be renewed in the existential moment of choice, but Torah as *halakhah,* law, is not susceptible of the same unshackling. This was the crisis and called forth from Rosenzweig an impassioned plea that his friend not forsake his obligation to give an answer that would do more than offer a reverential nod towards the Law "which can effect no practical difference in our lives or to our person."[10]

For Rosenzweig this search for the relevance of Torah not only as the Teaching but also as the Way was crucial. His foundation work *Der Stern der Erlösung* (The Star of Redemption) was written to dispose of theoretical philosophical problems so that he could proceed to the practical matter of living in that pattern of existence which preceded and was the source of the theory. It was within the rhythm of practical Judaism that the living relations of Creation, Revelation, Redemption between God and the World, God and Man, Man and the World were most clearly seen and fully grasped. The problem was then to find the means of possessing the deed of Judaism in the same living fashion in which Buber had shown the thought of Judaism could be grasped.[11]

The attempt of western European Neo-Orthodoxy under the leadership of Samson Raphael Hirsch to provide an undergirding for the Torah as *halakhah* was for Rosenzweig too narrow. "The problem of the Law cannot be dispatched by merely affirming or denying the pseudo-historical theory of its origin, or the pseudo-juristic theory of its power to obligate, theories which Hirsch's orthodoxy made the foundation of rigid and narrow structure, unbeautiful despite its magnificence." And liberalism simply would not take the problem seriously. Thus Rosenzweig, proceeding by way of analogy to Buber's rediscovery of Torah as Teaching, sought the meaning of Torah as Way for himself and his generation. He was determined to break down distinctions, to reaffirm the whole of the Law as "do-able." "As in the *teaching,* the rigid difference between the essential and the non-essential, as outlined by liberalism, should no longer exist, so in the sphere of what can be done the difference between the forbidden and the permissible (that which in Neo-Orthodox terms is outside the scope of Jewish law) ... must cease to exist."[12]

Once the do-able character of the whole tradition is re-established, then, as in the field of knowledge, some dynamic is needed which will enable the individual to *do*. "Whatever can and must be done is not yet deed; whatever can and must be commanded is not yet commandment. . . . Like *teaching* it must come into being consciously where its content ceases to be content and transforms itself into dynamic." Continuing the analogy with teaching, Rosenzweig suggests that this recognition of the realm of the do-able and the thrusting of oneself into it makes the individual not merely one who wishes to do but one who is able to do. "This choice (by which the stuff of the Law is transformed into the doing of the Law) because it is not dependent upon wish but upon ability, is entirely individual. . . . Thus, whether much or little or indeed anything at all will be done is of infinitely less consequence than that it be done dynamically. . . . The deed is created at the boundary of the merely do-able, where the voice of the commandment causes the spark to leap from 'I must' to 'I can.' The Law is built on such commandments, and only on them." The decision to act is the response not to an external demand that one act but to an internal recognition that one can act. "For this reason no one can take another person to task, though he can and should teach him; because only *I* know what *I* can do; only my own ear can hear the voice of my own being which I have to reckon with. And perhaps another's non-ability does more for the upbuilding of both teaching and law than my own ability."[13]

To this statement of the search for the Jewish deed, Buber would not give his consent. "I agree to everything that follows from the letter's premises, but not to those premises themselves. It is my faith that prevents me from doing this." Rosenzweig was not willing to let it go at that. "As far as faith is concerned, the difference between us is a small one. . . ." But Buber was adamant in the face of Rosenzweig's continuing effort to bridge the chasm. The Law for Buber is entirely human and can never be interposed between man and God. Here the echoes of the mystic's judgment drawn from his own experience of the divine, although expressed in the cooler language of dialogic thought and the existentialist's moment of decision, make themselves heard. Rosenzweig, on the other hand, while not equating revelation with law-giving, nonetheless asked only that the question be left open for proof not in theory but in existence.[14]

However unresolved the issue between them may be, its magnitude overshadows the tension, for the reality of the question of the Jewish deed is thrust forward as a challenge that cannot be ignored. Its fearsome demand is not to be answered in general and institutional terms, but is addressed directly to the "single one" as "What can *I* do?" It is to be answered by his whole being, not in isolation from but in tension with the whole community in which he inevitably stands.

V   The impact of taking seriously the questions posed in the confrontation of the contemporary Jew by his tradition was not limited to the European scene. Although the most influential answer offered in America moved in quite other directions from those just discussed, Mordecai Kaplan's attempt was grounded in the same seriousness as were these. While judgment as to the enduring value of his work necessarily involves partisanship, the recognition that it was a serious attempt to discuss Judaism in terms relevant to the naturalistic philosophic temper and the sociological analysis of the twenties and thirties of this century, involves no partisan commitment.

Kaplan, viewing the American scene, found the institutional answers offered, in so far as the questions raised by the situation were taken seriously, inadequate, despite individual insights found within one or the other. What he offered was a transvaluation of values such as his acknowledged master, the Zionist writer Ahad Ha-Am, had proposed. This transvaluation was demanded for Kaplan by the "scientific" understanding of the nature of religion as expressed particularly in the writings of the French anthropologists Levy-Bruhl and Durkheim; it was validated most particularly for Kaplan by the thought of John Dewey. The anthropological analysis accepted by Kaplan saw religion within the total complex of a society as the value-conserving structure that provides for the survival of that society. It corresponds to Dewey's understanding of the "religious attitude" as the affirmative response of man to his situation. Those ideas which affirm the society's existence in the highest degree are its ideology; those activities which contribute most effectively to its continuation are its "sancta," its holy deeds.[15]

Judaism was to be "reconstructed" to conform intellectually to this analysis. In so far as the complex ideas within the tradition pointed to an affirmation of the Jewish community, they were to be retained, although their previous meanings were to be replaced, for they no longer represented objective being but value judgment. In so far as the holy deeds—customs and ceremonies—continued to support and undergird the existence of the community, they were to be accepted as the pattern of communal and individual life.

It has been suggested that Kaplan's uneasiness about dismissing the entire metaphysical problem and his continuing attempt to provide a more substantial existence for God than the strict tenets of the Deweyan formulation require, indicate the basic unsoundness of his reconstruction. Granting this, there yet remains a relevance transcending the flaw. What Kaplan was concerned with was a reunion of "content and concept." He saw in Reform, emphasis on concept as against content and in Orthodoxy, the reverse, with intermediate positions revealing makeshift adjustments more or less irrelevant to the scene. It is then perhaps as a question-about rather than as an answer-to the American situation that Kaplan's thought is most effective. The failure to recognize this has all too frequently transformed it into an institutional or communal programme and strategy that ignores the theoretical problems it involves.[16]

VI The post-World War II scene has witnessed the emergence of an intellectual mood and temper more closely akin to the earlier European formulations. Out of these there have flowered contemporary statements, intent upon providing bases for modern man's acceptance of Judaism, not as a sphere apart from man's real existence but indeed as the interpretation of that very situation.[17]

World War I had brought to the European intellectual disillusionment with that optimistic perfectionism which had caught hold of man's imagination during previous decades and had made the Kingdom of Heaven a glorious possibility well on its way to realization on earth. Theologically this disillusionment was expressed through re-emphasis on the Reformation doctrine of man's total spiritual weakness and the futility of any of the works of his hands, heart, and mind.[18]

No doctrine could have been more uncongenial to the America of the twenties; and even the economic débâcle of the thirties was viewed by many as an unpleasant episode, frustrating to be sure, but not denying man's creative possibilities. Yet there were some who began to see the situation from another perspective and to question increasingly the portrait of man offered by the liberal position. To them the events of the forties made it clear that the demonic was not a momentary aberration but was a fixed and real aspect of man's life. For them the glorious visions and ecstatic dreams of the liberal era were but manifestations of sinful pride. Led by the distinguished Protestant theologian, Reinhold Niebuhr, this point of view, commonly called Neo-Orthodox, exerted ever more influence on American theology. Couched in traditional Christian terms, particularly those of Paul as understood by Augustine and the Reformation, this position was uncritically rejected or more frequently entirely ignored within the Jewish community. Sin and sinfulness were not to be taken seriously, even in the face of the *hurban Europa*, the devastation of the Jewish communities of Europe. Thus, paradoxically, German guilt is an article of faith for many within the Jewish community, but the source and dynamic of that guilt is never probed. When Will Herberg, an educational leader of the American labour movement, embraced the Neo-Orthodox position for Judaism, he opened himself at once to misunderstanding and attack. This was inevitable, for his statement of the insights derived from

Niebuhr continued for the most part to be expressed in the language of traditional Christianity, refurbished and garnished by references to Jewish sources. Instead, then, of precipitating a full-dress debate concerning the nature of man, Herberg's critics were content to focus their attack upon the language which could not help but distort the thought when viewed from the Jewish perspective. A false polarity was introduced to the discussion on both sides.[19]

Again, the crux is not Herberg's solution of the problem of sin and man's sinfulness, but his raising of the question. How is moral evil to be understood? Is it to be dissolved in economic determinism? glandular behaviourism? political opportunism? or is man's rebellion against God real in the sense that it represents an act rooted in his very nature? In a post-Hitlerian, post-Marxian, post-Freudian world, this is not an unreal question and cannot be avoided by such polite evasions as the philological explanation that the Hebrew word for sin, *het*, has as its root meaning "to miss the mark." The stark and brutal facts of the generation make it unquestionably clear that sin is not necessarily angelic failure but may well be demonic success. It is this perspective Herberg has re-introduced into Jewish thinking today with increasing subtlety and he has indicated how rebellion can express itself in disguise, so that religion itself may become the supreme act of irreligion. Most important, however, is the recognition, growing out of the question raised, that man and God are not static terms in an abstract system but are persons in a crucial and living relationship.[20]

VII   It was to this relationship Buber had turned to understand the meaning of religion. Rosenzweig's entire system, too, was rooted in the nature of the relationships existing between God, World, Man. It is on the fact of relationship that Abraham Joshua Heschel erects the structure of his comprehension of the nature of religion. In his case, as in the others, the approach is through man's situation to God. Thus religion is not unnatural, that is, unconnected with man's existence, but rather the clue to God is found in the experience of the ineffable which is the burgeoning of man's looking out at the universe in wonder, or as Heschel prefers, in "radical amazement." "The ineffable inhabits the magnificent and the common, the grandiose and the tiny facts of reality alike. Some people sense this quality at distant intervals in extraordinary events; others sense it in the ordinary events, in every fold, in every nook; day after day, hour after hour." What one encounters in Heschel is, on the one hand, a particularly sensitive formulation of that strand of philosophic thought given impetus in modern times by Bergson; on the other hand, and this is undoubtedly the fountain-head of

Heschel's position, it is a proclamation in terms appropriate to time and place of the way of Hassidism. Its fundamental claim, put philosophically, is that knowing is not exhausted by rational thought. Thus Heschel is concerned to exhibit the intricacy of knowing and to demonstrate not only the possibility but the actuality of an object of knowing "immediately given by way of an insight that is unending and underivable, logically and psychologically prior to judgment, to the assimilation of subject matter to mental categories, a universal insight into an objective aspect of reality, of which all men are at all times capable; not the froth of ignorance but the climax of thought, indigenous to the climate that prevails at the summit of intellectual endeavor, where such works as the last quartets of Beethoven come into being. It is a cognitive insight, since the awareness it evokes is a definite addition to the mind."[21]

Such an approach to or such a foundation for religion is by no means to be discounted easily or airily waved away as "mysticism." The profundity of the way of knowing included in this term has been pre-eminently demonstrated by Charles Bennett, Evelyn Underhill, and Rufus Jones; its place in Judaism—despite nineteenth-century strictures—cannot be ignored; Bergson's description of it as the source of dynamic religion must be reckoned with. It is all too seldom recognized, and perhaps Heschel's form of statement—theme and variation—is at fault, that he offers a philosophic system in the strict sense of the word. He moves out from the experience of the ineffable to the actuality of the ineffable; he poses the question put by it to the man who experiences it, "who are you?" The answer to the question, the recognition that "ultimately man is not a subject but an *object*," raises the further question, "whose object?" This leads through an examination of the "God of the Philosophers" at last into ". . . the Presence of God," and "from an intuition of His presence to an understanding of His essence." This last phrase is important, for it sets the unfolding goal of Heschel's endeavour. The affirmation of God does not spell the answer to the question. The meaning of the affirmation is in the strictest sense of the word, theology, the word about God; and Heschel does not evade the challenge of this word. Even here the inner demand of the dialectic of his thought continues, bringing him at last to the concrete situation or religion. "We are taught that what God asks of man is more than an inner attitude, that He gives man not only life but also a law, that His will is to be served not only adored, obeyed not only worshipped. . . . A pattern for living— the object of man's most urgent quest—which would correspond to his dignity . . . must be a design, not only for the satisfaction of needs, but also for the attainment of ends."[22]

In academic terms, theology gives rise to anthropology, the word about man, which is ultimately concerned with man's doing in response to God. "Our task is to concur with His interest, to carry out His vision of our task. God is in need of man for the attainment of His ends, and religion, as Jewish tradition understands it, is a way of serving these ends, of which we are in need, even though we may not be aware of them, ends which we must learn to feel the need of."[23]

Yet Heschel is writing not only within the situation of man, but within the situation of the Jew. Hence his philosophy of religion must be as well a philosophy of Judaism, which means not "a critique of Judaism," but "Judaism as a source of ideas which we are trying to understand." There is an interesting parallel here with Hermann Cohen's endeavour, for he too transformed philosophy into philosophy of Judaism. But in Heschel's case, although the philosophy of religion is chronologically and systematically anterior to the philosophy of Judaism, in the personal reality of Heschel's thought the contrary is undoubtedly the correct sequence.[24]

VIII   A friendly critic has suggested that "Heschel's philosophy does not offer the *non-observant* modern Jew sufficient links to enable him to make the transition, or 'leap of action,' from the universally human sense of the ineffable to an acceptance of the unique authority of the Bible and the sacredness of Jewish law in which the voice of God becomes identified with objective tradition." If one generalizes this tension, one finds oneself face to face with what may indeed be the twofold problem and task of contemporary Jewish theology. Put as a question, it is: Is the problem of the contemporary Jew religion or is it Judaism?[25]

In the case of Rosenzweig, for example, it was the latter. He did not ask whether there was a relationship between God and man, but whether Judaism had anything meaningful to say about that relation. Having in the moment of decision said "yes" to his question, he was then compelled to look at the universal structure of that relation in the light of that affirmation. Here theology follows after faith and the subsequent decision about the Law is made not as a prerequisite for entrance into the community but, as we have seen, out of one's ability since he is already within the community.

Again, as in Kaplan's thought, it may well be that fundamentally the problem is religion. Here the task is that of providing a statement which points to the cogency of the ideas and attitudes comprehended within the term. But whether a total transvaluation of religion is the solution is another matter.

Perhaps both religion and Judaism are for most of us problematic, so that the twofold question must be given a twofold answer, an answer in which both parts interpenetrate one into the other. What strikes one most forcibly as one surveys the scene is the aliveness of the possibilities—the aliveness of the possibilities as against the stubbornness of the situation. Herein lies both the challenge and the danger. To take the gesture for the deed, the enthusiasm for the fulfilment is to sacrifice concern to convention and commitment to conformity. To face the reality of the situation, to know the desperate hope, the dreadful trust that asks to be saved from stasis or mere empty motion, and listening to those who speak to our urgent need, answer with an unyielding yea, is to know that bone shall come together, bone to its bone with sinews upon them; that flesh shall come up and skin cover them above, and breath come into them, so that they live and stand up upon their feet.

NOTES

[1] Quoted in the Introduction to *The Book of Doctrine and Beliefs*, ed. Alexander Altmann (Oxford, 1946), p. 11.
[2] Julius Guttman, *Die Philosophie des Judentums* (München, 1933), pp. 342–343.
[3] *Ibid.*, p. 362. Hermann Cohen (1842–1918) was born in Coswig, Germany, the son of the cantor of that community. He studied at the Breslau Rabbinical Seminary and at the Universities of Berlin, Breslau, and Halle. His rise as a professor at the University of Marburg was rapid in the face of the anti-Semitic prejudices of the time. In 1912, after nearly forty years of university teaching, he went to Berlin to devote himself to Jewish studies and lectured at the Lehranstalt für die Wissenschaft des Judentums. For a brief account of his life, see the work by Agus cited in note 16, pp. 57–61; for a description of his impact as a teacher, see Glatzer's work on Rosenzweig cited in note 17, p. 29.
[4] Albert Lewkowitz, *Das Judentum und die geistigen Strömungen des 19. Jahrhunderts* (Breslau, 1935), pp. 452–568.
[5] Guttmann, *Die Philosophie des Judentums*, p. 361; Martin Buber, "The Idea of Deity and the Love of God," *Israel and the Nations* (New York, 1948), p. 65.
[6] Martin Buber, *Ich und Du* (Leipzig, 1923), English trans. by Ronald Gregor Smith (Edinburgh, 1937); M. Friedman, "Martin Buber's Concept of Education," *Christian Scholar*, XL: 2 (June, 1957), 109–116; R. G. Smith, "The Religion of Martin Buber," *Theology Today*, XII: 2 (July, 1955), 215; Malcolm Diamond, "Martin Buber and Contemporary Theology," *Union Seminary Quarterly Review*, XII: 2 (January, 1957). Maurice Friedman, in *Martin Buber* (Chicago, 1955), writes (p. 8):

"Martin Buber was born in Vienna in 1878 and was brought up until the age of fourteen in the Galician home of his grandfather, Solomon Buber, one of the last great scholars of the *Haskalah* [Jewish enlightenment]. He studied philosophy and the history of art at the University of Vienna and the University of Berlin, and in 1904 he received his Ph.D. from the latter University. In his twenties he was the leader of those Zionists who advocated a

Jewish cultural renaissance as opposed to purely political Zionism. In 1902 Buber helped found the Jüdischer Verlag, a German-Jewish publishing house, and in 1916 he founded *Der Jude*, a periodical he edited until 1924 and which became under his guidance the leading organ of German-speaking Jewry. . . . From 1923 to 1933 Buber taught Jewish philosophy of religion and later the history of religions at the University of Frankfurt. In 1938 Buber left Germany to make his home in Palestine, and from that year through 1951 he served as a professor of social philosophy at the Hebrew University, Jerusalem. After he became emeritus, the government of the state of Israel asked him to double the size of the Institute for Adult Education that he founded in 1949 and directed until 1953."

[7]M. Buber, *The Prophetic Faith* (New York, 1949), p. 55; 'The Question to the Single One," *Between Man and Man* (New York, 1948), pp. 79 ff.

[8]M. Friedman, "Martin Buber and Judaism," *CCAR Journal*, no. 16 (October, 1955), p. 18; M. Buber, "The Two Foci of the Jewish Soul," *Israel and the Nations*, p. 28.

[9]See N. Glatzer's Introduction to F. Rosenzweig, *On Jewish Learning* (New York, 1955), p. 21.

[10]*Ibid.*, pp. 72–92. I have departed from Glatzer's translation in a number of instances and have used my own rendering of "Die Bauleute" in F. Rosenzweig, *Kleinere Schriften* (Berlin, 1937).

Franz Rosenzweig was born in Cassel, Germany, at the end of 1886. He studied medicine at the Universities of Göttingen, Munich, and Freiburg during 1905–1907 but then turned to modern history and philosophy. He received his Ph.D. in 1912. The following year, after earnest consideration, he decided to leave Judaism and become a Christian. However, on Yom Kippur, 1913, he changed his mind and determined to devote himself to Jewish learning. He served with the German army during the First World War and began the writing of his foundation work, *Star of Redemption*, during that period. On his return to civilian life he went to Frankfort and participated in the establishment of the Freies Jüdisches Lehrhaus; he became its director in 1920. In 1922 it was discovered that he was fatally stricken with a progressive paralysis. During the next seven years, although his physical condition grew increasingly worse to the point that he was completely helpless, he continued to work with the assistance of his wife and remained a creative and productive thinker until his death in 1929. For a detailed account of his life see Glatzer's book cited below in note 16.

[11]F. Rosenzweig, *Der Stern der Erlösung* (2te Aufl., Frankfurt a.M., 1930).

[12]*On Jewish Learning*, pp. 79, 81–82; concerning the position taken by Hirsch and his school, see M. Weiner, "Judah Halevi's Concept of Religion and a Modern Counterpart," *HUCA* XXIII, Part One (1950–1951).

[13]*On Jewish Learning*, pp. 86, 91.

[14]*Ibid.*, pp. 111, 113–118.

[15]M. M. Kaplan, *Judaism as a Civilization* (New York, 1935); John Dewey, *A Common Faith* (New Haven, 1934).

Mordecai M. Kaplan was born in Lithuania in 1881 and came to the United States at the age of eight. He was educated at the City College of New York, Columbia University, and the Jewish Theological Seminary of America. After serving as rabbi in New York, in 1909 he became principal and later dean of the Teachers' Seminary of the Jewish Theological Seminary and in 1910 was appointed professor of homiletics in the Seminary. As founder and leader of the Reconstructionist movement and as editor of its journal *The Reconstructionist* as well as teacher and author, he has had a widespread influence on American Jewish thought.

16Jacob Agus, *Modern Philosophies of Judaism* (New York, 1941), pp. 298–315.

17The first full-length study in English of Buber is found in the work by Agus cited in the previous note, and dated 1941. John Tepfer dealt with an aspect of his thought in a paper before the Central Conference of American Rabbis in 1934, "Martin Buber and Neo-Mysticism, *CCAR Yearbook*, XLIV, 203–219. The earliest references in English to him, noted in the bibliography of Freidman's *Martin Buber*, are in a book by Ludwig Lewissohn published in 1927. Rosenzweig's introduction to the English reader was even later; see the bibliography in Glatzer's *Franz Rosenzweig: His Life and Thought* (New York, 1953).

18D. D. Williams, *What Present-day Theologians are Thinking* (New York, 1952).

19W. Herberg, *Judaism and Modern Man: An Interpretation of Jewish Religion* (New York, 1952); "Christian Apologist to the Secular World," *Union Seminary Quarterly Review*, vol. XI, no. 4 (May, 1956).

Will Herberg holds the B.A., M.A., and Ph.D. degrees from Columbia University. He has served as educational director for the Garment Workers Union and is now Adjunct Professor of Judaic Studies and Social Philosophy in Drew University.

20W. Herberg, *Protestant, Catholic and Jew: An Essay on American Religious Sociology* (Garden City, 1955).

21A. J. Heschel, *Man is Not Alone* (New York, 1951), p. 5.

Abraham Joshua Heschel, scion of a distinguished Hassidic family, was born in Poland in 1907. He received his Ph.D. at the University of Berlin in 1932 and taught in the Freies Jüdisches Lehrhaus in Frankfort. He came to the United States at the end of the thirties and for a time was a member of the faculty of the Hebrew Union College. He is now Associate Professor of Jewish Mysticism and Ethics at the Jewish Theological Seminary.

22*Ibid.*, pp. 67–68, 175–176; for a discussion of mysticism see in particular C. A. A. Bennett, *A Philosophical Study of Mysticism* (New Haven, 1923), for Jewish mysticism see G. Scholem, *Major Trends in Jewish Mysticism* (New York, 1946); for Bergson's discussion see his *The Two Sources of Religion and Morality* (New York, 1935).

23Heschel, *Man is Not Alone*, p. 241.

24A. J. Heschel, *God in Search of Man* (New York, 1955), p. 22.

25M. Friedman, "Reform Judaism and Modern Thought," unpublished.

Faith

Isserman / Weinstein /

Kagan / Feinberg

THE ESSENTIALS OF REFORM JUDAISM / Ferdinand M. Isserman

In an essay on "Halacha" read before the Central Conference of American Rabbis, Professor Alexander Gutman, Professor of Rabbinics at the Hebrew Union College, established the thesis that, with the exception of a few decadent periods, Judaism was a changing religion, changing in accordance with historical circumstances and environmental demands. When the Temple fell, the rabbis made no attempt to transfer the sacrificial ritual from Jerusalem elsewhere because of their belief that sacrifice as a method of worship of God had outlived its usefulness. Hillel, the historic rabbi of the first century of the Christian era, who was one of the formulators of the golden rule, declared inoperative the law of the Torah requiring the cancellation of debts in the sabbatical year. The rabbis suspended all Mosaic legislation that depended on the land of Israel, and declared that the civil law of the state takes precedence when it conflicts with the civil law of the Torah. Kaufman Kohler, America's most distinguished Jewish theologian, in his book on *Jewish Theology* wrote, "We too must do as Maimonides did—as Jews have always done—point out anew the really fundamental doctrines and discard those which have lost their hold upon the modern Jew or which conflict directly with his religious consciousness. If Judaism is to retain its paramount position among the powers of thought, and to be clearly understood by the modern world, it must again reshape its religious truths in harmony with the dominant ideas of the age."

Golda Meier, Foreign Minister of Israel, had an experience with a Yemenite woman, a new settler in Israel, which illustrates change in Torah laws. In her earlier capacity as a government official, Mrs. Meier had announced the plan to build one hundred thousand new homes for new settlers. She was accosted by a Yemenite woman who asked her if among these new homes she would not build one with an extra room for herself and her child. Her husband had two wives. She did not want to live in the same room with the other wife. Though polygamy is illegal in Israel, the government has recognized polygamous marriages which were contracted by Jews when living in Moselm countries where they were legal in accordance with Jewish and civil law. For Jews living in the Western world, polygamy, though sanctioned by the Torah, was abolished in the year 1000 by Rabbi Gershon Ben Juda, founder of Talmudic studies in France and Germany, under threat of excommunication. He also required that a wife must give her consent to a divorce. His changes of Torah laws were accepted as binding. Most of the laws of the Torah and the Shulchan Aruch are not observed by any large body of Jews today. The very fact that some call themselves *modern* Orthodox reveals that changes have been made even by this group.

The right to make changes is sustained by Jewish history, and is at the heart of the Reform movement in Judaism. Reform, therefore, is not a unique phenomenon in Jewish history. Unique rather was the freezing of Jewish practice in the ghetto period caused by a lack of contact with the world and by a fear of the dissolution of the Jewish community. The attempt to keep Judaism rigid was a break with Jewish tradition. Reform Judaism marks a return in western Europe to the old Jewish tradition that change in religion is valid.

THE USE OF THE VERNACULAR   One of the departures of Reform has been its readiness to use the vernacular in prayer. When in 1750 Moses Mendelssohn in Berlin translated the Pentateuch into German, using the letters of the Hebrew alphabet for the German language, use of his translation was forbidden by the rabbis of his time who did not recognize the right to use the vernacular in Torah study. Yet there were many precedents for it. One of the most popular prayers in Judaism is the Kaddish, which was written in Aramaic when it had supplanted Hebrew as the spoken language of the Jewish masses. The Torah also was translated into Aramaic by Onkelos. For the Greek-speaking Jewish community in Alexandria, the Septuagint translation was made. This became an important factor in the rise of Christianity. In 1808 Israel Jacobson, living in Westphalia, Germany, used the German language at Jewish services. He thus became one of the pioneers of reform. Lily Montagu, one of the founders of Reform Judaism in England, introduced prayers and hymns in English for children in religious schools. For this, she states in her book *The Faith of a Jewish Woman*, she was bitterly attacked.

The use of the vernacular in Holy Blossom Temple was begun before the advent of Rabbi Brickner to Toronto in 1920. Rabbi Jacobs and his predecessors had given sermons in English, and had used English in their prayers. Their reforms had followed the pattern of congregations like the West London Congregation of British Jews. Today the use of the vernacular in worship is accepted in Orthodox synagogues in France and England, as well as in the United States.

THE ERA OF EMANCIPATION   The Reform Jewish movement, as a revolt against the blind acceptance of the authority of the past and a vindication of man's right to use reason in his religion, followed in the pattern of the Renaissance, the Protestant Reformation, and the French and American revolutions. That the first attempt at reform began in sections of Germany conquered by Napoleon during the Napoleonic period indicates the impact of the liberalism of the end of the eighteenth and beginning of the nineteenth century on Judaism. Wherever the armies of Napoleon went, they carried with them French revolutionary ideals. Prior to his advent, a French parliament, under the leadership of a cleric, Abbé Gregoire, and an aristocrat, Baron Mirabeau, had declared that the declaration of the rights of man applied to Jews. Jews therefore could have full civil equality and rights in France, could become French citizens, and share in every aspect of French national life, including service in the military forces. Napoleon questioned the wisdom of this declaration, but dared not challenge it, as he ostensibly was the guardian of French revolutionary ideals. He hoped by convoking a Jewish Sanhedrin to induce Jews to make statements about their allegiances which would give him justification for repealing the declaration of previous parliaments with reference to the emancipation of Jews. But this conclave of spiritual leaders which he convened did not give him the answers he sought. It affirmed the French Jews' desire to live as citizens of France and to disavow Jewish nationality for themselves.

The assertion that Jews were members of a religious community and not of a national minority in Western lands subsequently became a cardinal plank in the platform of Reform Judaism, as formulated in Pittsburgh in November, 1885, at the meeting of the Central Conference of American Rabbis. Its fifth article stated: "We consider ourselves no longer a nation, but a religious community, and therefore expect neither a return to Palestine nor sacrificial worship under the sons of Aaron, nor the restoration of any of the laws concerning the Jewish state." Today there exists a Jewish state in the land of Israel, but Jewish citizens of Canada, the United States, as well as of other democratic nations of the world, do not consider themselves citizens of that state, though all Jews were invited to become such. They have elected to remain citizens of Canada, the United States, Great Britain, and France. Thus by their actions they have declared themselves not members of a Jewish nation but of a Jewish religious community.

THE MISSION OF ISRAEL AND THE MESSIANIC HOPE   Isaac Mayer Wise, who had come to the United States from Bohemia in search of freedom, was forcibly ejected from his congregation in Albany in 1858 because he asserted that he did not believe in the coming of a personal Messiah, in the restoration of the sacrificial cult, and in the physical resurrection of the dead. He organized a new congregation in Albany and subsequently became the founder of the Union of American Hebrew Congregations, with which Holy Blossom Temple is affiliated, the Hebrew Union College, many of whose graduates have served in Holy Blossom pulpits, and the Central Conference of American Rabbis, of which all senior Holy Blossom rabbis for the past two generations have been members. The views of Isaac Mayer Wise about the Messiah, the sacrificial cult, and the resurrection of the dead became important in the development of Reform Judaism in America, and references to them were eliminated from the prayer-book.

They centred about the messianic belief which had been for centuries a cardinal doctrine of Judaism. It held that God would in His judgment send a redeemer who would gather in the Jewish exiles from all parts of the world, reunite the scattered members of the Jewish nation, re-establish the rule of the royal family of David, rebuild the Temple, and restore the sacrificial practices under the descendants of Aaron. Then the dead would rise out of their graves and live in this restored Jewish commonwealth. Reform Judaism has modified this messianic concept. It denies that Jews are living in exile in states where they enjoy full rights and citizenship. It asserts the belief in the coming of a messianic age of universal justice, love, brotherhood and peace, which will be achieved by the co-operation of peoples of many races, of many nations, and of many faiths. In this achievement, the Jew, by virtue of his being an heir of the ancient Covenant and custodian of the belief in one God and one humanity, would be a leader. This idea is rooted in the prophetic traditions of Judaism and found expression in the disarmament vision of the prophets Isaiah and Micah. "And they shall beat their swords into plowshares and their spears into pruning-hooks, nation shall not lift up sword against nation, neither shall they learn war any more. But they shall sit, every man under his vine and under his fig-tree, and none shall make them afraid, for the mouth of the Lord of hosts hath spoken" (Micah 4:1-4). "They shall not hurt or destroy in all my holy mountain, for the earth shall be full of the knowledge of the Lord as the waters cover the sea" (Isaiah 11:9).

Such a faith in universal peace based on universal security, representing the plan of God for man, became central in the messianic hope of Reform Judaism. To realize these visions of the prophets became the dominant social goal of Reform Judaism. This was no departure from the best in the past traditions. The rabbi did state that whoever recites the Shema[1] assumes upon himself the yoke of the kingdom of heaven. Reform emancipated the messianic hope from outworn dogmas. In article 6 of the Pittsburgh Platform, 1885, it found expression in the words: "We extend the hand of fellowship to all who operate with us in the establishment of the reign of truth and righteousness among men." This was the mission of Israel which became central in Reform Judaism.

The mission is being challenged in our time by the pessimistic mood of some theologians; by fears concerning the dwarfing of man by mammoth technical inventions and the destruction of our civilization in nuclear conflicts; by the mass murder of Jews in Nazi Germany and the ruthlessness within totalitarian states; and by the cynicism in international relations, the open and greedy desire to manipulate the resources of the earth in the interests of national power, the disappearance of pacifist movements, and the renewal of the belief in the taint of man. The myth of man's expulsion from paradise has gained fresh sway over men. The mission of Israel is regarded as a vain hope which grew out of a perverse faith in man's capacities. Sinful man is incapable of building a perfect society. World justice and world brotherhood and world peace are noble goals that cannot be achieved by imperfect human beings. The realities of history must compel moderns to reconcile themselves to their tragic lot, to bear with heroism and dignity the burden of suffering, and to await the inevitable doom. Man is a helpless creature, like the person about whom Edgar Allan Poe wrote in "The Pit and the Pendulum."

Judaism has always rejected such defeatism. In ages just as critical and more so than ours, such as the expulsion from Spain in 1492, Jews were not crushed. History records that a group of these exiles, leaving their homes, their possessions, their careers, chanted the prayer, "With great love hast thou loved us, O our God." They did not succumb to eternal pessimism because of their own tragic circumstances. They retained their faith, rose to moral heights, moved on to Holland, helped make it the mistress of the seas. Their descendants were pioneer inhabitants of the Western hemisphere. Some of them still live in the islands of the Caribbean, and others were the first Jewish settlers in New Amsterdam, now New York. In the darkest periods of persecution, Jews survived because of their faith in God and hope in a messianic age. A people without hope perishes. Modern pessimists who have abandoned their faith in man, and therefore their faith in the justice of God in history, question the belief in the mission of Israel. This is no time to join in the chorus of lamentations over man, but rather to affirm his infinite capacity, and this Reform Judaism does.

There comes to mind a passage from the Torah (Deuteronomy 30:19), part of the required reading at services on the morning of the Day of Atonement: "I call heaven and earth to witness against you this day, that I have set before thee life and death, the blessing and the curse, therefore choose life that thou mayest live, thou and thy seed, to love the Lord thy God, and hearken unto His voice, and to cleave unto Him, for that is thy life and the length of thy days." Here is affirmed faith in man to make good moral choices and his capacity to be master of his destiny. This is also a time to remind ourselves of the verses in the first chapter of Genesis, "And God created man in His own image. In the image of God created He him, male and female created He them." Here too is the assertion of the perfectibility of man made in God's image. Man is godlike and can attain godlike stature. Genesis did not distinguish between the sexes, even as Reform did not by declaring women eligible for confirmation. God created the world of nature, and man is to create the social order, "Let them have dominion over the whole earth." This is Judaism, the belief in man's obligation to hold dominion over the earth. Its chief festival is the Day of Atonement when we are held accountable for our sins, because we have freedom of the will, and contain within us the potentialities of perfection. God calls us to give an accounting, and hopes that we will realize our stature of being but little lower than the angels. With such qualities has He endowed us. Man is not a fallen creature, but a potential angel.

For our time the mission of Israel has great relevance and has been given fresh vitality and centrality in the Reform movement. Orthodoxy had become too involved in ritual punctiliousness. Reform minimizes the significance of practices, and emphasizes prophetic teachings. The prophetic tradition is in orthodoxy: sections of the prophets as well as portions of the Torah were read at services; the book of Jonah with its supreme ethical ideal of serving one's foes was put in the Yom Kippur ritual by orthodox rabbis, and is part of the authentic Jewish tradition. But in a decadent period of history the externals of religion, its scaffolding, had become central. The good Jew became synonymous with the faithful observer of dietary laws and other traditions irrelevant in our time. Reform Judaism protested against recognizing various externals as being as compelling as the moral law: the wearing of a hat at worship, a practice not indigenous to Judaism, but copied from other peoples; the ideas that the Torah may be approached only by those who wear a scarf, and by men; that the priestly blessing may be voiced only by those of Aramaic descent, that to ride to a house of worship on the sabbath to experience prayer with fellow-believers is sinful; and that a young widow whose husband is lost at sea during a war may never remarry until his body is found.

The late Rabbi Judah L. Magnes, one of the noble spirits of our time, who was rejected because of his loyalty to prophetic ideals, as well as because of his recognition that universalism transcended nationalism, said that for the practice of ritual the Reform Jew had to substitute acts of social justice. Certainly in the United States of America and Canada, in movements for international peace and social justice, the Reform rabbi, and following him the Reform Jewish layman, has played a significant and important role. The very fact that Reform Jewish congregations have committees on human relations, on peace, on social justice, is evidence of the awareness of the obligation to better social order. The passion for righteousness of Reform Jews has made its impact. *Justice in Judaism*, the title of a textbook issued by the Union of American Hebrew Congregations, the parent organization of Reform, lists many acts of social justice performed by American rabbis and congregations. No individual has done more towards educating and improving the Negro's status in America than the late Julius Rosenwald of Temple Sinai, Chicago. A rabbi in New Orleans led in the plea to desegregate the schools. A congregation in Missouri founded an interracial nursery, the first interracial school in that state. A rabbi in Alabama protested against the execution of five Scottsboro Negroes. That attempts have been made to bomb Jewish congregations by those who opposed integration is indicative of the strength of the ideal of social justice in Judaism. When Margaret Sanger could secure no platform in Chicago, Sinai Temple opened its doors to her. When a politician rode roughshod in Kansas City, Rabbi Samuel Mayerberg successfully aroused the community and brought about his downfall. Before a congregation of steel magnates and coal operators, Rabbi Goldenson demanded justice for workers in mine and factory. During the steel strike of 1920, Rabbi Stephen S. Wise championed the cause of the strikers. The president of his congregation resigned in protest, and a new temple building was delayed. No wonder that Harry Overstreet said that in evaluating the liberalism of the United States, the contribution of Reform rabbis cannot be ignored. My most eloquent predecessor in my present post, Rabbi Leon Harrison, whose services were thronged by non-Jews and Jews, was a factor in making St. Louis a liberal religious centre. Among those who heard him regularly while a student was Reinhold Niebuhr, America's leading theologian. Negro preachers have appeared in Reform pulpits as an expression of brotherhood.

INTERFAITH RELATIONS It was as a result of this emphasis on social justice, interracial brotherhood, and world peace that Reform rabbis began to form friendships with Christian clergy and their congregations. The writer can testify to this, from his own experiences while rabbi at Holy Blossom in Toronto. In accordance with the urgings of my *alma mater*, the Hebrew Union College, I preached the social imperatives of the prophets, and endeavoured to relate them to the challenging problems of our day. Finding swollen wrists on children, I was moved to lead a citizens' committee, unsuccessfully, to request the abolition of corporal punishment in the public schools of Toronto. When an individual accused of blasphemy was sentenced, I rose to defend his right of freedom of speech, though not his wisdom, in attacking the Bible. Frequently laymen were timid. They believed that the forthright insistence on the fulfilment of prophetic but unpopular ideals would jeopardize the status of the Jew. Their concern was personal security, not the fulfilment of prophetic imperatives, nor the mission of Israel. My own experiences proved them wrong. I made friends among the Christian clergy of Toronto because they too recognized that prophetic teachings were primary and creedal allegiances and ritualistic observances secondary. Preaching of the mandates of prophetic Judaism opened to me pulpits of Canadian churches, and led to a historic exchange of pulpits in 1928 between Reverend E. Crossley Hunter and myself. Subsequently, Reverend E. Crossley Hunter became the national chairman of the Canadian Conference of Christians and Jews.

What can be seen so clearly in Toronto took place all over the United States. The clergy of Christendom saw in the rabbis who spoke about Isaiah and Jeremiah and Micah and Amos and Hosea kindred spirits, and thus the abyss between Judaism and Christianity was bridged, and hurts centuries old were healed. This was most magnificently illustrated recently in a statement by Reinhold Niebuhr recommending that Christians abandon their efforts to convert Jews, and in a similar vein Bishop Arthur Lichtenberger of the Episcopal Diocese of Missouri spoke at Temple Israel, St. Louis, on October 12, 1956. He asserted that it was the duty of the Jewish congregation to enrich the religious life of the city by emphasizing the Jewish approach to God, and that it must give Jewish testimony about faith, as his church must give Christian testimony. "Both of these witnesses, Jewish and Christian, would strengthen religion in the community," said he.

As a result of friendship with Christian clergy and congregations, rabbis and other Jewish scholars began to study the life of Jesus and the significance of the New Testament. The provost of the Hebrew Union College–Jewish Institute of Religion, and its professor of Hellenistic Literature, secured his doctorate at Yale University, majoring in the New Testament. He chose this field at the suggestion of a distinguished Christian educator. Professor Sandmel has since written a book, the research for which was done with a grant from Brown University, entitled *A Jewish View of the New Testament*. A generation ago Rabbi Hyman G. Enelow, the rabbi of Temple Emanu-El of New York, published *The Jewish View of Jesus*. The late Rabbi Emil Hirsch of Chicago composed an essay on "A Jewish View of the Crucifixion." A sermon on "The Jewish Jesus and the Christian Christ," given over the Message of Israel radio network, received more favourable response than any other sermon in the history of this programme. At the Hebrew University in Jerusalem Professor Klausner wrote a book on Jesus in Hebrew. These are evidences of a new mood in interfaith relations, the climate for which was created by Reform Judaism.

WITHIN JUDAISM   The reforms in ritual and in doctrine were followed by changes in the attitude towards the Torah. In 1912 at the annual meeting of the Central Conference of American Rabbis, Professor Julian Morgenstern, then a professor of Bible at the Hebrew Union College, later its president, and now its president emeritus (the author was the first rabbi he ordained, in June 1922), read a paper on "The Foundation of Israel's History," in which he declared that Judaism must accept the basic principles of historical criticism, that the Torah, for example, is the work of many men over many ages, that it was woven together by skilful editors out of many manuscripts, that the editors tried to insinuate their own point of view, and that it was written to preserve Judaism for Jews, and the faith about one God for humanity. The Torah was to be the textbook to win the world to allegiance to one God. He likewise pointed out that many traditional concepts about the heroes of the Bible had to be revised in the light of new researches, that the prophetic teachings preceded much of the Mosaic law, that Isaiah and Micah influenced the legislation in Deuteronomy, that King David did not write the Psalms, nor Solomon Proverbs. Dr. Morgenstern's views were bitterly opposed by some of the rabbis then. They have now been accepted in principle, and are taught to religious school teachers and pupils and preached from pulpits. They have helped to make meaningless the conflict, for, example, between evolution and Genesis, and they have enabled modern men and women to appreciate the moral and spiritual majesty of the Bible without compromising their intellectual convictions or scientific knowledge. Today they see more clearly than ever the importance of the Torah and the Bible for our time, and how its message of one God is tailor-made for the need to establish one world and one humanity. To fulfil this ideal remains one of the dedicated goals of all Jews who recognize what is central in Judaism and primary to God.

The right to change, to modify, to eliminate, or to add ceremonies or doctrines; the use of the vernacular in worship; the conviction that Jews constitute a religious and not a national group, but are nationals of many lands; the mission of Israel; the duty to labour for a messianic age through social justice, international peace, and good human relations in co-operation with all people of goodwill; the acceptance of the principles of historical criticism of the Bible: these have been essentials of Reform Judaism. It has saved many Jews for the faith. It has moved other interpretations of Judaism towards liberalism. It has liberalized other faiths. It has helped to build a better world, and deepened and strengthened universal religion. Its teachings are an antidote to modern defeatism, because of its unshakable confidence in man, created in God's image, who shall build the perfect society in accordance with the Divine plan. History is the record of man's march to the messianic goal which, despite temporary setbacks, will ultimately be achieved.

NOTES

[1] The ancient watchword of Jewish faith, "Hear O Israel, the Lord our God, the Lord is One."

REFORM JUDAISM RECONSIDERED / *Jacob J. Weinstein*

It is good for a congregation to take stock of itself. For an old congregation it is important to take these inventories in order to keep from moving only within ruts or from being addicted to the *status quo*. For a young congregation, it is even more important. Religious congregations set precedents much more readily than other institutions. Perhaps this is so because many who come to them are searching for an anchorage of certainty. They are ready to make any directive into a tradition, any straw into a raft. It will take many years to undo what may be carelessly accepted in the first formative years of a congregation's growth.

The sector of Judaism to which Holy Blossom synagogue belongs, is Reform Judaism. It has also been called liberal and progressive Judaism, but Reform is by far its most general label. As other essays have indicated, it took its origins in Europe in the late eighteenth and early nineteenth centuries and was the Jewish counterpart and consequence of three great liberating factors. There was, first of all, the Emancipation conferred by Napoleon on the Jews. He made them for the first time eligible for citizenship in the country of their residence. For this he exacted a heavy price, insisting that the Jews denationalize their faith, that they overtly sever the ties of historic fellowship and ethnic kinship which tied Jew to Jew. Jew must be related to Jew by faith and faith alone. In doing so, as we shall see later, Napoleon furnished the precedent and rationalization for some rather crude neural surgery to be performed on Judaism. Yet this act was no more psychologically inept than the peculiar departmental attitude of Moses Mendelssohn, who even earlier had asserted that he was a Jew at home and a man abroad.

The second liberating force was Rationalism. Whether by way of the French Encyclopaedists, or the German Kantians, or the Russian Jewish Maskilim, reason became the measure of man. The Jewish community jettisoned the heavy cargo of myths, superstitions, folkways, mystical conjurings which the fears, the emotional hunger, the relentless oppression of the people had heaped upon the religion of Judaism. Darwin and the Biblical critics together stormed the ghetto Talmud towers and converted a divine saga into a pedestrian human enterprise. Marx explained that enterprise in brittle deterministic terms. He allocated to religion a rather unworthy role: opiate and police force to dampen the rebellion of the masses against the yoke of their economic exploiters.

The third force was primarily a mood. It was a mood of superb optimism. The young Samsons—Science and the Industrial Revolution—seemed to have no limits to their progress. The achievement of Utopia on earth was practically around the corner.

These liberating forces received a serious setback in the reaction that followed the defeat of Napoleon, but the Reform movement which began among the Jews in Germany was wafted across the ocean and, like the Jack pine, found congenial soil in America. Here the opening of the frontier, the attitude generated by the settlers' background of religious persecution, the optimism of the Transcendentalists, all conspired to confirm the pious hope of Lessing in *Nathan the Wise* that the era of universal tolerance and inter-faith fellowship was at hand. This faith was strengthened in the early Jewish settler in America by his sharp hunger to be a man among men, a citizen among citizens. Thus his needs and the climate of opinion in nineteenth-century America were felicitously joined. He was eager, therefore, to adapt his religious practices to the prevailing Protestant norm. A service almost entirely in English, often held on the Christian Sabbath, wherein the major emphasis was on the sermon discourse was evolved. It was easy to imitate the majority for the feeling was general that majorities and minorities were soon to be absorbed in the larger fellowship of a universal faith.

The Pittsburgh Platform of the Central Conference of American Rabbis of 1885 crystallized this mood. It divorced Judaism from nationalism and the folk. It gave the answer that Napoleon demanded of the Sanhedrin in 1806: "We totally disapprove of any attempt to establish a Jewish state," and it went on to declare that any such attempt would be in contravention of the Mission of Israel, which was to be a light unto the Gentiles. The great majority of the rabbis whose views were contained in the Pittsburgh Code looked upon the dispersion of the Jews as a blessing. Washington was to be the New Jerusalem. Detached from the land of Israel and the people of Israel, Judaism would be free to spread the truth of pure monotheism to all mankind. By personal example and by preaching the ethical beauties of prophetic Judaism, Jews would bring to pass the vision of Isaiah, "that the mountain of the Lord will be established as the top of the mountains and all nations shall flow unto it."

As the Reform rabbis of 1885 cut the delicate nerves and muscles which bound the faith, the land, and the people of Israel together, so did they cut away the swaddling bands of ritual from the child of faith. "Rituals intended exclusively to keep the Jew apart from his environment must be abandoned." In the exuberance of their young powers, the rabbis cut and cut away; not only the Payoth and the

Tzizith, the Kapota and the Sheitel, but the Mezuzah, the Kiddush Cup, the candelabra and yes, the Torah. Emil Hirsch, the most learned and forceful of the radical reformers, was opposed to the building of an Ark in the Sinai Temple on Grand Boulevard in Chicago. He considered the traditional enshrinement of the Torah scroll as a kind of mummy fetishism. Confident that the practice of the religion of humanity was soon to come, he advised his congregation to fling their old orthodox garments into the fires of the new spring and become the vanguard of those who would leave behind the enclosures of the sects and ascend to the unwalled meadows of the higher faith. There are still a goodly remnant of the disciples of Hirsch who wait, naked, for the Messiah of the religion of humanity. They often resent their "weaker brethren" who later decided that they had mistaken a swallow for a summer and returned to the warmth of the ancestral fold and to a Judaism that had a local habitation and a specific, even differentiating, content. Yet it is not our intention to accuse the radical reformers of emotional ineptitude or shallowness of spirit. They were lured by their hopes to credit humanity with more virtue than it had and evil with less persistence than it had. Those of us who have the advantage of the hindsight of these past fifty years must be temperate in our criticism and remember Thornton Wilder's admonition: "The mistakes of generosity are never so terrible as the gains of caution."

Classic Reform as represented by the C.C.A.R. Platform of 1885 thrived in several ways. It established institutions in every large and medium-sized urban centre of the United States, Canada, England, Australia, and South Africa. It gave a reasonable, sometimes noble, interpretation of Judaism for Jews largely of German origin, many of whom would undoubtedly have drifted into some liberal Protestant denomination or into no religion at all. When Reform is accused of having opened the gates to Christianity for some Jews, it must in fairness be given credit for having hindered the desertion of even more Jews.

Reform Temples became unwittingly effective agencies of inter-faith goodwill. Thousands of Christians gained for the first time an appreciation of Judaism. Unable to penetrate the strange ways and language of the ghetto, non-Jews had come to look upon Judaism as a strange, fossilized cult destined to warn true believers of the fate of the stiff-necked infidel. It was the boast of many of the early Reform rabbis that they had more Christians at their Sunday morning services than Jews. The Boards of the temples which these rabbis served were equally proud and considered a rabbi's salary well earned for his role as an ambassador to the Gentiles. The Reform Temple soon gained a position of highest prestige in these communities. Membership in it was a definite aid in entering the charmed circle of the affluent merchants, bankers, and professional men who belonged to it.

Although there was much in traditional Judaism that Reform failed to convey, one concept it honoured much more in the observance than in the breach. This was *Zedakah*, or perhaps it would be better to say *Gemillat Chassadim*; organized charity is not quite equivalent to social righteousness, which is the basic meaning of *Zedakah*, and it is a bit too impersonal to represent the acts of loving-kindness which are encompassed in the term *Gemillat Chassadim*. But however their activity may fall between the boundaries of these major directives of the Jewish ethic, the members of the Reform Temples of America made of the half-loaf of charity as sustaining a support for the stranger and the needy as could be made by any single group within the framework of a free enterprise economy. The orderliness of the German, the social sensitivity and conscience of the Jew, the administrative know-how of the American, all combined to make the federations of Jewish charities true models for implementing man's responsibility to his fellow-man. It is no wonder that to this day a considerable portion of Reform Jews consider philanthropy not only a major directive of Judaism but an acceptable substitute for it.

A quarter of a century after the adoption of the Pittsburgh Platform, it became obvious that the architects of that platform had miscalculated. There was, first of all, a vague dissatisfaction with the in-breeding of the Reform community. Its own numbers were not appreciably growing. The children of Reform families were not as enthusiastic as their parents. Many of them drifted into the Jewish fellowship of the city club and the country club and equated their Jewish loyalty with a sizable contribution to the charities. Some accepted ethical culture, humanism, unitarianism, as a non-surrendering form of assimilation to the Gentile community. Surprisingly few of the children of Reform families entered the rabbinate.

While Reform rabbis were almost exclusively recruited from the homes of Orthodox, East European Jews, the membership of Reform congregations was not being equally sustained by the Jews from eastern Europe who now—at the end of the First World War—constituted 2 million of the 2½ million Jews in America. Even when the rational basis of Reform became acceptable to the East European Jew, he felt that his emotions were not involved. He felt somehow that the atmosphere of the Reform temple was "goyish." It did not satisfy his nostalgia for the *shtetl* folkways, nor his sense of kinship with his fellow-Jews. Conservative Judaism came to fill this vacuum between the rigidity of Orthodoxy and the too great permissiveness of Reform. Never has shrewd opportunism been endowed by circumstance with so noble an aspect of inspired moderation.

By 1937, at Columbus, Ohio, the Central Conference of American Rabbis was ready to analyse these developments and re-evaluate the platform of 1885. How much of this re-evaluation was due to the fact that now the vast majority of American Jews and an even greater majority of Reform rabbis were of East European origin and therefore sympathetic towards a return to earlier practices and how much was due to a genuine re-thinking of basic premises can never be determined. As with all other facts of life, so with religion—the best that man can achieve is a weighted average, a viable balance between reality and hope, soness and oughtness. It is no derogation of the deliberations of the 1937 Conference that they reflect the changed structure of American Jewry. Rabbis are not ivory-tower philosophers, nor saintly hermits, nor itinerant, raven-fed prophets. With them, as with any leaders who must work with mixed groups of men and women and children, the failure to accept the better because it is not the best is a sure way of bringing about the worst. So there emerged what we now call the Columbus Platform. Twenty years of trial and testing have confirmed the validity of this re-evaluation.

The world of 1937 was one considerably changed in emotional and intellectual climate from that of 1885. For one thing, political emanicipation of the Jew had stopped at the eastern border of Germany. All the guarantees of minority rights of the Treaty of Versailles had proved of no avail. The East European Jew was still a pariah, at best a second-class citizen. Mendelssohn's pious hope that the Jew could be a man abroad had not been honoured in Russia, Poland, or Roumania.

Then, too, serious flaws had been revealed in the rationalism of Darwin and Marx. Their self-contained universe was not so self-contained. The march of man was not uninterruptedly forward. Economic power did not disperse itself inevitably downward. Behavioristic psychology did not explain behaviour. Depth psychology uncovered hidden places of the psyche where human motivations were more completely determined than in all the configurations of the environment. Marxian economics ran into unyielding psychological barriers. Lenin's "locomotive of history" was derailed by unseen switches. Science itself departed from the certain pattern of the contained atom to take up relativistic time-space. Chance and probability were recognized as inherent in the nature of things. Speculations about the nature of God and the soul were no longer considered as hostile to the scientific spirit, as trespassers on the territory of reason—but rather as necessary means of discovering the true meaning and purpose of life.

Just as certain imponderables would not succumb to the microscopic analysis of the scientific method, so the Jewish people would not be submerged in the ocean of humanity. By a peculiar, almost mysterious power it transmuted hostility into the stuff of life and, *lehachlis,* insisted on reading academic and authoritarian decrees of extinction as charters of independence. Sometimes conscious of a mission, sometimes only obedient to the instinct to survive, sometimes affirming God's will, sometimes asserting only its own, the people was maintained through one crisis after another and at long last determined to hasten the plan of redemption.

It was between 1885 and 1937 that the Jews of eastern Europe, led by a brilliant Viennese intellectual, Herzl, converted religious Messianism into a political mass movement, determined to become the collective Messiah and gather the dispersed of Israel from the four corners of the earth and plant them again in the land promised to Abraham, Isaac, and Jacob. Any objective historian will recognize that political Zionism was as normal and rational a reaction to the conditions of East European life as Rabbi Hirsch's plea for a religion of humanity was to the conditions of American life. It was part of the obtuseness of the classic Reformers that they insisted on reading the circumstances of Western existence into the East European picture, as it was the obtuseness of those who believed in *Shollel Ha-Galut*—the final hopelessness of the diaspora—to read the conditions of East Europe into the Western scene.

The Columbus Platform avoided both extremes. Mellowed by fifty years of experience with the Pittsburgh Platform, acquainted with the insights of depth psychology, conscious of its obligation to Jews who were not as fortunate as the Jews of America, the Platform reunited the peoplehood of Israel and the faith of Israel. Zionism was seen as the necessary prelude to the fulfilment of the Messianic dream of the gathering of the dispersed and the sovereignty of the Torah. The old dichotomy between universalism and nationalism fell by the wayside. Thanks to the insights of depth psychology, the prophets' addiction to both concepts was understood not as self-contradiction but as an intuitive comprehension of the need to belong and the need to reach out. The development of the people of Israel to its highest potential through the revival of its God-centred culture was seen as an aid to the ultimate universal fellowship of nations under the one God of humanity. The prophets who had so blithely been divorced from Zion by the zealots of classic Reform were now restored to Eretz (the land of Israel). This was a magnificent act of spiritual restitution by which Amos, Isaiah, and Jeremiah became again something much more than patron saints of the philanthropies of the New Jerusalems of Berlin, London, and Washington!

Thanks to the Columbus Platform, Reform Jewry could now accept its obligations to help move the rejected Jews of East Europe to the rejected land of Palestine. And they could do this with benefit of clergy. For now the Union Prayer Book, formerly purified of Zionistic aspirations, embodied this prayer:

. . . Uphold also the hands of our brothers who toil to rebuild Zion. In their pilgrimage among the nations, Thy people have always turned in love to the land where Israel was born, where our prophets taught their imperishable message of justice and brotherhood and where our psalmists sang their deathless songs of love for Thee and of Thy love for us and all humanity. Ever enshrined in the hearts of Israel was the hope that Zion might be restored, not for their own pride or vain glory, but as a living witness to the truth of Thy word which shall lead the nations to the reign of peace. Grant us strength that with Thy help we may bring a new light to shine upon Zion. Imbue us who live in lands of freedom with a sense of Israel's spiritual unity that we may share joyously in the work of redemption so that from Zion shall go forth the law and the word of God from Jerusalem.

The Columbus Conference also took a second look at the problem of ritual and ceremonies. The rabbis could now see these matters more objectively. They were not worried about being separated from their fellow-Americans, being aware of the slag in the American melting pot and conscious that it was intellectually respectable to talk about cultural pluralism. Randolph Bourne, Horace Kallen, I. B. Berkson were formulating the stimulating concept of America as a symphony of cultures, a nation of nationalities, a federation of races. The Anglo-Saxon Protestant norm was seen as only one of several cultural patterns in the great fabric of the American civilization. The preservation of distinctive values was seen not only as an aid to the psychological health of the various constituent groups in the American population, but as a real contribution to the depth and richness of our common American life. Dr. Mordecai Kaplan had published only a few years before his *Judaism as a Civilization*, where he had profoundly analysed the nature of the cultural interaction between the American and the Jewish civilizations. His concept of "otherness" had helped to remove the fear of conflicting differences from those who attempted the burden of loyalty to both cultures.

Formidable evidence for this reassessment had also come from the experience of each rabbi with his religious school. Teachers were reporting that even the children were becoming restive with textbooks and curricula largely concerned with what our fathers and grandfathers did, but which we liberal Jews were not doing any more. The Reform religious curriculum was taking on the aspect of a museum of antiquities. When some imaginative teachers asked the children to act out some of these ceremonial practices, such as the blessing over the lights, the waving of the *lulov* and the *esrog*, the *havdalah*, they found that the children loved these ceremonies and claimed them for their own. The vast interest in the techniques which the schools of education had popularized in America was beginning to register in the religious school. Authentic studies of vocabulary levels, learning habits, concept formations, were beginning to reveal how little of the ethical distillate of classic Reform was making its way into the mind and the emotions of our children. It became painfully apparent that if for no other reason, then for pedagogical necessity it was imperative that Reform recapture a considerable part of the ritual and ceremony which the rabbis had eliminated at Pittsburgh.

But there were other reasons, too. They were adult reasons; and they were not altogether accounted for by the depression and the ominous rise of Hitlerism —though these events certainly had their impact. There was simply the recognition that man lived by more than the bread of reason alone. A reading of the sermons of John Haynes Holmes and John Dietrich, a re-reading of Bertrand Russell's *Free Man's Worship*, revealed the brittleness of their unassailable logic. There were just too many pockets of the psyche which these humanistic rationalists did not touch. Freud and Jung's brilliant explorations of the unconscious helped us to understand why, but even more they helped the rabbis of 1937 to emancipate themselves from fear of the rationalists.

It no longer became *lèse-majesté* to question the sovereignty of reason. With this bitterly gained humility, it was possible to appreciate the profounder wisdom of the mytho-poeic tales of the Bible or of the Hassidim. It was possible to understand that the language of ritual had an evocative power not given to descriptive language. Sensitive men, disturbed by the growing alienation of the scientific and the business world, needed the symbols of common belonging and aspiration which the rituals and ceremonies of religion provided. It was seen now how the rationalists who dominated the thinking of classic Reform had preserved the libretto of Judaism but had discarded the music. The Columbus Conference heard the report of its standing Commission on Ritual and Ceremonies and renewed its directive to encourage the return of meaningful ritual to the synagogue. The Commission has acted more as a clearing house than as a propaganda agency. It has faithfully collected the records of the experiments and practices in each congregation and made them available to one another. It has published some of the more successful rituals and prayers and has encouraged artists, architects, and musicians to give form and beauty to the symbols in their various media. The actual acceptance of these rituals and symbolic forms has been vested, of course, in each congregation. It is remarkable, however, that there has been so considerable a degree of unanimity in the recasting of Reform practice.

Almost all congregations (only seven exceptions have been noted) have returned to the Sabbath Eve or the Sabbath Morning service as their main worship service. A great majority of Reform congregations have introduced more Hebrew in the services. Many have engaged a cantor to chant the traditional music. Most Reform congregations have accepted the ritual of the lighting of the lights, the Kiddush, and the Torah service. They have encouraged the rabbi to wear a robe and a tallith. They have brought Purim and Hanukah back to the synagogue and in this practice have returned to folkways which combine ritual and peoplehood, thus restoring that ethnic bond which Dr. Kaufman Kohler insisted was inalienable from Judaism.

The illuminating survey made by Rabbi Morton Berman under the auspices of the Union of American Hebrew Congregations details many other ritual and ceremonial practices which have been adopted by the overwhelming majority of Reform congregations, either in imitation of one another or by spontaneous reaction to the felt needs of the membership. The conviction that this return need not be a retreat to orthodoxy or a surrender to reaction is best expressed in the architecture of the new temples. They demonstrate better than any treatise that modernism and tradition can be harmoniously combined. There is no inherent reason why reverence for tradition and love for the clean functional line of the modern cannot be happily married.

Reform Judaism, and its rabbis particularly, need to remember, however, that eternal vigilance is the price that must be paid for a workable synthesis. There are indications that a return to tradition may be an escape to the past; that the modification and supplementation of reason may be used as an excuse to throttle reason. If the Nichomachean mean was difficult for the emotionally more balanced Greeks, how much more difficult is it for the passionate sons of Israel. Kohelet's admonition for moderation aroused no great enthusiasm in his time. But the admonition is nevertheless pertinent.

Our times have seen the grim failure of international morality. This must not be made the occasion for the recrudescence of tribal nationalism. The rebuilding and the security of the State of Israel do not automatically mean the renunciation of Jewry's future in the rest of the world. The fact that science has failed us in bringing automation without salvation does not imply that we must renounce science or the reasoned disciplines on which it is based. Existentialists, Neo-Orthodox zealots, rabid nationalists in our midst testify to the Jewish failing for being forever in pendulary movement between extremes. We who glorify Yeshivah should echo Nerissa's wise opinion: "It is no mean happiness, therefore, to be *seated* in the mean: superfluity comes sooner by white hairs, but competency lives longer."

There is a tendency to excess in a religious philosophy that is dependent more on profession than on experience. The happiest control, therefore, is that which is to be found in the scene of human action where the living deed rubs off the excrescences of partial judgment. In Reform's new-found emphasis on social action may be found the real testing ground which will refine religious directives to meet the fundamental needs of man. In the findings of the Commission on Social Action, as they become duplicated in the life of each congregation, will be found the real antidote to that kind of ritualism which becomes formalism and that kind of nationalism which becomes parochialism.

The rabbis of Pittsburgh often claimed exclusive rights for the profession of prophetic Judaism. While they concentrated on pointing out the superiority of prophetic over priestly and Rabbinic Judaism, they left little time or effort to the implementing of these prophetic truths. Their names and the names of their congregants are seldom found beside those of Henry George, or Samuel Gompers, or Eugene Debs. The rabbis of Columbus could boast of a better record of involvement in those struggles which were concerned with basic justice in the affairs of men. Their younger colleagues and disciples are more concerned with the building of effective techniques by which a congregation may put its professions to the test of life.

The Report of the Joint Commission on Social Action of the Central Conference of American Rabbis and the Union of American Hebrew Congregations at the Biennial Meetings in Toronto (May, 1957) was a significant sign of the growing maturity of American Reform Judaism. It indicated at least that the return to the ritual of synagogue has been but the dynamic emotional counterpart of a greater concern for light and truth and justice in the world; that the symbolic love of Zion has been but a sacred prototype of a greater love for that Jerusalem which is to be built without walls.

PSYCHOLOGY AND RELIGION / *Henry Enoch Kagan*

The individual genius, working alone, illumines the way to truth. The path he has lighted up is then broadened and lengthened by followers who come from different disciplines but who work together in the glow of the new insight. This team approach is more characteristic of our times than any previous age. The accumulation of knowledge in the twentieth century is so vast that any one person can grasp only a small fragment. At the same time, when our particular approach to an inquiry is conditioned by limited information, we may tend to rationalize prejudices in favour of our partial knowledge, and blind ourselves into believing we possess the whole truth.

Because true knowledge in our day results from combinations of learning, new hyphenated terms have been created. Today we speak of bio-chemistry, geo-politics, socio-economics, psychosomatic medicine, and cybernetics. Discoveries are made because separate scientists have joined together in their pursuit. Indeed, the anticipated voyage of manned space-ships to the planets millions of miles away will be the direct result of such a development: the intellectual revolution which turned physics away from a rigid deterministic view of the nature of the universe to an uncertain, inexact, probable and contingent view. The great mathematician, Nobert Wiener, who has traced this revolution in physics not to Einstein but to Gibbs, has written: "One interesting change that has taken place is that in a probabilistic world we no longer deal with quantities and statements which concern a specific real universe as a whole, but ask instead questions which may find their answers in a large number of similar universes." One set of knowledge which excludes all others cannot survive in the Space Age.

The specific sphere of religion is the knowledge of God or theology. The specific sphere of psychology is the knowledge of the nervous and mental functions of man. However, both ask questions about the general nature of man and how he lives as well as ought to live, and the area wherein they overlap may be defined as the psycho-religious experience. When, through prayer or ritual, man has a religious experience, it is irreverent as well as futile to inquire about the effect of this experience on God; but it should not be irreverent to study the effect of this experience on man. To my knowledge scientific research on the psychological effect of prayer upon man has never been attempted, but such a study could fittingly challenge the combined talents of the theologian and psychologist.

In any team approach each member must surrender the idea that he possesses a monopoly on truth. This is especially difficult for the religionist for he is committed to a dogma and vested ecclesiastical authority. When Copernican astronomy in the sixteenth century disproved the centrality of the earth, it took the Catholic Church more than a century to accept the new modest place of our small earth in the cosmic, planetary system. When Darwinian biology in the nineteenth century denied man's self-glorifying claim of miraculous separateness from the animal kingdom in the evolutionary scale, fundamentalist Protestantism reacted violently and in many places still refuses to assimilate the new knowledge. The intellectual challenge to religion in the twentieth century is Freudian psychology which took from man divine will and made him subject to primordial instinct. The second half of this century finds this conflict in a new phase in which, in all probability, religion will make adjustments to Freud as it did to Darwin and Copernicus.

The effect of Sigmund Freud on the spiritual thinking of our times is as revolutionary as the effect of the new science on physics. As the new physics has made it possible to explore formerly inaccessible regions of space, so Freudian psychoanalysis has made it possible to explore previously inaccessible regions of the mind. By investigating the "unconscious," the deeply hidden and largest area of the mind, depth psychology has laid the foundation of a new science of human relations which, although it is still in its early stages of development, has already vitally affected religion.

At first, religion was antagonistic to depth psychology, not because of its methods, but because of its theory. Freud's emphasis on sexuality and its sublimation as the primary civilizing motive, as well as his contention that man created God instead of vice versa, blinded religion to the significance of his therapeutic method. When Freud's theories were radically modified by the rebellion of his former students, Alfred Adler and Carl Jung, who pointed out, respectively, the importance of the inferiority complex and of the collective unconscious, religion passed from the phase of belligerency to peaceful co-existence and is now in active co-operation. Such influential theologians as the Christian Paul Tillich, who encourages the use of psychiatry when it differentiates between pathological and existential anxiety, and the Jewish Martin Buber, who advocates a psychosynthetic method in which the private man-to-man counselling situation becomes in itself the best way to an awareness of God, have both become rallying points for the alliance between religion and psychiatry. Dr. R. Finley Gayle, in his inaugural address as president of the American Psychiatric Association, took note of this common interest religion and psychiatry have in guiding the unconscious motives of man when he said: "For the clergyman as well as for the psychiatrist the question is not so much *whether* he will deal with some of the unconscious material as it is *how* he will deal with it."

Because Freud was not only born a Jew but was also proud of his Jewishness, it is ironic to find that his influence has been taken more seriously by Catholicism and Protestantism than by Judaism. In 1956, when the world was celebrating the centenary of Freud, no Jewish organization but at least one important American Christian Church formally commemorated the birth of this "infidel Jew," as Freud defined himself. Protestant thinkers find in Freud's concept of the instinctual *id* a confirmation of their doctrine of the inborn sinfulness of man; Catholic thinkers concern themselves with the differences between the confessional booth and the analyst's couch. There are extenuating circumstances which might explain the hesitancy of Judaism to make adjustments to the psychoanalysis of the individual. While Christianity continuously emphasized the salvation of the individual soul, the virulence of anti-Semitism concurrent with the rise of Freudianism made it so necessary for Judaism to be preoccupied with sheer group survival that it had little time to devote to the emotional needs of the Jew as an individual.

It is much more important for the welfare of man, that religion arrive at a working alliance with psychiatry than with astronomy or biology. The revolution of the earth about the sun and the evolution of the human species deal with external material aspects of life, but psychiatry deals with the functioning of man's inner life—with his very being. The problem of the twentieth century is no longer the science of matter. The problem of our age is the science of human relationships. As Charles De Gaulle aptly remarked, "We may as well go to the moon but that's not very far. The greatest distance we have to cover still lies within us." We know very much about the atomic structure of nature and more and more about interplanetary communication. We know very much less about the structure of personality and how humans may control their inner selves to achieve a happy life in a more harmonious society.

The popularity of books on psychology demonstrates how desperate is the need to find a pattern for harmonious living. "Peace of mind" and "peace of soul" have become household terms. When the late brilliant rabbi, Joshua Liebman, wrote a widely read book in which he sought a reconciliation between religion and Freudian psychoanalysis, he called it *Peace of Mind*; when the forensic bishop, Fulton Sheen, wrote his rejoinder, which is a declaration of war against psychoanalysis, he called his book *Peace of Soul*. Liebman's book with its liberation of the individual may seem to be more in the right direction than Sheen's book with its subordination of the individual. However, both books commanded wide attention not so much because they have the right answers, but because so many are asking the right question—How can I find peace of mind or peace of soul?

Many are the causes advanced to explain why there is so little peace of mind in our time. The obvious cause is fear, but fear is not necessarily incompatible with a feeling of security. My peace of mind is not disturbed by the knowledge that I should be afraid of a deadly snake. The fear of the known does not profoundly upset normal people. On the contrary, such fear leads to action, to flight from the snake or to destruction of it. The action is avoidance or aggression. The fear of the unknown, on the other hand, does upset emotionally, for when a person fears the unknown he remains inactive, since he does not know what to avoid or fight. Not knowing what to do blocks the release of his fear which action can accomplish and when the release of fear is blocked outwardly it turns upon him inwardly, producing tension. Unrelieved tension is anxiety.

The most pervasive mood of our day is anxiety. A catastrophe that has not yet happened but which we doubt we can prevent keeps us in a perpetual condition of tension and worry. The threat of atomic annihilation of the human race; the uncertainty of the cold war which could continue for generations; the revolutionary awakening of the coloured races at home and around the world; the new industrial automation which threatens the worker with uselessness; the increasing urbanization by which the individual is swallowed up into the faceless masses of the city; the daily brain-washing by commercial advertisements which thrive on producing discontent; the business organization of man into a commodity personality whose only value is his marketability as a seller or a buyer; the compulsive obsession of making money even if it kills prematurely with heart attacks; the frantic way in which leisure is dissipated with purposeless motion—these are only some of the factors which give the fear with which we act our individual roles. This anxiety of the individual is evident in the rise in divorce, suicide, crime, juvenile delinquency, and above all in the frightening increase in mental diseases which fill our hospitals and for which we need five times as many psychiatrists as are now available.

Another demonstration of the anxiety of the individual is the attraction that political authoritarianism of both the fascist and the communist type have for fear-ridden people. In place of the challenging responsibilities of freedom they prefer an authority which deludes them with an imaginary security. These people cling to totalitarian leaders out of their desperate need to be relieved of anxiety. On the democratic side, anxiety expresses itself in acts of hysteria to meet these present threats to freedom.

Anxiety is also the central theme in much of the writings in modern philosophy and religion. Here the so-called crisis-writers declare that our civilization is threatening man with the loss of his entire sense of being. Existence is meaningless and man is rapidly losing an awareness that he even possesses a self. The reply comes in existentialism, the philosophy and the psychology which deal with the attempt to recapture the very feeling of existence.

The cumulative effect of all these forces is a mounting feeling that the individual as an individual is really a nothing and at the same time a fierce drive to become a somebody. The greatest cause for anxiety is the individual's feeling of not belonging anywhere, not even to himself. The psychologists correctly diagnose this most threatening of all emotional diseases as alienation of self. In its psychotic form, it is schizophrenia, the splitting off of personality where the complete loss of identity causes the victim even to call himself by another's name.

Frequently we hear three routine answers to the problem of the anxious soul in our society. The first platitude is, let him be religious. If one has confidence in God, one is freed of anxiety. Faith is the answer. No person with it suffers a nervous breakdown. It is true that an effective religious faith can be important in mental health, but it should not be thought that the incidence of emotional problems is any less among religious people.

The second platitude is, he should be practical. All he needs is to become better adjusted. Certainly, an individual can fit into an environment like a cog into a machine, but are there not certain conditions of society adjustment to which will mean the loss of freedom and the achievement of mediocrity instead of maturity? For slaves to the environment there may be no emotional illness, but there would also be no social justice or progress. The individual needs to be a person, not a machine. Religious leaders should use most guardedly that popular phrase of our day, peace of mind, if religion is not to become merely a tranquillizer. Religion must also be a daring disturber of the mind on behalf of the unfinished struggle for the peace of one's fellow men. As Rollo May has pointed out, those who recommend the soft approach—just have faith—or the hard approach—you should adjust—are not dealing seriously with the emotional illness in our society.

There is the third platitude, used by the cynic, who says let us be humorous. He would laugh off the serious attempt of modern psychology to come to grips with the sickness of the modern soul by contending that analysis only leads to further paralysis. Much fun is poked at psychoanalysis on this score. *Punch* once pointed out that today "when a man thinks a thing, the thing he thinks he thinks is not the thing he thinks he thinks, but only the thing he thinks he thinks he thinks." Yet humour is only the other side of tragedy; we must learn to understand what makes us move if we wish to walk with calm dignity. Unless we try to understand how the unconscious does work, we can heal today neither medically nor spiritually.

What psychiatry through its knowledge of the unconscious, and religion through its knowledge of the soul, have to contribute to mental health, they can give now as allies and not as enemies because of the progress both disciplines are continuing to make in the understanding of each other. That the healing of sick souls involved not only medicine and psychology, but also religion, Dr. Freud eventually understood well. His first publication was "Studies in Hysteria" but his last was "Moses and Monotheism." Freud started as a medical man and ended as a theorizer about religion. It is true that Freud called the religion of a father god the "illusion" of infantile minds and said that it had no "future." In his earlier period, he believed religion was on the wane and probably hoped that psychoanalysis might replace religion to keep men from falling back into primitive savage instinct. Theodore Reik insists that Freud was anti-religious whereas Ernest Jones holds Freud was non-religious. Probably Freud who understood ambivalence so well became ambivalent himself on the subject of religion. Unsound as his Biblical exegesis is in his last work, "Moses and Monotheism," this Jewish genius nevertheless has written there: "Judaism is a triumph of spirituality over the senses and a self confidence that accompanies progress in spirituality."

As he grew older, Freud himself believed his most significant contributions to be in the psychology of religion, and these were not entirely negative. About his book, *The Future of an Illusion,* he wrote later, "I expressed an essentially negative valuation of religion. Later, I found a formula which did better justice to it. While granting that its power lies in the truth which it contains, I showed that truth was not a material but a historical truth." Liberal Jews, who believe in the evolutionary inspirational and not the static revelational development of our Judaism, will agree.

The authority of Freud cannot be quoted to disprove the real existence of God, but only to prove man's need for the existence of God. In this regard it would be helpful to the religious critics of Freud, including Jewish ones who strangely prefer the mysticism of the anti-Semitic Jung as a means of substantiating their attacks, to read Freud's correspondence with the Reverend Oscar Pfister, the first clergyman who tried to incorporate Freud's views. Freud called him "a true servant of God, the very idea of whose existence seemed to me highly unlikely."

Pfister was much interested in the psychoanalytic principle of the transference of love by the patient to the analyst. In his correspondence with Pfister on this subject, Freud came to recognize how a religion that emphasized the ethics of a loving God could be valuable in sublimating the primitive libido in man. I choose three of the many letters which Freud wrote to Pfister over a ten-year period. In 1909 he answered: "In itself psychoanalysis is neither religious nor the opposite but an impartial instrument which can serve the clergy as well as the laity when it is used only to free suffering people. I have been very struck at realizing how I had never thought of the extraordinary help the psychoanalytic method can be in pastoral work, probably because wicked heretics like myself are far away from that circle." In that same letter this strictly moralistic heretic suggests that it is because most people are no longer really religious that those who cannot endure their suffering must needs turn to psychoanalysis to master their "obdurate instinct." He even admires proper religious sublimation but he adds (and this is important) that such religious success depends on the maturity of the person-to-person relationship between pastor and parishioner. "You," referring to Pfister, "are in the fortunate position of leading them to God and reconstructing the conditions of earlier times, fortunate at least in the one respect that religious piety stifles neuroses."

What has been the practical effect of the modern psychological definition of the unconscious in making religion itself a more effective instrument for mental health? I wish to point out three important positive effects of the influence of psychiatry on religion. In all three areas, I wish to indicate that the influence is great *not* because psychiatry has made new discoveries but because it has rediscovered with greater clarity old insights into human nature. Psychology has been rediscovering a wisdom particularly old to religion but which organized religion has been forgetting that it ever once possessed. First, modern psychoanalysis has revived our interest in the ancient healing method always inherent in classic religion. Secondly, it has clarified and reaffirmed religion's ancient contention that character depends on parent-child relations. And thirdly, it has given scientific substantiation to what religion long ago declared to be the only road to personal happiness and stability, namely, the capacity to hope and love.

II All of us are subject to unconscious motives and some of us carry around physical evidence of it in a variety of bodily illnesses. In the early days of his career, Freud had greater opposition from doctors than from theologians, because he asserted that diseases could originate not in organic pathological disorders, but out of emotional psychological conditions. Today, the more advanced practice of medicine based on the pioneer investigations of Walter Canon and Flanders Dunbar, approaches disease psychosomatically or by the study of the influence of the psyche, the soul, upon the soma, the tissues. Eminent authorities now tell us that one-third of the sick people who consult physicians do not have any bodily disease to account for the illness. The diseases that originate in and become aggravated by such emotions as anger, anxiety, a feeling of loneliness and unlovableness, may extend from headaches to high blood pressure, from indigestion to ulcers, from asthma to arthritis. Disease states are no longer either physical or psychological—they are both. Medicine has rejoined body and soul.

Psychiatry by revolutionizing medicine has actually brought it back to ancient classical medical concepts. Socrates, 2,500 years ago, returning from the Thracian campaign, reported that the Thracians realized that the body could not be cured without the soul. "This," he said, "is the reason why the cure of many diseases is unknown to the physicians of Hellas, because they are ignorant of the whole." This appreciation of the influence of the spirit upon the body was never confined to philosophers. People have always intuitively felt it and it is dramatically reflected in folk language. For instance, our daily use of the word "heart," which is a physical organ to pump blood, illustrates, as a psychiatrist has shown, a sound knowledge of how our emotions affect it. When we want to say, "Be kind and merciful," we might exclaim, "Have a heart"; "It does my heart good" means it makes me feel better; "To break the heart" is to crush with sorrow; "To make the heart bleed" is to cause extreme anguish; "To eat one's heart out" is to pine away with longing; "To wear one's heart on one's sleeve" is to expose unnecessarily one's feeling to everyone; "To have one's heart in one's mouth" is to be frightened; "to take heart" is to pluck up courage. In this common use of our own language we unconsciously admit the profound connection between our bodies and our emotions.

It is remarkable to observe that just because classic Biblical Judaism wisely did not separate body and soul, as did some other religions, it arrived in ancient days at an understanding of man's illnesses that is surprisingly modern. Some passages in the Book of Proverbs read like a text in modern psychosomatic medicine. Do you wish to avoid indigestion? Then, "Better is a dry morsel and quietness therewith, than a house full of feasting with strife." Do you wish to control a disposition for arthritis? Then, "A merry heart doeth good like medicine, but a depressed spirit drieth up the bones."

Modern psychiatry tells us certain emotions affect our body because we repress them, and that the cure is talk them out. Two important things occur in this healing method: catharsis, or getting repressions out into the open, which relieves a person of his tensions; and transfer, by which he develops a close attachment to the counsellor. This gives him a feeling of complete protection so that he feels free to say anything without fear of punishment. Eventually this confidence builds up self-acceptance and respect and the patient is cured when he frees himself of his dependence on the analyst and assumes full responsibility for his own life.

This method of talking-out also goes back to classical religion. Is not this remarkable insight of modern psychotherapy for aiding emotionally disturbed people given in Proverbs 12:25. "If there is worry in the heart of man, let one talk it out." "Yea, a good word will even make it glad." Psalm 32 presents advance knowledge that unless we get rid of feelings of guilt as soon as we can by talking them out, they dig deeper into our souls and weaken our bodily strength the more. "When I kept silence, my bones wore away through my groaning all the day long. Then I said, I will make confession and Thou didst forgive." Here is both catharsis and transference—not to an analyst, but to God.

Religion at least owes this to modern psychiatry. Psychiatry has restored our awareness of the profound insight religion has always had about the therapeutic importance of talking out emotions which trouble our souls. And as far as Judaism is concerned, it is of more than passing interest to note that the recent revival of Jewish interest in Chassidism is concurrent with this impact of psychiatry upon religion. Chassidism even devised a technique a century before Freud for a talking method to aid a person to achieve renewed confidence in himself and in life. To quote one Chassidic leader, Rabbi Simcha Bunam of Parshisha who lived 150 years ago, "It is highly necessary for every human being to have at least one sincere friend. One true companion. This friend must be so close to us that we are able to tell him even that of which we are ashamed."

It is perhaps a comment on the failure of a religion to perform one of its classic functions, when we hear it is impossible to get an appointment with reasonable reputable psychiatrists because their offices are over-crowded, while in painful contrast clergymen, who for centuries were regarded as physicians of the soul, are only infrequently consulted by people needing help and counsel. Of course, serious mental illness is the province of medical psychiatry, but most people need only counselling to help them to understand their emotions. As a preventive measure against emotional strain, all of us could use another person to whom we could turn and receive complete confidence. This person would not be one who would take our responsibilities away from us and tell us what to do, or one who would sit in critical judgment upon our actions, but one who in a permissive counselling situation would help us gain insight into ourselves, into our own worth, our own capacities for strength, so that we could ourselves solve our emotional problems.

The time may yet come when the office of the modern clergyman and rabbi will take up not a new but an *old* function and he will change from a *talking* preacher to a *listening* pastor. I say old, because apparently we have overlooked one important personage of Biblical days. We know much about the priest and the prophet but have forgotten the Chacham, the wise men, whose wisdom literature in Proverbs and Psalms shows what effective counsellors they must have been for the individual soul. Jeremiah recognized their value as equal to that of the priest or the prophet when he said, "The Torah shall not perish from the priest, nor the word from the prophet, nor counselling from the Chacham, the wise." In recommending this counselling function to the modern clergyman or rabbi, who should have for it training in psychology, I do not refer to what is popularly known as the "confessional," or "faith healing" in religion, but to pastoral counselling, which can become an important additional aid in halting the modern alienation of self. The Psalmist was referring to this type of religious counselling when he said, "He restoreth my soul."

III In addition to providing a method of talking out for the healing of souls, religion has also concerned itself with strengthening character to resist breakdowns. And here, modern psychology has helped make us aware how the personalities of parents unconsciously affect the development of their children's character structure. It is not necessary to accept the Freudian theories of Oedipus complexes to understand that a father who is submissive and feminine, or a mother who is masculine and dominant, will adversely affect their children who identify with them. Judaism long ago understood these psychiatric insights into parent-child relations, as exemplified in the Bible story of the sibling rivalry between the brothers Jacob and Esau. It is as modern as any case history in dynamic child psychology.

The Bible says the father, Isaac, loved Esau; but the mother, Rebecca, loved Jacob. This division in family love resulted from the personalities, not of the children, but of the parents. Isaac was dominated in his own childhood by his strong father, Abraham. Abraham rebelled against his own father and left home. But he dominated his son, Isaac, even to the point of sacrificing him, if this had been necessary. At the same time, Isaac was over-protected by his elderly mother, Sara, and chided by his half-brother as a mama's boy for his delayed weaning. Isaac accepted the wife chosen for him by his father. When Isaac first met his wife, Rebecca, he considered her, the Bible says, to be a comfort for his recently deceased mother. Isaac, in other words, was an over-maternalized, submissive person, who was looking not for a wife, but for a mother. In contrast, his wife Rebecca was an active shepherdess—aggressive in welcoming strangers at the well, you will recall. Her father had to seek her consent to the marriage. She ran the family afterwards and planned the advantage of her own favourite, Jacob, which involved deceiving her husband. The boys might have been equally loved by both parents had the parents considered the needs of their sons. Instead, the parents projected into their sons compensations for their own frustrations. The submissive father, Isaac, liked in Esau what he was not allowed to have in his childhood—the freedom of the hunter. The aggressive mother, Rebecca, liked Jacob more because she could not dominate the freer Esau. Each of the twins was only half-loved. Insufficiently loved by his feminine father, Jacob was filled with fear. Insufficiently loved by his masculine mother, Esau was filled with hate. The Bible clearly shows that Isaac's home life was unhappy because the father and the mother were in conflict over what should be their own roles in the family.

The quest for a healthier parent-child relationship receives clearer guidance through psychiatric insights which clarify the roles which are *appropriate* to the father, to the mother, and to the child. Religion can readily accept this knowledge in working towards the goal the Jewish prayerbook describes, "when the hearts of the parents will be turned toward the children, and the hearts of the children to the parents, strengthening the bonds of devotion and love in the home and making it a sanctuary worthy of God's presence."

IV Finally there is the third area—the way to happiness—to which the cooperative effort of psychiatry and religion can direct in this age of anxiety. This area is the most important for if it were understood, the need for healing methods would be reduced, and healthy parent-child relations would be almost automatic. All religions have held that a person can be happy only if he has the capacity to love. Without this capacity to establish a relation of affection with another person, he condemns himself to the most deadly of all woes—loneliness. The Bible, with profound psychological insight, actually declares that a person cannot love himself unless he can love another. I wish to point out two aspects of this capacity to love: one by which religion can learn from psychiatry, and the other by which psychiatry has much to learn from religion.

Psychiatry correctly emphasizes the significance of sex in the capacity to love and has contributed greatly to the understanding of the importance of sex education for happy marital living. But there is a popular misunderstanding that accuses psychiatry of advocating sexual license. The contrary is true. Any competent psychologist knows that mature happiness involves the acceptance of limitations; that promiscuity is a neurotic sickness; that self-centredness is unhealthy and is the basis of sadism, the perverted pleasure of paining others, or of masochism, the perverted pleasure of putting oneself in a position to be pained by others. All these are attention-getting devices, characteristic of those adults who feel like unwanted children, and are appropriately called "regressions to infantilism."

Only a person completely untrained in psychology like the zoologist, Dr. Kinsey, could assume that because he found a great decline in chastity among his interviewees, these people were *ipso facto* happier. Dr. Kinsey's only measurement of happiness was the presence of a physical orgiastic reflex. The word "love" seldom appears in either Kinsey reports. To be sure, sex can be separated from love. However, modern psychology takes the position that the separation of the physical from the psychological is not the sign of happiness, but a symptom of emotional sickness. Religion has frequently been accused, as Dr. Kinsey accuses it, of placing unrealistic restrictions on sex. Speaking for Judaism, I find nowhere in this religion, the view that sex is sinful. On the contrary, our Bible makes a healthy effort to lift the conception of sex from mere animalism or body chemistry, as does the Song of Songs, in which love is both sexual and sanctified for the glorification of God.

As a matter of fact, our problem today is less one of recognizing the *physical reality of sex* than it is one of restoring our confidence in the *psychological reality of love*. And here is where religion can help psychiatry. I contend that the reality of human love is never fully experienced unless a person has faith in life, which religion defines as believing in God's love for mankind. For proof, examine those who write about love—the novelist and the poets. When the writers believe life has meaning, then they also write affirmatively of human love. When they are disillusioned about life, they write bitterly, as though love were an obscene joke.

Compare Ernest Hemingway's two novels, *Farewell to Arms* and *For Whom the Bell Tolls*. The themes are identical: a hero and his beloved against the background of a military blunder. The first was written in the bitterness and disappointment at the failure after the First World War to achieve a just peace; in *Farewell to Arms* the beloved girl dies and the hero lives on in desperate futility. The second was written at the beginning of the Second World War, when there seemed hope of defeating Fascist animalism, and in *For Whom the Bell Tolls* the hero dies but the beloved lives on to hope for a better world. In the first novel love was treated as a mere physical act: in the second, Hemingway actually says, "I never really believed in such a concept."

We might also contrast the poets Robert Browning and T. S. Eliot. The Victorian age was prudish about the mention of sex but it was hopeful about the future and a better world; therefore Robert Browning could write in his "Love among the Ruins," "Oh Heart, Oh Blood that freezes, Blood that burns, Earth's return for whole centuries of folly, noise and sin. Shut them in with their triumphs, their glories and the rest, Love is best." But in our Age of Anxiety, which knows all about sex but has lost a faith in the future, what does T. S. Eliot write about love? In his poem-play *The Cocktail Party*: "Love is the noise of an insect, dry, endless, meaningless." The wife and husband in the play decide not to separate; the husband thinks he cannot love any woman so that he might as well stay with this one, and the wife thinks no man could love her so that she might as well stay with this one and make the most of a bad job. The heroine, instead of marrying, dies as a martyr because, she says, "All are unloving and unlovable, and marriage is two people who know they do not understand each other breeding children whom they do not understand and who will never understand them."

It is only when we have confidence that life itself has meaning that love can be affirmed as being more than sex. And there is no better book to read in order to revive belief in life and, therefore, in love, than the Bible. There the prophets have such a high opinion of the capacity of man and woman to love one another that they compare such love to the love of God for His people saying, "For thy Maker is thy Husband, for the Lord has called thee to Himself, a wife of love in His youth." That is why the Hebrew for marriage is *Kiddushin*, in which married love becomes the religious art of making life holy.

The soil in which healthy personality grows is this feeling of relatedness to another. As Kurt Lewin has shown, what a person can do, and how well he will do it depends on how secure he feels in being wanted and loved. This applies to everyone—to the child's achievement in school; to the worker's efficiency in the factory; and to the happiness of the aged in the community, as well as to the husband-wife relationship.

The reader of psychiatric literature is compelled to think mainly of hostility, hate, fear, and guilt. We cannot understand light without the presence of darkness, but if we stay in the dark, we will never see the light. The dark unconscious needs the light of a religious consciousness which emphasizes the brighter aspects of human nature. The wickedness we see about us is not inherent in man either as original sin or its Freudian counterpart, the instinctual id. I think the healthier assumption of our religion, Judaism, is the goodness of life—"and God saw all that He had created and behold it was very good." The newer schools of psychiatry are beginning to concede this positive religious attitude to life. They admit now the therapeutic value of ceremonies, of public worship in companionship with others, and of prayer because a man can through them recapture a sense of his own personal worth and regain a feeling of belonging with others and of at-homeness in the world. Certainly, nothing can equal religious faith in its power of holding one over the period of grief in order to keep faith with life while accepting the sorrows of death and to achieve a recathexis of love.

Psychiatry can never replace religion. Religion is superior to psychiatry because it extends the love that a person needs for another person to a love that the same person needs for life as a whole. Religion is a constant therapeutic approach to the whole of life, while psychiatry deals with breakdown episodes in life. Psychiatry is an aid to help cure the sickness of anxious souls; against this sickness the best preventive is a mature religion not of infantile fears or of authoritarian condemnation but of such love of God and man as will inspire tenderness and compassion—those qualities which are incomparably the most healing of all agents.

A LIBERAL SYNAGOGUE TODAY: ITS PURPOSES AND PRINCIPLES /
Abraham L. Feinberg

The function of church and synagogue in a society rocked by revolutionary change must reflect that change. No institution can remain rigid in such a tumultuous era as the middle of the twentieth century. Even orthodox faiths, proud of undeviating loyalty to their pristine past, have been forced into an awareness of turmoil behind their facade of doctrinal fixity. There is a need for organizational equilibrium and for personal tranquillity in a world from which man is being increasingly alienated. This may explain the alleged "religious revival" of our desperate time, a revival which yet hesitates to venture beyond the cozy ramparts of naïve belief.

Dogma, however jealously preserved, provides an illusion of conservatism only to theologians and philosophers. Beyond the formal phrases of faith and the ritualistic incantations, the active clergyman "in the field" knows that parish must meet the need of people, and that people need far more from parish than ever before. These are days of routine and rote—but not for religion with a conscience! In the universal spiritual malaise of our time, it would be suicide to offer mankind the ivied stone of ancient assumptions for the bread and wine of honest guidance—even if this is admittedly subject to inadequacy and error. Only a flexible, courageous church alerted for combat in all areas and forms can fulfil its purpose on a darkling beachhead "where ignorant armies clash by night." Instead of an attic storehouse for out-moded antiques, religion, to survive and to serve, ought to be a lighthouse for the buffeted, a power-house for the faint of heart—as well as a House of God. This is no mean order of business, but priest, minister, and rabbi can receive no more eloquent tribute to their dignity.

The Jewish "situation" underscores with special eloquence this bond between external facts and internal function. Every crisis in Jewry intensifies the challenge to Judaism. Like King David's legendary harp whose strings sang the mournful melody of midnight, the synagogue quivers to the pain and peril of Jews throughout the earth. The fears and frustrations of the individual Jew, who, like a barometer, records with mathematical certitude the general psychic climate of society and the tensions and conflicts on the global battle-ground of nations, all converge on the pulpit and study of the rabbi. Every alarm—whether in Treblinka, Tel-Aviv, Toronto, or the secret chamber of a congregant's confused spirit—finds echo in the sensitive radar mechanism of the synagogue. Far from being an "island unto itself," it is a deeply involved "part of the whole." Nothing which affects the Jewish people, near or far, is beyond the purview of its spokesmen.

The synagogue has always had a triple role: house of worship, house of study, and meeting-house of the people. The uniquely Jewish blend of folk and faith, of historic experience and hallowed aspiration, of tough realism and tougher idealism, of material necessity and mystic ecstasy, of the love of life and the love of God, has never permitted the synagogue to withdraw from the practical world of contemporary events or to become a medium solely of the divine mysteries. During a period marked by stress, the intimate involvement of the synagogue in the actual life of the people was intensified. At no time since the Dispersion nineteen centuries ago could it relax or rest on a lotus bed of stability. As a Talmudic sage once declared, the suffering of the Jew is all the more real when it emanates from the suffering of humanity. Surely, then, in the cockpit of competitiveness and war into which our civilized, scientific age has descended, to be a mirror of the world is no trivial destiny!

A complete list of Holy Blossom Temple's aims, therefore, would be a *précis* of the life of this generation—the most dramatic, and traumatically affected, since the Dispersion—and a case report of its problems.

II   In a series of concentric circles, the vineyard of Holy Blossom's husbanding expands to the far horizons; nothing human is alien to it. The centre, however, is the alienated individual wrestling with the complexity and loneliness of modern life, harried by personal dilemmas, asking for an answer and anchorage.

Increasingly during recent years, the pin-point hub of a rabbi's sphere of activity has retreated to the desk of his private study where he counsels people with problems. Emotional pressures have been intensified by a high standard of living which sharpens ambition to "make the grade," by the "doom-psychology" of H-bomb warfare, by the deflation of man's egoism with his awareness of an inexorably enlarging physical universe, by the demotion of the family from its role as a sure haven for the harried, and by the gradual sunset of the Father image from which earlier times derived unshakable serenity. The rabbinate is shifting the balance of its energies from a vocation whose core was preaching to one whose care is personal counselling.

Although the customary pastoral role of the clergy has never been dominant in the hierarchy of rabbinical duties (for example, the routine practice of calling on congregants can scarcely be said to exist), the current stress on stress, the psychosomatic relationship, the practical value of religious faith for mental health, and, above all, sheer human need, climaxed perhaps in bereavement by death, have led the rabbi into active partnership with the psychiatrist.

Amateur psychiatry can be dangerous. Common-sense wisdom and mature understanding of human nature, verbalized and guided by the techniques and principles of counselling, define the strict limitations of the average rabbi's therapy. Often his study is merely the first stage in a questioner's journey to the psychiatric interview—if the distraught congregant (or non-congregant) can be persuaded to overcome a lingering reluctance to become a patient.

It is clear, however, that the absolute trustworthiness and sagacity which are implied in a rabbi's ordination make him an ideal recourse for spirits enmeshed in any of the numerous tensions related to business and personal faith which beset men today.

The next sphere of activity for the synagogue, beyond the individual microcosmic soul, is religious training of children and youth.

Adequate school education in Holy Blossom for Jewish middle-class youngsters in an environment of diverse alluring social and cultural interests, with a few class-room hours a week, is a herculean assignment. Our total objective is to communicate the saga of the thirty-five centuries of the most ancient people in Western civilization, a people seemingly fated always, as now, to be caught up in the vortex of world events and to be engaged dynamically in the action and reaction of history; to convey a rational, yet deeply devout, religious life-philosophy through the exploration of Judaism from the Biblical to the atomic age; to encourage valid and relevant ritual practices in the home, and worship in synagogue; to cultivate fine moral character and future communal leadership; to inculcate sympathetic understanding of other faiths; to create a sense of fellowship with Jews throughout the globe, especially in the State of Israel; to nurture self-respect without arrogance, pride without chauvinism, humility without obsequiousness and self-knowledge without self-segregation.

Obviously, these utopian ends have been tempered by stern reality. Yet, under unflagging, sacrificial, and imaginative supervision, and with a dedicated staff and resources made possible by trustees who realize the centrality of the educational process, Holy Blossom has become a pilot-project for fruitful and well-conceived experimentation in pedagogical method and policy, and is regarded as one of the most effective Temple schools on the continent.

Jewish youth in suburbia is exposed to well-known spiritual hazards—yet that very material security which breeds enervating "softness" and laxity also establishes a seed-bed for concern with the more introspective matters of faith. Adolescent youngsters propound questions about God, the soul, and human destiny which their counterparts of immediate immigrant ancestry would not have considered germane to lives preoccupied with earning a livelihood and preserving their liberty. Middle-class Canadian Jewish teen-agers of sensitive temperament take "groceries and civil rights" for granted; an integral part of Canada by birth and choice, they seek the spiritual security of integration with the universe and with Judaism.

It has been said that grandchildren want to remember what their parents tried to forget. Whether the reason be A-bomb jitters, a revival of loyalty to personal religion, or the strong fillip administered to Jewishness by the State of Israel, the third generation evinces a kind of wistful piety closer to the mood of the first generation than to that of their parents who grew up between the two World Wars. And Holy Blossom can be the loam wherein that reverential and receptive mood comes to flower and fruit.

Jeremiah admonished the Jews of Babylon to pray for the well-being of their city. The immediate community, then, is the next circle of synagogal obligation.

Institutions of social welfare and charity drives absorb such a large share of passionate endeavour among Jews that philanthropy threatens to wag religion. A cheque book and a pledge card are a moral zero without the compassion and assurance of human worth which are the ethical aspect of the religious outlook and thus the ultimate incentive to charitable enterprise. Lacking the values and virtues of church and synagogue, projects for the underprivileged will wither at the root. The crucial initiative which enabled Holy Blossom members to launch the organization of Toronto's early Jewish charities emerged from the recognized mandate to serve God by serving man.

In the Bible, aid to the poor was a command addressed to the individual. After the Dispersion, the desperate plight of Jewish communities thrust into sudden exile or persecution required a collective system which enabled settlements far removed from each other to engage in mutual assistance. The idea of Federation, or Community Chest, was a Jewish invention mothered by necessity. Every village synagogue had its bureau of social welfare; even the marriage dowry of an indigent maiden became a communal chore (albeit frequently a joyous one).

At all levels of civic association, Holy Blossom must open supply-lines for the feeding of constructive agencies in the general community. Among them the philanthropic is most native to Jewish tradition.

The next orbit of Holy Blossom is World Jewry, particularly the State of Israel, with which it is important that the link of spiritual kinship be tightened.

In the credo of Reform, as adopted by the Central Conference of American Rabbis in 1937, the first paragraph categorically terms Judaism "the soul of which the Jewish people is the body." The peoplehood of Israel is a desideratum clearly etched by the facts of history and the history of our faith. Without the religion, the people would have no justification for existence; without the people, the religion would have no instrumentality for existence. Saadia, a tenth-century sage, left behind an oft-quoted epigram: "Israel is a people only because of the Torah." In 1954, a Reform professor of theology wrote that "Judaism represents the universal religious consciousness expressed in the Jewish *people*."

The atheist who yet considers himself a Jew by "nationality" cannot be expunged from the ranks; he is indeed abnormal and truncated—but only the deliberate espousal of *another* faith would make him a gentile. Yet folksy sentiment, an accent on "Jewishness," which may exalt culinary customs into a sign of belonging (gefillte-fish or lox-and-bagel "Yiddishkeit"), enshrines particularism and ignores the spiritual end to which it is dedicated. On the other hand, exclusive emphasis on "ethical monotheism" and denial of ethnic folkways, drain Judaism of vitality and doom it to slow suffocation in the strait-jacket of a creed.

The form of Jewish peoplehood varies with geography and historic conditioning. East European Jewry, before its erasure by Hitlerism, often got official recognition as a culturally autonomous local minority; in Canada, Jews enjoy the status of a primary religious denomination acculturated in a pluralistic and permissive milieu; the State of Israel has resurrected independent political sovereignty on the soil to which song and prayer have been directed for nineteen centuries.

From the Babylonian Exile in 586 B.C., Jews dwelt beyond the borders of Palestine. Merchants, artisans, and missionaries dotted Egypt, Asia Minor, Greece, Italy—and even the Rhineland and Britain—with colonies of voluntary "exiles." It is likely that two-thirds of the Jewish people were strewn over the Roman Empire at the time of Jesus. These inhabitants of the ancient Diaspora, like those of today, owed no political allegiance whatever to the homeland. They did send a regular token subsidy for the maintenance of the Jerusalem Temple, until its destruction in the year 70 A.D.

The tiny State of Israel is, and will be for some years, harassed by economic burdens arising from the influx of usually impoverished immigrants which doubled its population in a decade, from the urgent requirements of defence, and from the paucity of natural wealth. Its chief role is temporarily being shaped by emergency: a refuge. With the consolidation of almost-miraculous material progress, however, its meaning for homeless Jews will develop into that of a mission for hallowed Judaism, and the particularistic passion which engendered it on the graveyard of six million martyrs to Hitler will ripen into the universalism of service dreamed of by the prophets.

From free, enlightened Canada, only a splinter of the Jewish population will migrate to Israel. For the overwhelming majority of Jews in Canada, however, the *spiritual* tie is close and deep. Towards Canada, they feel the unfailing love of a man for the spouse he has chosen; towards Israel, the love of a child for the mother who cradled his culture and character. Both can co-exist, and are mutually enriching.

The peoplehood of the Jews must be covenanted anew before they can renew their consecration to the brotherhood of peoples. Although the early pioneers of Reform combined intellectual liberalism and the imperatives of nineteenth-century science with the anti-nationalistic Messianism kindled by the supposedly imminent dawn of universal emancipation, Reform Judaism today welcomes the rejuvenated Israeli republic, and would build a bridge between the State of Israel and the children of Israel in other states.

III These four areas, in successive enlargement, describe the crucial spheres of Holy Blossom's concrete *purpose*. Let us now analyse four basic *principles* that have moulded, and continue to mould, its course. First, *it seeks to enable and encourage Jewry and mankind to worship God in dignity, with the beauty of ritual and prayer, enveloped by a sense of holiness.*

More than a house *of* God, a religious institution must be a link *with* God. The concept of the sanctuary, the dwelling-place, implies remoteness, a transcendent, static condition of sacredness—apart from man. A view of church and synagogue as a meeting-place of the Divine and the human, with prayer as the bridge between them, introduces life and movement, opens up the dead-end to spiritual traffic, and breaks mass into energy.

The vaulting dimensions of Holy Blossom architecture suggest Deity ensconced in cosmic grandeur, King of the Universe. Yet, since outer space has become an area for supra-mundane imperialism instead of a golden celestial paradise and the inner realm of the human spirit shrinks into a wasteland parched with thirst for a personal God, the majesty of the Almighty's throne is less desired than the touch of His hand. A spacious, abstract cathedral no longer reflects universal and unquestioning faith; the Root and Ground of all things is a swift "Hound of

Heaven" who eludes our quietly desperate search. More than a Royal Potentate, fragmentized man needs a Friend.

Faith has been defined by Samuel Hugo Bergman, Professor of Humanities at Hebrew University, as "experience of the great moment and the exclusive possession of the individual." The popularity of existentialism—even for those who but dimly understand its rationale—stems from its emphasis on personal encounter, the confrontation of man and Maker. An act of worship is a transaction, an exchange of doing between each person in his solitude and God.

Obviously the formal ritualism of organized, collective prayer is hard put to provide such communion. Deep whispering to deep, the lonely dialogue of the soul and its Source? To extract such felicity from the routine formalism of public worship would require the mystic technique of a self-absorbed yogi, or a magic quality in the service beyond any which a highly structured machinery can ordinarily provide or the modern sophisticate readily accept.

Perhaps by its very nature, planned prayer for the group cannot satisfy the hunger of people who have no other, more private, access to the spiritual domain. The inability to pray has evoked fervent prayer in many hearts unmoved by Temple prayer-book and service. The over-extroverted synagogue, the chill rationalism to which English translations are subject, classical Reform's inflation of formal dignity into fatal "decorum," the executive and institutionalized routine of rabbis in large congregations: all these influences have intensified the pathetic rigidity, the ankylosis of the spiritual joints induced by a materialistic world.

Recent lay conventions indicate that the Reform movement stirs on the threshold of a resurgent quest for the recovery of "the power to pray." Our "best" people are far from naïve—yet they thirst for an experience many of them have never known: the prayerful liberation of the soul.

When a person implores God for guidance, he is no longer alone—God takes up residence within him; he is no longer afraid—God illumines his pilgrimage on earth; he is no longer in servitude—God loosens him from enslavement to the self; he is no longer weak—God endows him with redemptive strength; he is no longer trivial—God has marked him with the Divine image; he is no longer adrift —God is an immovable anchorage; he is no longer without hope—God warms his heart with joy. Like a captain who posts his sentinels at night, that man can sleep!

It is this assurance of the Divine Presence and Partnership that the more sensitive young people increasingly want from the synagogue. Third- and fourth-generation Jews have been emancipated, at least subjectively, from obsessive concern about group status. In the free air of Canada, the focus of their Jewish consciousness has shifted from security as Jews in a gentile milieu to serenity as human beings in a revolutionary epoch undergoing such rapid change that the old gods perish long before new ones can be born.

Ritualism provides a prelude to prayer. During recent years Holy Blossom has revived many rituals dear to tradition, and created others. In Judaism, ceremonial practices can be justified by the bond they symbolize and forge with the Jewish people (defined by a great Conservative leader as "Catholic Israel"), and with the historic past. We are a people in time—and timelessness; only a percentage, the Israeli, will ever be a people in space. Synagogue (and home) customs are the poetic distillation of Jewish history.

Reform Judaism reaches into the vast, cumulative treasure of Jewish ceremonial and liturgy to select what is viable and valid for the present. The ultimate criterion is not literal adherence to a supernaturally revealed law but rather adaptation to the spiritual needs of life. At every moment in the twenty centuries of dispersion, the orthodox *siddur* (the Hebrew word for prayer-book, meaning "order") has been fluid and flexible, reflecting the contemporary mood and need of the people—and in this it differs from the Bible, fixed by canon statute.

More crucial than a particular ceremony, is a study of its purpose. Holy Blossom Congregation has its own traditions, among them the courage to challenge itself. Are the rituals we espouse an aesthetic auxiliary of Judaism, a means of emotional catharsis and "the living garment of divinity"—or are they an anaesthetic which mutes a sense of frustration, an escape from outmoded doctrine, merely another aspect of American "know-how" activism? Are they the language of piety, which, like any other language, can be light-heartedly changed for convenience—or, as Abraham Heschel hinted, the "homage of disbelief to faith"? Is elaborate ceremonialism a sign of health or of waning moral passion, as in other historical religions? Is it a retreat from the grave risks of reason in a clouded world?

At the beginning of its second century, the basic predicament of Holy Blossom reveals itself to be the union, through public worship, of God's love and man's need. Indeed that is, and must increasingly become, the universal human predicament, and the primary function of any religious body. Whatever arithmetical success may be garnered, such as growth in numbers, physical structure, and "activities," the ultimate test in the future will be the extent to which the sanctuary *of* God effects encounter *with* God.

The second principle of Holy Blossom must be *to vitalize the verities of*

Judaism, place them in the twentieth century, and affirm the role of reason, and of man, in religious thought.

Orthodox Judaism demands absolute observance of the total Torah ("Teaching") as the revealed word and will of God. Even the Oral Law, which proliferated in the Talmud and subsequent commentaries to implement in detail the written code of the Bible, was considered implicit in the Sinaitic theophany. No prescription, however trivial, is unimportant. All issue alike from Deity. Conservative Judaism relies on the principle, if not the full practice, of the legalistic heritage. For the lightning on Sinai's mount, it substitutes the historic voice of the people, the consensus of custom, as authority. The law changes—but remains the same.

Reform approaches the past with a clear-cut, uncompromising rejection of a single revelation through Moses. God unveils His truth constantly; man's insight evolves; altered conditions render certain laws irrelevant; the needs of *life* are paramount; only the mandates of morality have eternal significance; the prohibition of *shaatnez* (the mixture of linen and wool in clothing) does not enjoy equal rank with the admonition to love one's neighbour, even though they are found in the same chapter of Leviticus.

Male head-covering at worship provides an apt illustration. The origin of this observance is obscure. Sages and scholars generations ago (for example, the Gaon of Vilna) regarded it as a custom, rather than a divine fiat. According to liberal Judaism, an article of raiment belongs to the category of external detail, not essential principle. A Holy Blossom Temple by-law, which evoked considerable controversy among the members when first proposed about forty years ago, *permits* men to worship with bare heads; it does not *compel* them. The question is beyond the realm of ethics, morals, or basic tradition and can be left to voluntary choice. "Yesterday is necessary—but it cannot displace today, dominate tomorrow" or become a sanctified relic.

At many cross-roads Judaism survived by its ability to meet and match the grim challenge of life (thus fulfilling Toynbee's qualification for viability—although he dismissed Judaism as "Syriac fossil"). When the Jewish state and the formalized worship on Jerusalem's height vanished in flame under the armed might of imperial Rome, teachers and rabbis replaced the sacrificial offerings with penitential prayers, the altar of priesthood with the piety of the home, the centralized sanctuary with humble synagogues which sprang up throughout the dispersion—and the static Torah with a portable and continuous revelation of God for Jews wherever they may be.

Reform Judaism was begotten by a similar process of adaptation, under far different circumstances. The French revolution in 1791 offered political equality to Jews. Thenceforth, with intermittent retreat to oppression, the spirit of enlightenment flickered across Europe, then to England, and rose to a luminous torch on the North American continent. In the year 70, the walls of the Temple in Jerusalem had tumbled down. Now it was the walls of the ghetto that crashed. For fifteen centuries Israel had been isolated from the culture and commerce of expanding Western civilization. The Sanhedrin, or high rabbinical court, which alone could authorize new adjustments in the Torah, had disappeared. Suddenly the barriers were gone—and the Jew walked from mediaevalism into the modern world, bringing to it a love of learning, a mind hungry for wider vistas, and a soul steeped in the pursuit of godliness.

A way of life suitable for the segregated ghetto could not be carried over into a world where the Jew participated, at least theoretically, as a partner. Many ritualistic observances seemed antiquated, incompatible with standards of the new age. Like many gentiles, Westernized Jews floundered in conflict between sentiment and realism, between rigidity and reason.

For that crisis, Reform Judaism was born. From the depths of the great ocean of Judaism, it brought forth what was needed, utilized an ages-old pattern of adaptation and showed Jews how they can retain their loyalty to the basic and beloved religion of their forefathers and also enjoy liberty as equal and enlightened citizens.

This has been the immemorial Jewish answer to history. Even the Pharisaic rabbis, who created "normative" Judaism, were motivated by the desire to make their religion work. The New Testament's prejudice has converted "Pharisee" into a by-word for rigidity, but they had only one changeless idea: the external mechanism and material of faith exist for man, not man for them. The Talmud itself records eight centuries (300 B.C. to 500 A.D.) of endeavour to fit the law to life by ceaseless interpretation of the written Scripture. It actually admonished Jews to heed a prophet "who bids thee transgress a commandment of the Torah; do according to the needs of the hour"! Did not Rabbi Jochanan say that "every sound of the revelation on Sinai was uttered in seventy tongues"? All fresh truths discovered in any generation by the wise are part of the divine truth. Maimonides counselled the abolition of certain rites to save the rest, "even as a physician amputates a limb" to save life.

The Eighteen Benedictions of our prayer-book speak to "Our God and God of our fathers." God is an ancestral heritage and also the achievement of our own personal need; the past plus immediate insight; the security of ancient prestige plus the liberty to live one's own way; at times a ponderous ocean liner of authority and at other times a solitary raft on the open sea of individual experience— tradition tested by reason.

Reason itself needs unreserved affirmation, in an age when the "something inside all of us that yearns . . . not for clear thought but for the whisperings of the irrational" (as Karl Jaspers described it) has brought a deepening twilight of the mind. The anti-intellectual path marked out, paradoxically, by the intellects of Kierkegaard, William James, Bergson, and Buber has led to a form of Know-Nothingism, with reactionary political and social ramifications, and on a lower plane to pseudo-religious Couéism harvested in Norman Vincent Peale.

The hard-headed rabbis and their lay disciples turned away from the leap in the dark. No Jewish thinker ever recommended "sacrificium intellectus," sacrifice of the intellect, or scorned seeking and inquiring as "wisdom of the flesh," desire for truth as "dissolution," and striving for knowledge as "a kind of brutality" (quoting Novalis). Confidence in man's mind led Saadia, the great Jewish sage already quoted, to declare that even without revelation man would ultimately understand the existence and nature of God, and Maimonides exempted the first two commandments of the Decalogue from Mosaic mediation because they can be perceived without divine assistance. No more than a man cuts off his feet after falling into a pit, does Judaism banish reason because its abuse in the atomic age has brought man to the brink of an abyss. The Jew cannot know all of God— but he is bound to know all he can!

The encounter of God and man poses the crucial challenge to reason. Confronted by the twentieth-century "fall" of man, Western religious thought more and more espouses "the dismal dogma that nature is sin, the intellect the devil and man depraved." Whereas the Enlightenment which begat Reform forgot that man is capable of evil, this post-Hitler era forgets that man is capable of good. The messianic progressivism of the nineteenth century was a theological version of Swinburne's hymn to "Man as the master of things" and veered close to humanism, where man is all; the melancholy pessimism of the twentieth would convert man into a hopeless, helpless zero, God into an arbitrary dispenser of salvation, and the quest for truth into a subjective, trance-like moment of revelation.

The pendulum has swung to the view of man alienated, "a haunted soul lost in lonely monologue amid the immensities of space and the obscenities of matter," the doomed hero of Kafka's *The Castle*. Once release from authoritarianism was the liberal's pride; now man wants security through authority, hopes for serenity from intellectual suicide, is afraid of the loneliness that freedom offers him and longs to be a cipher. His disillusion with himself, rooted in the dogma of original sin of fundamentalist Christianity, has been fed by shallow interpretation of three Jewish intellectuals: Marx, who allegedly termed man a machine; Freud, who according to the "short-cut" reading thought man a marionette of the subconscious; and Einstein who, it is said, conceived man as ultimately a mathematical syllogism. Now this deflation is being sped by the existentialist.

A Hassidic saint declared that everyone must have two pockets, so that he can reach into one or the other according to his needs. In his right pocket are the words, "For my sake was the world created." In his left pocket is the confession, "I am dust and ashes." The basic challenge to liberal religion (and Holy Blossom) is to turn mankind towards the assurance of dignity and worth in the right pocket, rather than too often to the self-abasement in the left. To the sceptic, liberalism says that truth is possible; to the fanatic, that truth is difficult.

The third principle of our congregation is *to establish a vigorous, progressive Jewish life in this vast, forward-looking land, to contribute to the constructive shaping of Canada's destiny and to promote inter-group goodwill based on mutual equality and respect.*

For nineteen centuries, the key to the Jewish psyche has been minority status and millenial oppression. Today freedom has opened a new door to an understanding of the Jewish mind.

In earlier times not only was the Jew keenly conscious of himself; Christendom also had profound awareness of his unique position. Whether the Jew dwelt apart voluntarily behind the ramparts of religious separation or was herded into a ghetto, whether equipped by mediaeval superstition with Satanic horns or by George Eliot with a heroic halo, whether blamed for the Black Plague in the thirteenth century or capitalism in the nineteenth or Communism in the twentieth, his continued existence—contrary to logic or precedent—was a constant enigma.

One-half of 1 per cent of the world's population, we are still the dramatized and "different" Number One minority—expelled two hundred times during twenty centuries, often from lands where we had dwelt for generations, and still wearing under the skin a fragment of the Yellow Badge decreed by the Fourth Lateran Council in 1215 and revived by the Nazis seven centuries later.

Sometimes I ask myself if I would prefer to have been born into a gentile household. Being a non-Jew would be easier and more serene—but lacking in colour, challenge, and zest. It might blunt the sword of struggle, tempt one to contentment, conventionality, and worship of the right thing rather than the right.

It would mean a smoother path, a softer bed, a safer voyage, by "just being a human being"—but there is also the danger of spiritual smugness and narrower horizons. Not being a Jew would bring more opportunity for peace of mind, in a world where I was like the others—but being a Jew in this growing, generous land brings the privilege of inhabiting two worlds and the chance of wedding the best in Canada and the best in Judaism.

My Ohio birth-place offered a childhood mildly reminiscent of the world of Huckleberry Finn: rowing a hand-made john-boat, poling a raft out into the river to ride the stern-wheeler waves, hopping freight-trains, sliding down the muddy "crick" bank into the old sycamore swimming-hole, raiding orchards, pitching horseshoes, picking paw-paws, hooking cat-fish with a stick and string. Yet those days also saw brawny dullards from the coal-pits who shouted "Christ-killer," doused me under the fountain, and rubbed my face in the snow to scare me away from a gentile competitor's news-stand. And every night my pillow heard a prayer for the return of the Jewish homeless to Palestine (although I had not yet even heard of Zionism). When "Onward Christian Soldiers" was sung in school, I fixed my inner eye on the Red Sea, Joshua, and the Maccabees; come Christmas carol time, I changed the words under my breath.

In *heder* (the rear room of the drab little wooden synagogue) the Jewish boys were drilled mercilessly in Hebrew by a cadaverous *melamed* ("teacher") who avenged himself on fate by pulling their ears. How different it was from the bright, clean, brick public-school, where the lady teachers cocked their heads sideways like pink birds, and we romped at recess with gentiles, who dressed up for Sunday church and ate butter with meat. Yet the sight and sound and smell of *heder* could not always quench the grandeur of the Book we read there, and the smudgy lapels of the *melamed*'s black coat often faded into the silver radiance of the High Priest's breast-plate.

Today, the psychological trammels of timidity and pain in the old-fashioned *heder* are broken. Jewish youth takes first-class citizenship for granted. The external stigmata of Jewishness have vanished; our teen-agers dress, talk, giggle, and jive "Canadian." Suburbia and security remove the sting not only of mediaeval affliction, but of the new Dark Age which descended on Jewry but a few years ago; to many Canadian-Jewish youngsters, Dachau and Buchenwald are only nasty words.

"Holy Blossom" is the English translation of the Hebrew words *Pirchay Kodesh*, engraved on a Torah ornament donated to the congregation in 1857, only a few months after it was founded; they may refer to the young apprenticed priests ("holy blossoms") in the Jerusalem sanctuary. Our Temple began as an Orthodox congregation and has traversed successive periods of change. Yet throughout its career, it has followed certain built-in imperatives, among them the mandate to serve Canadianism while preserving Judaism—in war and in peace, in calm and crisis, through communal endeavour and civic responsibility, testifying that patriotic Canadianism and proud Judaism can be fruitfully merged.

Always the basis for and condition of co-operative goodwill has been equality. Repeatedly the rabbinate and lay leadership of Holy Blossom has refused to condone sectarian religious instruction in the public schools; their protest is a document of courage and essential confidence in the ultimate fair judgment of the Canadian people and affirms mutual respect as a condition of mutual fellowship. Harmony purchased by subservience or silence is a sham! A half-century ago the Holy Blossom pulpit rebuked Christian missionaries for an especially humiliating and self-righteous campaign to obtain Jewish converts—again establishing a precedent for the defence of Jewish dignity which has received further reaffirmation.

Canada is equipped by history and geography to be a clinical laboratory for an experiment in group relations, of which the central theme is acculturation, not assimilation, and the aim an Irish stew, wherein each racial ingredient retains its own identity and flavour, rather than a melting-pot of uniformity. It was born in a compromise between two opposing forces, the need not only to live, but let live. The arranged marriage of Frenchman and Briton, sealed in the British North America Act, became a permanent formula for the nurture of the young dominion —a pattern which has encouraged a kind of cultural autonomy among all the ethnic elements that make Canada their home.

In fact, this is a nation of minorities. Less than half of Canadians are British by descent, 30 per cent are French, 18 other Europeans, and the remainder an agglomeration of Asiatics, Africans, Indians, and Eskimos. Scattered over a huge land, they are bound together not so much by propaganda slogans or textbook ballyhoo as by a common life and destiny.

The bulk of Canada's population dwell in a narrow ribbon from sea to sea, close to the southern border. Yet what diversity: the Cape Breton cod-fisherman in his lonely dory; the coal-miner of the Maritimes, digging three miles out under the ocean; the Arctic seal-hunter scanning the icy wastes; the parish farmer of Quebec, loving the land which sustains the body and the church that comforts the spirit; the blue-denimed mechanic in the automobile plants of southern Ontario; the Americanized city-dwellers along the soft southern rim; the research-scientist probing cancer or soil-erosion in a university laboratory; the prairie wheat-king reaping his golden domain from a tractor to feed the world; the fruit-grower of the Okanagan Valley; the frontier missionary carrying God's word to Indian and Eskimo and white prospector; the gold-seeker in Yellowknife, the bush-pilot around Hudson Bay, the lumber jack of British Columbia, the fur-trapper and trader and nurse and physician and mounted police all of whom free a sprawling continent from the clutch of the primitive, hew out a path for civilized living, build a nation and keep it intact over thousands of miles of stream and mountain and forest and plain!

For the future maturation of Canada, its Jewish citizenry offers a hoary culture and a hallowed faith, in a contemporary setting, but with essence intact. For that alchemy of spirit Holy Blossom is a catalyst.

Its fourth principle of action should be *to engage in expanding areas of common effort with non-Jews for social justice, through a free, liberating pulpit, in accord with the message of Hebrew prophecy.* Social passion has never been absent from the arsenal of liberal Judaism. It is noteworthy that the late Kaufmann Kohler, scholarly head of the Reform rabbinical seminary (Hebrew Union College), who wrote the classic work on *Jewish Theology,* forsook his ivory tower and called on Reform to "mount the watch-tower and unfurl the banner of high idealism before the world." The Hebrew prophets, by their thunderous challenge to "let justice flow as water and righteousness as a mighty stream," to free the oppressed and curb those who "add field to field," have lured many followers, particularly among the liberal rabbinate, into a struggle often dubbed "radicalism." Yet these prophets were actually arch-conservatives. The bitter opposition to the abuses of private ownership and personal gain which sharpened their invective originated in memories of clan-owned communal property: the supplanted pastoral-agricultural economy of past generations.

No less than the message of the prophets, has the alertness of Holy Blossom's pulpit to social problems been an inevitable outgrowth of traditional Jewish belief. It has not by any means been a radical departure from that belief. The fight against war, racism, economic exploitation, suppression of freedom, and religious bigotry which has marked the Temple's preachment for generations has mirrored the flux of contemporary events and would constitute a history of the social struggle during that period—but at its centre lay the inmost kernel of Jewish teaching.

Judaism has always been at odds with the Greek view of reality as a static thing, cast in an eternal and changeless Form. The Hellenic ideal visualized a perfect balance of beauty frozen for serene contemplation, like a piece of statuary in space which man sees with the eye; the Hebraic spirit responded to the Voice, for which one listens with the ear, the troubling Word in time that cries battle again and again, hurls God's command to collaborate with Him for a better world and bans contentment with anything less than His Kingdom on earth. Jewish thought has been dynamic, militant, timeful—directed to the stream of the temporal order, namely, *becoming*, rather than to a state of "absolute" *being*. Perhaps this concept of God as intimately involved with phenomena and seeking His own oneness through nature and man spurred the Jewish rejection of Paulinian Christianity. Even the super-mystical Kabbalah summoned man to reunite by his moral acts two aspects of the Divine: *elohut*, remote Being of God, and *schechinah*, which wanders astray and scattered in creation. By contrast, the church, as R. H. Tawney pointed out, gradually abdicated from leadership in the area of social and economic improvement and clung to personal salvation by grace.

The synagogue has been a ferment, a creative minority, rather than an established power. Rabbi Leo Baeck called the Jews "sons and daughters of the revolution." Judaism is a religion of the way—of march and movement. To liberal Judaism, history is assuredly not a "fill-in between the resurrection of Christ and his Second Coming (after the "nihilism" of Barth) nor a cradle for the rebirth of "Christian love" (in accordance with the modern activism of Berdyaev, who denounces withdrawal from the world as a refined form of egoism and declares that "bread for myself is a material question, while bread for my neighbour is a spiritual question"). It is an instrument whereby man can hold back or hurry forward the Messianic era of the Hebrew prophets. Although one might agree with Emil Fackenheim that progress need not be deemed certain, no authentic Jewish thinker would abandon its possibility.

The coupling of conventional religious faith and a reactionary social ethic is a miscegenation based on a historic accident. Marxism was linked with antireligion because it arose in the era of industrial and technological revolution, which also witnessed the onslaught of scientific rationalism against the church. Reinhold Niebuhr testifies that a "crisis" theology need not blunt sensitiveness to the continuing social crisis, and such ecclesiastical pronouncements as "Christian Principles and Assumptions for Economic Life," issued some years ago in Amsterdam by the World Council of Churches, even questioned the spiritual validity of capitalism. The Federal Council of Churches of Christ in America (condemned for non-orthodoxy by fundamentalists) has repeatedly affirmed that religion "cannot be concerned with the highest development of human personality and yet be unconcerned with slums, unemployment, racial injustice and war." Even if man survives death and is destined for individual salvation, constructive and socially minded activity in this world is the best preparation for the next. Through "politics," an extension of the pulpit, the church and synagogue may help to prevent such monstrous evils as war, which Clausewitz termed an extension of politics.

The Divine Power first worked *for* man, to begin creation, and now must work *through* him, to complete it. The most disciplined and enduring rationale for a programme of social justice is not transient moral indignation, nor even a sense of empathy with the wronged—but rather the communion with, and confrontation of, God which sped the prophets on their path. Before they saw "plowshares and pruning-hooks," they visualized a God whose purpose was peace (not peace of mind!).

The progression from the Jewish concept of God *and* man to the duty of man *to* man is clear. Basic Judaism may be condensed into a chain of affirmations which lead directly to the battlefield of social issues. This gamut begins with the dual concept of a God dwelling in, yet transcending nature, close to man at need yet beyond comprehension, allied with man, who is created from earth after the divine image, sacred in both body and soul, limited in power yet free to shape his spiritual development; it continues with the assurance that all men are equal in potentiality for realizing the greatness and goodness of life, which is God's supreme gift, and that the conquest of evil condenses the meaning and adventure of our earthly experience; it ends by envisioning a golden age of universal justice, brotherhood, and peace, expedited by the endeavours of human beings, whose primary obligation should be towards life on this side of the grave.

Within that framework, Reform Judaism has still further emphasized the orientation towards social justice by exalting prophet rather than priest, righteousness in preference to ritual, universalism as a counter-balance to particularism, and collective action instead of compulsory belief.

Liberalism as a political creed has undergone many changes of mood, content, and balance in recent decades. There is in religion more secure rootage, more dogged staying quality for constructive social protest! The documentation for anti-racism lies not so much in a British North America Act or Declaration of Independence as in the scriptural mandate of "one law for the stranger and the home-born"; its rationale is the categorical enunciation of God's colour-blindness by Amos when he declared unto the Children of Israel, "Are ye not as the children of Ethiopia unto me?" It is because "men were created in the image of God" that they may not be herded into concentration camps, hounded by witch-hunters, handled like an inanimate commodity or index-number, and humiliated by discrimination because of colour, caste, or creed.

Martin Buber has ascribed to Judaism one central achievement: not a single God, but rather that "men can say 'Thou' to Him." He has also reminded us that "Israel has accorded to spiritual inwardness its rightful place. Inward truth, however, must become real life—a drop of Messianic consummation." The "Thou" addressed to God in solitude is transmuted by social passion into "Thou" for all mankind. As a Talmudic precept puts it, "Guard ye justice, and I (the Lord) will guard your souls." Like the atoms which together and innumerably comprise the physical energy of the universe, every human individual is a minute bearer of moral energy which, when finally and fully released, will produce the Messianic Age. To that fulfilment, its fourth and final principle, turns the heart and hand of Holy Blossom.

This book has been set in Linotype Times Roman with Weiss italic display type and printed on Velvalur English Finish Book paper. Design is by Harold Kurschenska. He has taken as his theme a menorah hand-carved on a linoleum block. The book is bound in red Sundour cloth.

www.ingramcontent.com/pod-product-compliance
Lightning Source LLC
Chambersburg PA
CBHW020408080526
44584CB00014B/1224